Ethnicities and Global Multiculture

Ethnicities and Global Multiculture

Pants for an Octopus

Jan Nederveen Pieterse

ROWMAN & LITTLEFIELD PUBLISHERS, INC.
Lanham • Boulder • New York • Toronto • Plymouth, UK

ROWMAN & LITTLEFIELD PUBLISHERS, INC.

Published in the United States of America
by Rowman & Littlefield Publishers, Inc.
A wholly owned subsidiary of The Rowman & Littlefield Publishing Group, Inc.
4501 Forbes Boulevard, Suite 200, Lanham, Maryland 20706
www.rowmanlittlefield.com

Estover Road, Plymouth PL6 7PY, United Kingdom

British Library Cataloguing in Publication Information Available

Library of Congress Cataloging-in-Publication Data

Nederveen Pieterse, Jan.
  Ethnicities and global multiculture : pants for an octopus / Jan Nederveen
  Pieterse.
        p. cm.
  Includes bibliographical references and index.
  ISBN-13: 978-0-7425-4063-7 (cloth : alk. paper)
  ISBN-10: 0-7425-4063-4 (cloth : alk. paper)
  ISBN-13: 978-0-7425-4064-4 (pbk. : alk. paper)
  ISBN-10: 0-7425-4064-2 (pbk. : alk. paper)
  1. Multiculturalism. 2. Ethnicity. 3. Globalization. I. Title.
  HM1271.N46 2007
  305.8009'045—dc22   2006101219

Printed in the United States of America

♾ ™ The paper used in this publication meets the minimum requirements of
American National Standard for Information Sciences—Permanence of Paper
for Printed Library Materials, ANSI/NISO Z39.48-1992.

Contents

Box and Tables

Acknowledgments

The chapters in this book that were published in earlier versions have been completely overhauled. Nevertheless, these texts have a history and I should credit their earlier versions.

Chapter 1 is new, and I thank Fazal Rizvi and Jan Ekecrantz for their insightful comments, and Takamitsu Ono for references. Chapter 2 originally grew out of a paper for a conference at Rhodes University, Grahamstown ("Ethnicity, identity and Nationalism in South Africa: Comparative perspectives (1993). Earlier versions appeared in a volume edited by Ed Wilmsen and Patrick McAllister (*The politics of difference*, 1996) and in *Nations and Nationalism* (3, 3, 1997). I gave versions of this paper as talks at Utrecht University; Bergen University; the International Centre of Ethnic Studies in Colombo, Sri Lanka; and the Center for Afro-Brazilian Studies in Salvador, Bahia. I thank Livio Sansone for comments. Chapter 3 was presented at an Institute of Social Studies seminar in The Hague and at a LOS Centre conference at Bergen University ("Investigating social capital," 2000). The mailing list on Immigrant Entrepreneurship was a useful resource. An earlier version appeared in *Ethnicities* (3, 1, 2003). I thank Alev Cinar, Des Gasper, Ivan Light, and journal reviewers for helpful comments. Chapter 4 originates in contributions to conferences on multiculturalism at the Catholic University Louvain and Bilkent University, Ankara. Earlier versions appeared in *Social Identities* (7, 3, 2001) and in a volume edited by Barbara Saunders and David Haljan (*Whither multiculturalism?* 2003). I benefited from conversations with Hermann Schwengel in Germany and representatives of multicultural centers in Freiburg and Stockholm and the Islamitisches Zentrum in Freiburg. Chapter 5 originates in a conference presentation at Bristol University ("Nationalism, identity and minority rights," 1999). An earlier version appears in a volume edited by Stephen May, Tariq Modood, and Judith Squires (*Ethnicity, nationalism and minority rights*, 2005). I thank Stephen May, Emin Adas, and a reviewer for comments. Chapter 6 originates in talks for the Deutsche Gesellschaft für Völkerkunde (Leipzig, 1993), the National Ethnological Museum in Osaka (International Museums Conference, 1994), Yokohama National University, and the Ethnographic Museum in Antwerp. I thank participants and, in particular, Wolfgang Mey for comments. Working at the Museum of the Tropics in Amsterdam, the Netherlands' major ethnological museum, to prepare a major exhibit has made me sensitive to this side of the politics of representation. Earlier versions appeared in *Theory Culture and Society* (14, 4, 1997) and in Dutch translation in the Boekmancahier. I thank Ineke van Hamersveld and referees for comments. Chapter 7 was presented at conferences at the University of California, Berkeley ("Islamizing the Cosmopolis," 2005) and Prince of Songkhla University (Pattani, Thailand). An earlier version was published in a volume edited by Björn Hettne. Chapter 8 was presented at several conferences (at South Florida University, Tampa; Utrecht University; and the International Sociological Association in Durban) and universities (Stockholm, Gothenburg, Freiburg, Yunnan, Ferris in Yokohama, Delhi University, and National College of Arts, Lahore) in 2006. I thank participants for comments, in particular, Daniel Beltram, Don Kalb, Lisa Chason, Markus Schulz, Meng Aegean, and Imtaz Ahmad. I thank Ken Cuno for references. An earlier version was published in the journal *Globalizations*.

This work has benefited from conversations with colleagues in Brazil, China, India, Pakistan, Sri Lanka (in particular Jayadeva Uyangoda), South Africa, Sweden, and Thailand. Some colleagues have taken the time to comment on the entire manuscript, and I express my warm thanks to Fazal Rizvi, Jan Ekecrantz, and especially my dear friend Bhikhu Parekh. The usual disclaimer applies.

Introduction

Most literature on ethnicity deals with ethnic conflict, and nearly every recent study opens with sentences such as these:

> Over the past decades, ethnonationalist conflict has become the dominant form of mass political violence.[1]
>
> More than any previous age, ours is marked by ethnic conflicts. In recent decades, domestic conflicts and wars have greatly exceeded interstate conflicts.[2]
>
> Since the end of World War II most wars have been internal conflicts, a trend that accelerated in the aftermath of the end of the Cold War. The majority of these internal conflicts had a strong ethnic dimension.[3]

Several studies observe that ethnic conflict now comes second only after international terrorism as the main global security problem and note that international terrorism and ethnic conflict overlap, for instance, in Sri Lanka, Palestine, Kashmir, India, Bosnia, Chechnya, Iraq, and Thailand.

The persistence and salience of ethnic identity and conflict might be viewed as anomalous at a time when the scale of social cooperation is generally widening, when many speak of global citizenship and post-nationalism, and when identities seem increasingly flexible and wider allegiances are taking shape. But let's note that multiethnicity is common throughout the world and practically all societies are now culturally diverse. It follows that cultural diversity does not necessarily involve conflict or violence. Ethnicity becomes salient when it leads to conflict, but how do we regard it when it doesn't? To what extent is the salience of ethnic conflict and violence an optical illusion? The pessimism prompted by episodes of ethnic cleansing should not be transposed to cultural diversity in general but should prompt examination of the circumstances that produce conflict. Since conflict isn't necessarily a feature of multiethnicity, it follows that specific conflicts don't concern ethnicity per se but the conjunction of ethnicity with other circumstances.

Ethnicity as an issue keeps coming back in different forms. Iraq since the 2003 war has been undergoing a process of deconstruction and reconstruction of ethnicity and a shift of power from Sunnis to Shiites and Kurds. Iraq's new army, according to voting records of January 2006, comprises only 7 percent Sunnis, who make up 20 percent of the population, while Kurdish Pesh Merga are represented in greater numbers than their proportion in the population. In Afghanistan since the war of 2001 there has been a realignment of government power from the Pashtuns in the south (who formed the backbone of the Taliban) to a coalition in which the Northern Alliance plays a large part. War changed the power equation between population segments, activating different nodes of power, a different distribution of resources, economic opportunities, allies, and ecological niches, so different political and cultural affinities came to the foreground. Changes in ethnic power relations generally occur because of demographic dynamics, migration, new economic opportunities or constraints, changes in international power (such as the breakup of the Soviet Union and its ripple effects in the Caucasus and Eastern Europe), and civilizational shifts. There are lasting stalemates and precarious balancing acts, as in the African Great Lakes area and the Balkans, and emerging fault lines, as in the Caucasus and Central Asia. Political Islam has emerged as a fault line with familiar signal moments.

Ethnicity and multiculturalism are essential for understanding globalization, but in most treatments they are considered in national contexts. This book examines the tortuous relationship between multiethnicity and nation states. Multiethnicity precedes the nation state by centuries or even millennia. Nation states emerged from multiethnicity and represent the crystallization and institutionalization of interethnic relations as they exist at a particular stage, say, in the fourteenth, seventeenth, nineteenth, or twentieth centuries. Although nation states wield significant power, that power is limited. From the viewpoint of nation states, multiethnicity exists both within and outside the nation state, and while states seek to control borders and migration, they cannot oversee and control the multiple and fluid relations between multiethnicity in and beyond the nation. One could argue, by analogy, that the nation state stands to multiethnicity as the UN Security Council stands to world politics, as the victors of the last major war and the political dispensation that arose from it. The Security Council wields significant power, yet world power politics has moved on. Multiethnicity, likewise, has moved on in relation to nation states. It travels and makes use of new communication technologies, from satellite television to mobile phones and internet.

Multiethnicity has been an ordinary state of affairs through most of history. Multiculturalism, on the other hand, is an institutionalization of multiethnicity, a set of policies that usually imply a positive evaluation of multiethnicity. (Sometimes "multiculturalism" also loosely refers to cultural cohabitation as a demographic condition.) The term "multiculturalism" was at one time used exclusively in western countries, but increasingly countries in the global South—such as Malaysia, Singapore, Brazil, Mexico, India, and South Africa—have adopted the terminology, as well as some multiculturalism policies, in recognition of minorities and human rights. Multiethnicity, the condition, is wider than multiculturalism, the policy framework. Settlements of ethnic conflicts, such as autonomy and federalism, mediate tensions between diversity and the nation state. Many ethnic conflicts concern spatially concentrated groups, so land and ecology are often variables in autonomy arrangements, but they rarely figure in multiculturalism. And multiculturalism usually concerns relatively recent immigrants, whereas ethnic autonomy often concerns long-term internal differentiation.

Multiculturalism is a work in progress, an arena in which dramas of global inequality are being played out, a meeting point of nation states and unequal development, of poverty in the global South and deindustrialization, welfare cutbacks, neglected working-class neighborhoods and opportunities and life chances in the West. Films such as *La Haine* (Paris, 1995), about North African youths in the French banlieues, and *Tough Enough* (Berlin, 2006), about Turkish and German youths in a working-class suburb of Berlin illustrate the frictions in this arena.

Ethnicity occupies an odd place in social science because although it is intensively studied, much of the literature is noncumulative because ethnic studies are dispersed across many fields. Ethnicity is a classic theme in anthropology. Sociology studies multiculturalism, regional diversity, and autonomy movements in western countries. Economic sociology and geography study migrant economies (such as labor market segmentation and ethnic economies) and urban diversity. Diversity is an emerging theme in business and management. In political theory and philosophy, multiculturalism is viewed through the lens of theories of rights. Law focuses on immigration and citizenship. Cultural studies address cultural interplay in popular culture and representations of diversity in media, museums, and art. Ethnic conflict is the purview of political science, international studies, policymakers, and media. As Andreas Wimmer notes, this sprawl in research makes the literature segmented: "Journalists are rarely aware of the scholarly debate and the results it has produced; policy makers continue to discuss models that imply an understanding of conflict out of tune with the models that researchers have developed; academics often arrive at policy conclusions that are far off the accumulated experience of ethnic conflict management; scholars that evaluate policy options are sometimes unaware of the decades of research undertaken by their more academically oriented colleagues."[4]

What would it take to open up the debate and make the discussion of multiculturalism truly global? According to Norbert Elias, social science needs *Langsicht* (a long view) and *Breitsicht* (a broad view). A long view situates multiethnicity in a historical perspective, and a broad view adopts a comparative framework. Ethnicity, nationhood, migration, multiculturalism, and politics of representation take on different hues when viewed in the *longue durée*. Because concepts and analytics reflect particular periods and regions, adopting a comparative historical approach also holds theoretical and analytical implications.

William Roseberry noted that most studies of immigration around the turn of the century in the United States were done by recent immigrants (such as Florian Znaniecki).[5] This is also true now; many scholars of multiculturalism share a migration and diaspora profile. There is an emotional and existential texture to the migration-multiculturalism discussions stemming from histories of travel, often across generations. When migration is part of one's life history, one empathizes with newcomers' needs and anxieties, and after spending a lifetime in the destination country, one identifies with its needs too. One knows that world citizenship is acquired one step at a time.

I am of immigrant background, too; my family came from the Netherlands East Indies right before Indonesia's independence. They were a colonial family of mixed European and Indies ancestry that had spent some two hundred years in Java, Sumatra, and Sulawesi. I was born in Amsterdam eleven days after their arrival in the Netherlands, the only one in the family born outside the Indies for many generations, so I am Dutch by citizenship but emotionally connected to a wider world. I didn't relate to Indonesia in particular. Indonesia under the Suharto government was not an attractive place. I traded this affinity for, so to speak, global sympathy. Eventually I lived in Java for several months, shortly before the Suharto government fell. Living in the United States, I'm now an immigrant again.

As the delta of the Rhine and Meuse, the Netherlands originally was composed of a mélange population of Batavians, Saxons, Frisians, Burgundians, and many others. Since the eleventh century the Low Countries—where due to their seaside geography the aristocracy was relatively weak—competed with neighboring lands and princedoms by allowing trade with infidels, imposing low levies, and allowing ships to return in times of war. This "political economy of tolerance" became well established and led to conflicts with the Spanish Habsburg Empire when it wanted to impose the restrictions of the Inquisition. This prompted the independence struggle of the northern Low Countries, the United Provinces. In the seventeenth century this led to further waves of immigrants, refugees from religious oppression—Sephardic and Ashkenazi Jews, Huguenots, Pilgrims—merchants from the Baltic, and workers from neighboring countries.

Growing up in the Netherlands, I was happy to see the country gradually become more multicultural. Indos, Indo-Dutch, and Moluccans were the first to come in numbers from outside Europe after World War II, followed by Surinamese and Antilleans from the sixties on, along with Mediterranean peoples, Turks, and Moroccans in the seventies and eighties, and many more from across the world. Thus postwar multiculturalism was superimposed on and interacted with prior strata of diversity, such as Catholics concentrated in the south of the country and Protestants in the north. Eventually multiculturalism became a rollercoaster experience. I discuss some of these problems in this book.

I can't transcend all the barriers that separate the literatures, but my broad background in social science, political economy, development studies, and history crosses several of these lines.[6] By intertwining strands of social science and western and non-western bodies of research, this book attempts to overcome the disciplinary and regional segmentation in the literature. By adopting a comparative-historical and kaleidoscopic perspective, this book seeks to make an innovative contribution. It builds on research conducted in countries north and south, travel from the borders of Afghanistan to Central America, and recent research and interviews in Brazil, China, South Africa, Sri Lanka, Sweden, Thailand, and Germany.

"Putting pants on an octopus" is a proverb in the Baleares for doing something that is very difficult, indeed, virtually impossible. I think using concepts such as ethnicity and multiculturalism to do justice to multiethnicity and global cultural flux is like putting pants on an octopus. In this book I propose *ethnicities* and *global multiculture* as alternative concepts. Putting pants on an octopus remains a difficult undertaking, but it helps when the pants are large.

I take a historicizing approach in this study. Since perspectives on diversity reflect a particular time and region, taking a historical approach has theoretical implications, too, and unhinges concepts and paradigms. Many reflections on diversity are of a specific, regional nature and cannot be generalized to cultural difference as a whole. This book presents a sustained and organized argument, but this is not a systematic argument in the sense of analytical philosophy, building from concepts with stable definitions toward systematic propositions. I'm not a philosopher but a social scientist (I have nostalgia for philosophy but not for analytical philosophy). Second, bringing out the fluidity of social relations over time and the historical contingency of concepts is one of the key points of this study. An argument that runs through this book is that stable definitions in social science are in many cases fictional. We need a wide-angle take on cultural diversity, and thus I seek to open up the discussions of ethnicity and multiculturalism by highlighting the diverse and fluid character of cultural difference and the wide variety of circumstances in which it unfolds. I adopt a pluralizing approach, combining and contrasting varieties of ethnicities and multiculturalisms. Combining this wide-angle approach with typologies and tables brings some organization to the debates.

Chapter 1 presents a short history and *tour d'horizon* of multiethnicity, turns to the relationship between the nation and ethnicity, and closes with a reflection on ethnicity from a historical point of view. Chapter 2 takes up the varieties of ethnicity. Many discussions of ethnicity engage in generalizations, as if there is only one kind of ethnicity, but it is more realistic to think of ethnicity in the plural and as a continuum, with wide variations in terms of salience, intensity, and meaning. This chapter distinguishes four main types of ethnicity: domination, enclosure, competition, and optional.

Chapter 3 is concerned with the political economy of multiethnicity and social capital. I question the "ethnic economy" approach because it refers to national origin rather than ethnicity and diverts attention from social and economic relations *across* cultural boundaries. The role migrants play in national and transnational enterprise, formal and informal, involves extensive crosscultural relations. The chapter further considers interethnic enterprise in long-term perspective and with a view to policy. Understanding capitalism and accumulation in cultural terms, and taking into account crosscultural enterprise and interethnic relations, means taking into account the various types of social capital within and across cultural boundaries.

Chapter 4 opens a series of chapters on multiculturalism: chapter 5 on ethnicities and multiculturalisms, chapter 6 on multiculturalism and museums, chapter 7 on Islam and cosmopolitanism, and chapter 8 on global multiculture. Chapter 4 raises fundamental questions about multiculturalism as a moving target amid ongoing cultural flux and tenuous institutional arrangements. That multiculturalism is multifaceted and complex reflects the many streams, past and present, that multiculturalism is on the receiving end of and represents. We need a complex take on multiculturalism as a configuration of trends and as a contested notion. From a historical viewpoint, multiculturalism signifies a time of transition and reworking of local, national, regional, and global identities and interrelations. Taking a multiperspective view this treatment probes several vortices around which multiculturalism takes shape—cultural flux, everyday experience, politics of recognition, and class.

Chapter 5 juxtaposes ethnicities and multiculturalisms by taking up the underlying theme of boundaries—their discourses, representations, and politics. What underlie the varieties of ethnicity are different ways of drawing group boundaries, and likewise the key variable in different notions and practices of multiculturalism is an understanding of group boundaries and identity. Conceptions of multiculturalism derive from several sources: colonial society, settlements of the *Kulturkampf* in Europe, experiences in settler societies such as the United States and Canada, and corporate marketing strategies. Juxtaposing ethnicities and multiculturalisms makes the limitations of various perspectives on multiculturalism visible.

Ethnicities and multiculturalisms are embedded in representations; they exist and are negotiated through representations, so representation is a vital area of concern. Chapter 6 focuses on the politics of representation. Museums and exhibitions stage representations of the imagined collective self (particularly in history, art, and science museums) and others (in ethnographic museums, ethnic theme parks, and the margins of other displays). How do globalization and multiculturalism affect the strategies of display? Representations of self and others are interdependent. One view holds that representations of others tend to be either exoticizing or assimilating. Displaying ethnographic objects as art follows an assimilative approach, in situ exhibits tend to be exoticizing, and encyclopedic exhibitions follow mixed strategies. Philosophies of culture also inform display strategies. How these approaches are implemented in display strategies is affected by the *rapport de forces* in different settings. Accelerated globalization and new migrations destabilize the once-stable dichotomy between self and other. The Enlightenment subjectivities of the past are now refracted in multiple identities, and "the Other" becomes "others"—differentiated by, among other characteristics, ethnicity, class, gender, and lifestyle. These changes are articulated in various alternative display agendas: I discuss pluralism, dialogue, self-representation, hybridity, and reflexive representation as exhibition formats, each of which raises its own questions.

A deeper dilemma is that of exhibiting power, in the two senses of the power to exhibit and how to exhibit power. Representation tends to keep the power of representation out of view. Thus colonialism frames ethnographic exhibitions but is rarely addressed by it. Exhibitions fetishize rather than interrogate power because, surreptitiously or explicitly, they borrow rather than interrogate the charisma of power.

Chapter 7 on Islam and cosmopolitanism starts from the assumption that there is no globalization and no cosmopolitanism without access to collective memory as the threshold to a collective future. A cosmopolitanism that is informed from one part of the world only, that monopolizes the world through a single language and a single cultural style, is not cosmopolitanism but hegemony. Islamic cosmopolitanism is a major chapter in the history of globalization, and the cleavage between the worlds of Islam and the West ranks as one of today's major rifts. The first part of this chapter discusses the cosmopolitan character of Islamic culture and the second section asks how this fares when the Islamic world loses its intercontinental middleman role during the era of European dominance. The third section focuses on contemporary political Islam and its codependence with American hegemony, and the closing section reflects on how clichés about "Islamic fundamentalism" and the new trope of "Islamic fascism" relate to American national security perspectives.

Chapter 8 develops two propositions: multiculturalism has gone global and identification has become flexible. Multiculturalism is a global arena, yet most treatments still conceive of multiculturalism as a national arena. In contemporary global multiculture, far-off conflicts become part of multiculturalism arenas, which is illustrated with a discussion of two multiculturalism conflicts, the Danish cartoons mocking Islam and the murder of filmmaker Theo van Gogh in Amsterdam. Muslim women's headscarves from Istanbul and Cairo to Tehran and Lyon display a wide register of meanings, but in the French National Assembly they have been signified in just one. Multiculturalism means global engagement, and to engage with the world is to engage with its conflicts. Multiculturalism is neither a no-man's-land nor consensus. There is no consensus in Britain about the war in Iraq, and there isn't among immigrants either. The securitization of cultural difference confirms the interplay between global and multicultural frictions. Multiculturalism is one of the faces of globalization, and globalization, at its Sunday best, is human history conscious of itself, which by the way isn't always nice.

The conclusion rounds off the book with a discussion of global multiculture as a new social formation and a new phase of globalization.

Notes

1. Wimmer 2004, 1.
2. Ghai 2000, 1.
3. Lobell and Mauceri 2004, 1.
4. Wimmer 2004, 3.
5. Roseberry 1992.
6. My education as an anthropologist makes me sensitive to anthropological perspectives. Working in sociology I'm aware of these debates and social theory. Work in cultural studies has sharpened my awareness of representations, stereotypes, framing, and the labeling of "others." Because of work in development studies, I'm familiar with macro policy approaches as well as country studies and share a development approach to social issues. Work in political economy gives me a keen interest in the political economy dimensions of ethnicity.

1

❖

Ethos and ethnos

Different cultural groups have been interacting, mingling, and cohabiting since time immemorial. Population movements and social formations from tribe to empire predate the emergence of nations by millennia. To understand multiculturalism we should not take the nations for granted but also consider the time before nations arose. The area that is now Jordan was located on the caravan routes from the Red Sea, Aden, and Yemen to Damascus and straddled the old kingdoms of the Ammonites (hence Amman) and Nabateans. King Herod, who was appointed king of Judea by the Romans, was "by birth an Idumean (i.e., Edomite), by profession a Jew, by necessity a Roman, by culture and by choice a Greek."[1] Multiethnicity and multiple identity have a long history. It is a modern fiction that multiethnicity is peculiar to our times. In this opening chapter I first discuss a short history of multiethnicity and then turn to the relationship between nation and ethnicity.

The earliest episodes of multiethnicity include interactions between indigenous populations, usually hunter-gatherers, and later arrivals. Indigenous peoples are scattered through contemporary Asia, several numbering millions, such as the Santals (6 million), Bhils (6 million), and Gonds (3 million) in central India and Nagas (1.7 million) among the 80 million Adivasis in India;[2] some sizable, such as the hill peoples in Southeast Asia, Orang Asli in Malaysia, Igorot in the Philippines, the early island peoples of Indonesia and Micronesia, and indigenes of Taiwan and the Papuans; and some in tiny numbers (the Veddas in Sri Lanka were down to five families in 1995). Many are of Melanesian or Austronesian descent and share traits with Micronesians and Aboriginals in Australia and Maori in New Zealand. Indigenous peoples further include pygmies in central Africa, San in southern Africa, Saami, Inuit, and Native Americans throughout the Americas. Subsequent migrants settled among these groups, and in many cases agriculture and pastoralism enabled them to become dominant groups and in time form urban settlements and states, first alongside the world's great rivers. Nomadic pastoralists were interspersed with cultivators, such as Bedouins in the Arabic peninsula and Berbers in North Africa. Pastoralists moved across the Sudanic belt of Africa and south to the Great Lakes region, fore-bears of the Masai in Kenya and the cattle herders of Rwanda and Burundi.

The "archeology of ethnicity" indicates that in many parts of the world in the Neolithic and Iron Age, three formations coexisted, hunter-gatherers, cultivators, and pastoralists, establishing checkerboard ecologies of ethnic interaction. In time many indigenous peoples also became cultivators. Over time these groups were joined by traders, itinerant craftsmen, and artisans, and later still by scholars and pilgrims. Long-distance trade networks criss-crossed Asia and Africa for many centuries before the Europeans came, such as the gold trade to northern Africa, the Hausa in West Africa, and Arabs who settled along the east coast of Africa. Indonesians from Srivijaya allegedly established trade links with eastern Africa early on, and the Chinese did so during the fourteenth century.[3]

Consider the case of Japan. Japan is generally viewed as a homogeneous, monocultural society by Japanese as well as by outsiders, a pure, monoracial state founded by the "Yamato race." But archaeological findings document the richness and pluralism of Japan's past and trace its population history back to Paleolithic times and to the Jōmon period starting about 14,000 BP, when populations from Southeast Asia and southern China were the first to settle. The mainstay of Japan's population can be traced back to large-scale migrations from northeastern Asia during the Yayoi and Kofun periods, mixing with the indigenous inhabitants, whose contemporary descendants include the Ainu. The Ainu are of Siberian and Mongol stock. The history of the Japanese language is likewise plural and originally developed as a trade and contact language through pidginization of Altaic and Austronesian languages.[4] The historical and archeological records show a thoroughly mixed population. As McCormack notes, "The idea of a uniquely pure link between the modern Japanese and the ancient civilization of the Jōmon period cannot be sustained. The Japanese are, like all modern peoples, a 'mixed race.'"[5]

Kingdoms in the Ryukyu archipelago to the south and Hokkaido (formerly Ezo) and the Kurile Islands in the north began to be viewed as "frontier cultures" from the sixteenth century onward. Until the early eighteenth century they were regarded as foreign lands outside "Japan proper." Eventually they were incorporated into Japan and their populations forcibly assimilated. The eighteenth-century policy of Japanization of the Ainu was a response to the encroaching Russification practiced by the Russian empire: "In response to growing foreign pressure, the Japanese government redefined the nation's boundaries, in 1869 incorporating the Land of the Ainu under the new name of Hokkaido, and ten years later unilaterally declaring its control over the old Ryukyu kingdom (which was now to be designated Okinawa prefecture)."[6] Beyond the discourse of *minzoku* (Volk), "race" thinking (*jinshu*) played a major part particularly during the Meiji period.[7]

The Ainu Emancipation League, founded in 1972, claimed the status of indigenous people for the Ainu as a response to development projects in Hokkaido and built on the Burakumin rights movement in Japan and on international momentum. Japan recognized the Ainu as a minority only in 1991 and in 1997 as an indigenous people. Okinawans sought recognition for the Ryukyu archipelago as an "Okinawan cultural sphere." Hanazaki Kohei comments, "Ainu and Okinawan experience also suggests the need for a new look, not just at Japanese history, but also at world history from the viewpoint of ethnic groups who were conquered and controlled, and makes us reflect on the discrimination inherent in the ideology of assimilation born from the processes of civilisation and modernisation."[8]

Now, like all countries, Japan faces the challenge of internationalization (*kokusaika*) and globalization (*gurō baruka*).[9] Growing labor migration in Japan since the 1980s is viewed in terms of human rights, and multiculturalism is rarely talked about. McCormack, one of the editors of a volume on Japan's multiculturalism, observes that "the creation of a multicultural future depends on, and is fed by, the discovery of the multiculturalism of the past."[10] He further notes that "its deepening engagement with the world raises questions about orthodox formulations of 'Japaneseness' stemming from antiquity," and adds, "Japan's modern triumph was achieved at the cost of a series of negations and fabrications about its origins and essence which are now increasingly visible. . . . The myth of 'Japaneseness' as the quality of a monocultural, blood-united, preordained people confronts the historical reality of the emergence of the earliest Japanese states out of a complex of more or less equal communities, which traded, contended and communicated across the islands and peninsulas of the adjacent continent."[11] German observers, according to McCormack, share in some respects parallel experiences and are particularly sensitive to Japan's problem of isolation in the region and in the world. The challenge facing Japan is "to renounce the mask of 'Japaneseness' as a unique, imperial essence that it has worn for over a thousand years."[12]

The past is multiethnic, yet the *archeology of ethnicity* is a problematic enterprise because of the tendency to read the present backward, to essentialize identities and ignore the changes that have taken place over time. Each subsequent formation is a vortex in which previous relations are reworked and rearticulated. In identifying archeological "cultures," nineteenth-century archeology focused on either linguistic or "racial" lineages, and both approaches sought to conflate race, language, and culture. In the 1930s "race" was replaced by "culture," and "nationalist archeology" sought to achieve reconstructions of static "museum cultures." Contemporary ethno-archeological research finds, however, that "there is rarely a one-to-one correlation between cultural similarities and differences and ethnic groups . . . that the kinds of material culture involved in ethnic symbolism can vary between different groups, and that the expression of ethnic boundaries may involve a limited range of material culture, whilst other material forms and styles may be shared across group boundaries."[13] Also in Japanese archeology there is "an unhealthy preoccupation with the ethnic group" and an attempt to link past hypothetical groups to modern ethnic groups in a dubious "search for ethnic origins."[14]

China is widely viewed, in some ways like Japan, as a society that has been continuous over a long stretch of time and has been relatively homogeneous, clustered around the Han Chinese with ethnic groups such as Mongolians, Uyghurs, and minorities in Yunnan and southern China, at the margins. In fact, this matches the self-image of fifteenth-century Ming China. After the Chinese state expansion to Inner Asia in the seventeenth and eighteenth centuries under Manchu rule, China redefined itself as a multiethnic state.[15] Indeed, China has been ruled by non-Han rulers and dynasties more often, longer, and during more significant periods than by Han. Major dynasties have come from China's margins of Turkic-speaking peoples, Mongolians (Yuan dynasty), Manchurians (Qing), and other northerners (Liao).[16] China's centers of power shifted repeatedly in all directions, as did the size of the state. The "Han" are an ethno-linguistic category rather than an ethnic group, an ethnic canopy whose origins are lost in time. During several periods China consisted of multiple states. Through much of Chinese history what mattered was whether power centers, such as Chang'an, controlled the trade and caravan routes of Central Asia. Relations with Korea were another concern. Major considerations were conquest and vulnerability to conquest, notably by Tibet and Turkic-speaking peoples in the west, expansion toward the extreme west and extreme east, and protection against the nomadic peoples in the north.

Chinese culture evolved as a composite shaped by the general Asian confluence of cultures with major influences from India (including Buddhism and spices), Central Asia (trade links, music), Southeast Asia (spices), Persia, Turkic-speaking peoples and Mongolians. China coheres on cultural grounds, not on the basis of an ethnic definition. Confucianism emerged as the umbrella under which outlying groups were integrated. What mattered in relation to minorities, for instance, in Hainan, was whether they adopted Chinese cultural attributes in clothing, hair style, and language.[17] Thus it is appropriate to view China, like Japan, as a rainbow culture ethnically and culturally.

To return to general history, at times cultivators were conquered by subsequent groups. Seafarers established settlements wide a field such as Phoenicians in Carthage, Barcelona and Marseille, Greeks across the Mediterranean world, Berbers and Arabs during the Muslim hegemony of the Mediterranean, and Vikings and Danes from the British Isles and Bretagne to the Crimea and Sicily. Conquering peoples established cultures of rule or were assimilated over time, such as the Mongols in China, who established the Yuan dynasty (1206–1368 CE), and Manchus, who founded the Qing dynasty (1616–1911). Indo-European language speakers allegedly established the caste system in northern India.

Superimposed on and interspersed with this confluence of peoples were empires, in the sense of institutionalized conquest cultures of some duration. Egypt, Mesopotamia, the Athenian empire, the Achaemenid Empire, Alexander's empire, the Roman Empire, Byzantium, and the Mongols, Mughals, and Ottomans established trade networks, infrastructures, and institutions that wired geographies, cultures, and languages. Thebes, Luxor, Babylon, Persepolis, Athens, Rome, Constantinople, Istanbul, Toledo, Córdoba, Lahore, and Delhi were multicultural hubs at the confluence of cultures. The Tower of Babel and the Library of Alexandria are among the icons of early multiculturalism.

Cultural influences from Persia to Egypt brought the Mithras cult, Egyptian sun worship, and Babylonian and Greek gods to Rome. Tacitus contrasted the cultural mix of imperial Rome with the "purity" of the Germanic tribes and believed that Rome's cultural mix brought about its decadence and eventually its downfall. Echoed in Edward Gibbon's eighteenth-century study of the *Decline and Fall of the Roman Empire*, this conservative view deeply influenced European elites and aristocracies.[18]

Networks of power were also civilizational configurations—worlds of religion, art and science, language and learning, technological transmission, and symbolic exchange. Myths and legends, literacy, numeracy, writing, sciences, arts and crafts, and religions circulated in and across these civilizational networks. Some religions lingered as minority religions, such as the fire worship of the Zoroastrian Parsees; some vanished or were eradicated, such as the Manichaeism of the Cathars; some survived diasporas, such as Judaism; some were absorbed in dominant religions, such as Sufism, or merged with them, such as Bon which in combination with Buddhism generated Tibetan Buddhism; and a handful achieved the status of "world religions."

This checkerboard confluence of peoples and cultures comprises the second to the fourth multiethnicity in the historical schema of multiethnicity in Table 1.1. Each layer represents a stratum and dominant phase.

Table 1.1.   Layers of multiethnicity over time

	Multiethnicity	Key words
I	Indigenes, cultivators, pastoralists	Land, ecology
II	Plus traders, artisans	Trade centers, networks, routes
III	Conquest formations	Institutions of rule (helots, caste, estates)
IV	Empires	Slavery, colonial rule, law
V	Nation states	Borders, crossborder groups; law, minorities
VI	Multiculturalism	Immigration, law, policy, popular culture

The sequence and chronology are rudimentary and approximate and cannot be uniform across the world (in some instances conquest cultures and empires were a single formation; nation formation took place early on in old continuous nations such as Egypt, Persia, and China, though the dominant group and center of power within them shifted repeatedly).

Multiethnicity in India begins with the Adivasis (the collective name for the tribal peoples) in phase I, the formation of Dalits originally took shape during the phase III of conquest, and "communalism," the term commonly used for multicultural diversity, derives from the Hindu and Muslim "communities" distinguished under British rule during phase IV. The nation state formation of phase V came with the Indo-Pakistan partition, the problem of Kashmir, and, later, Assam. In Latin America, differentiation among the indigenes took shape during conquests in phase III, such as Aztec, Maya, and Inca rule. The division between the indigenes and those of European descent dates back to the colonial conquest phase IV, which introduced colonial slavery, mines, and plantations as another vortex of differentiation. With the nation state of phase V came policies of mestizaje, mestizos of many stripes, and regional and minority issues such as Miskitos in Nicaragua and Afro-Caribbean groups in Venezuela and Colombia. The contemporary phase VI includes new immigrants such as the Japanese in Peru and Brazil. In the United States, the status of Native Americans has been changing throughout from phase I onward. Phase IV bequeathed slavery, and the Civil War of phase V led to the spatial reorganization of multiethnicity in reservations, Jim Crow segregation, and ghettoes. The contemporary phase VI reframes old multiethnicity as multiculturalism alongside new immigrants. In Rwanda the relationship between cultivators and pastoralists of phase I was wired into wider networks during phase II, affected by conquest episodes in phase III, rearticulated under Belgian colonialism in phase IV (which categorized the fuzzy identities of cattle herders and cultivators as ethnic "Tutsis" and "Hutus"), politicized during the nation state phase V and influenced by International Monetary Fund (IMF) policies and regional and political dynamics during phase VI.

This means that the "pathos of difference" has long lineages with many twists and turns that are deeply engrained in local and regional history. Signs and rituals marking difference, distance, and rank, boundaries, markers, and stereotypes with many coded and layered meanings existed between cultivators and hunter-gatherers, between sedentary peoples and nomadic pastoralists, between skilled townspeople and country bumpkins, between rulers, warriors, and subjects, between locals and sojourners, between clean and unclean trades, between manufacturing and agriculture, between high- and low-tech industry, between finance and mere production, between high finance and retail money lending, between global cities and cities, between mega cities and global cities, and on and on. Each subsequent production threshold involves disdain for prior levels, not necessarily so, but as an overall trend because of the rearrangement of the pecking order—"all that is solid melts into air." This does not, however, produce a linear logic of "progress" and humiliation. First, each mode of production depends on earlier forms of production for inputs; the pathos of difference rather serves as a device to manage the terms of exchange. Second, even as the earlier production technique is disparaged it is also romanticized and is the object of nostalgia: hunters and fishers are "freer" than cultivators; country air is healthier, more restful and virtuous than urban life, and so on. Third, there are developmental stages to these relations (early, middle, late); post-industrialism relates to agriculture on different terms than does industrialism; the survival technology of the prior phase becomes the leisure technology of the next level of producers (the gentleman hunter, the fox hunt) or a premium or luxury product (organic farming). Fourth, what often matters is a gradient between ecological niches—such as cultivators in the valleys disparaging mountain peoples or the inhabitants of the forests and deserts (declared "wild" in many cultures). "Progress" is fraught with ambiguity and nostalgia; hence the profound ambivalence of representations of and attitudes towards "others."[19]

A basic reason many policies to address cultural difference fail and fall short is that they are conceived in *one* particular framework and address one type of conflict, assuming that this is the template for *all* differences, overlooking that diversity is historically layered and follows diverse templates.

Each form of discrimination served as a template for subsequent ones, though not in a linear manner. In the flow of cultures, categories were created, resignified, projected as pristine identities back in time, intersected, and resignified again. For example, it was "the geographical term 'Hindu,' coined by the Muslims, which was finally adopted even by the British rulers to describe all native Indians other than the monotheist Muslims. . . . It was as a response to Muslim rule in Sindh that Shankara Acharya set about structuring Hindu society around the basis of a caste system." Thus "Hinduism" took shape as a political construct in response to Muslim power; "the challenge-response syndrome of Hindu-Muslim revivalism intensified with the rise of foreign power."[20] To escape outcast status, many Dalits converted to Islam and in the twentieth century to Buddhism and Christianity. Hence the categories—Hindu, Muslim, caste, Dalit, India, or race, people, nation, tribe, ethnicity, religion, culture—derive from relational sets that are meaningful in certain contexts; from a specific viewpoint located in time and space they seem like hard, unassailable identities, whereas from a historical viewpoint they are floating signifiers.

The nation state is a recent vortex in which all these relations are refigured. The nation state does not erase old forms of multiethnicity but is superimposed on and interspersed with them, not in their pristine form but in dynamic forms that include prior rounds of change. The nation state reorganizes multiethnicity in political opportunity structures (elections, parties, factions, regional uneven development, crossborder links), which contemporary globalization alters anew (policies of international institutions, transnational non-governmental organizations [NGOs] and social movements, indigenous peoples networks).

Nation and ethnicity

Multiethnicity precedes the nation, but to understand the meanings of ethnicity now one must understand the nation. To understand how cultural difference is constructed is to understand the formation and politics of national identity. The categorization and interpretation of ethnicity, politics of difference, and politics of recognition follow from the nation. Understanding nations is a historical undertaking. Analytical frameworks such as the difference between civic and ethnic nationalism matter but are incomplete. National identity is a historical process; ethnicity, identity politics, and multiculturalism are phases in this ongoing process. From a historical point of view, nation formation is a dominant form of ethnicity. In short, nationhood is *dominant ethnicity* and minorities or ethnic groups represent *subaltern ethnicity*.

The establishment of boundaries and borders is a gradual process taking shape as an expression of state power and in relation to external threats. For a long time boundaries were fuzzy; the demarcation of boundaries and their geographical identification on maps is a recent development. In Europe the Treaty of Westphalen in 1648 inaugurated the modern state system; yet Germany and Italy took shape as nation states only late in the nineteenth century, and some of their borders were settled only after World War II.

The existence of crossborder cultural formations is a reminder of the recent formation of nation states. There are Malay Muslims in southern

Thailand and Tai speakers in Yunnan, China; there are Karen in Burma and Thailand. Bangladesh was East Bengal. Pashto is spoken on both sides of the border between Afghanistan and Pakistan. Baluchistan straddles Pakistan and Iran. Ewe live on the coast in eastern Ghana, Togo and Benin. There are Mayans in Chiapas, Mexico and Chiapas, Guatemala. Jívaros are in Peru and Ecuador. Siberian and Alaskan Natives were part of a large, dynamic indigenous region of Beringia. Basques are on both sides of the Pyrenees in Spain and France. Multilingualism in Belgium, Switzerland, Italy, Finland, and Estonia is a reminder of the composite nature of these nations. Crossborder bilingualism, kinship ties and shared cultures are universal phenomena, also on tragic borders such as the border created by the partition of India and Pakistan where cultures share well over a thousand years of common history.[21]

Geographic contiguity invariably means cultural contiguity and this transcends borders. Borders are expressions of power equations and ethnicities are expressions of cultural identities that are usually much older. This is sometimes evoked under the heading of "border consciousness."[22] Korea and Japan did not exist as distinct entities until the sixth century. Southern Sweden (Scania, Skåne) was part of the Danish-Norwegian union until 1658, and Finland was part of Sweden until 1809. Andalusia has been part of many realms. Yugoslavia was a geopolitical formation superimposed astride old borders of the Roman Empire and Byzantium, the Latin and Greek Church, and the Ottoman Empire and Islam. These prehistories shape local attitudes.

The world of the nations was a multiethnic world already. Nations, old and new, arose from and were superimposed on existing intercultural formations.[23] This applies to old nations such as China, to later ones such as Japan, and to more recent formations. To understand postnational multiculturalism we must understand prenational multiethnicity as the infrastructure of contemporary multiculturalism that infuses it with diverse meanings. This might not mean much from distant or global viewpoints but is profoundly meaningful locally. It might not matter from the standpoint of Paris, Madrid, Tokyo, Beijing, Bangkok, Sao Paolo, or Mexico City, but it does matter in Brittany, Andalusia, Okinawa, Yunnan, southern Thailand, Mato Grosso, and Chiapas.

National identity and consciousness are layered; the nation is an assemblage of regional differences. French cuisine is a confluence of regional cuisines and specialties: Elzas choucroute, bouillabaisse from Marseille, boeuf bourguignon, butter from Bretagne, Médoc from Bordeaux. The Burgundians are originally a people of Scandinavian origin. The center is a center by virtue of the peripheries; peripheries in turn are centers in relation to older or different radii. Nations typically unravel at the borders; they come loose at the seams. Sociologists now no longer take for granted that their object of study is the "society" (read: nation, state) but study social networks in which "societies" are zones of relative high-density networks.[24] In the border areas, however, crossborder networks may be denser than the links to the national center. Trieste is an Italian port but owes its character to its location adjacent to Slovenia, its history as the port of the Habsburg Empire, a frontier of the Roman Empire and headquarters of Attila (in nearby Aquila). National identity is layered like marble, and like a hologram it looks different when viewed from different angles, from the center and from the borders. Visit the national museum and it tells one tale; visit the regional or folk museum and it may tell a quite different story. The national history museum in Thessalonica does not show a shred of Ottoman influence; the Ottoman past is completely erased and plastered over with a solid layer of national pride. But the regional folklore museum nearby displays peasant costumes that retain obvious Ottoman influences and old maps that show shepherd mountain trails crisscrossing the national borders. Folk culture is the id of the nation and retains that which national culture suppresses. Prenational legacies inform local and national perspectives on contemporary multiculturalism.

The inner circle of national culture is in many cases the culture of monarchs and nobles, the clergy, the bourgeoisie and haute bourgeoisie. Guides to European capitals such as Stockholm and Copenhagen often start from the royal palace and adjacent churches and then move outward to artisan and merchant quarters, market squares and then working class neighborhoods and suburbs. In the center of Yogyakarta and Solo, two classical Javanese cities, the sultan's kraton is surrounded by the artisans' quarters who serve the court and in the next ring are the merchants' streets and market squares. Peasant culture is yet another strand.

Strata and strands of indigenes, nomads, cultivators, conquerors, traders, craftsmen, and pilgrims coexist and interact. From a political economy viewpoint they have been associated with "modes of production" in a convention that goes back to Adam Ferguson and the Scottish Enlightenment and was reworked in Victorian anthropology and Marxist stages theory. Typically this ignored ethnic differences. From this angle, multiethnicity refers to the coexistence of peoples practicing different modes of production, as social and cultural articulations of modes of production. This view tends to be static, ignores the dynamism of "tradition," is often deceptive, and has been manipulated to justify state and colonial policies. The depiction of "savages" in the Americas and Australia as hunter-gatherers and their representation as "contemporary ancestors" justified the *terra nullius* fiction of colonizers.[25] Indigenous peoples often were or became cultivators over time. Table 1.2 is a schematic, simplified rendition of relations among times, demographics, and technologies.

Table 1.2. Multiethnicity over time

Multiethnicity	Layers	Political economies
Premodern	Indigenes, settlers, nomads	Hunter-gatherers, fishers, cultivators, pastoralists
	Conquering peoples	Warriors, rulers, caste, estates
	Traders, sojourners	Trade centers and networks, craftsmen, skilled elites, urban-rural differences
Early modern	Colonialism	Colonial division of labor, slavery, race; craft manufactures
Modern	Imperialism, neocolonialism	Industrialism, unequal trade, transnational corporations
Postmodern	Contemporary globalization	Flexible accumulation, multiculturalism

European colonialism and imperialism gradually gained an edge over many formations because of its geographical and commercial scope (which included the gold and silver of the New World and the triangular trade) and industrial techniques. This configuration produced multiethnicity mark IV. J. S. Furnivall referred to this formation rather stiffly as the "plural society" (discussed in later chapters), but Anthony King notes,

> The cultural conditions of a so-called postmodernity—irony, pastiche, the mixing of different histories, schizophrenia, cultural chasms, fragmentation, incoherence, disjunction of supposedly modern and premodern cultures . . . were characteristic of colonial societies, cultures and environments on the "global periphery" (in Calcutta, Hong Kong, Rio de Janeiro or Batavia/Jakarta) decades, if not centuries, before they appeared in Europe or the US. . . . What this suggests, therefore, is that what some have labeled "postmodern" culture pre-dated what they have labeled "modern" culture, but then this is only possible if we look at modernity in terms of space as well as time.[26]

The multicultural confluence of peoples, styles, and times in the colonial ports and cities was "postmodern" *avant la lettre* and thus, with a delectable twist of irony, postmodernity in the colonies preceded the formation of modernity in the metropolitan world. This has been followed by and interspersed with two other dynamics. In the new nations taking shape in the former colonies, old identities have been reworked alongside new migrations in a setting of postcolonial multiethnicity, whereas in the metropolitan world this phase involves post-imperial and labor migrations, and both worlds meet in contemporary accelerated globalization.

Nations arise as cultural formations on the basis of language and other cultural commonalities or, alternatively, as political projects. A familiar distinction runs between cultural and political understandings of the nation. Johann Gottfried Herder, the German "father of nationalism," viewed the nation as a cultural entity founded in particular on a common language. Uli Linke's study *Blood and Nation* traces the lineages of ethnic nationalism to the middle ages and its foundations in the "historic unconscious."[27] But there is a much simpler explanation. The 1648 Treaty of Westphalen, the end of the Thirty Years War in Germany, is generally hailed as the foundation of the modern state system since it established the principle of territorial state sovereignty. What is rarely mentioned, however, is that "the peacemakers of 1648 also imposed upon Germany a political settlement that confirmed and legitimized the atomization of Germany by recognizing over 300 German states as sovereign entities. . . . German disunity and powerlessness thus became part of the natural European order, acquiesced to by all Great Powers, including the larger German states."[28] Thus modernization of the state system in Western Europe was obtained at the price of institutionalizing a system of princely states and staggering particularism in Germany whose consequences were to last into the mid-twentieth century. What the German states had in common was language. So German ethnic nationalism should be viewed not as a medieval relic but as an adaptation to externally imposed power politics, and Herder's argument on language as the foundation of the nation must be understood as a cultural politics that was prompted by and sought to overcome the settlement of 1648.

The Romantic nation, notes Van de Putte, is constituted under the sign of particularity and must be understood through its Volksgeist in which state and ethnicity are fused; since in this view "the fusion of demos and ethnos is precisely the natural foundation of the state . . . democracy must be national democracy."[29] This conception of the nation state spread from Germany to Switzerland and Sweden, to central and eastern Europe, and shaped Theodor Herzl's Zionism and Israel's career as the Jewish state. Japan has subscribed to ethnic nationalism notably since the Meiji period. In 1939, under the influence of western ideas, Siam changed its name to Thailand—land of the Thai, an ethnicization of national identity that marginalizes non-Thais (such as ethnic Chinese, Malays in southern Thailand, and hill peoples in the north) and continues to be challenged up to now.[30]

In Western Europe, the contrary trajectory prevailed, from the political to the cultural, not from the cultural to the political. "This was only natural," Cobban notes, "because . . . in their medieval origins, nations like the French, English, Portuguese, and Spanish were built up by the political power of strong monarchies."[31] This is the basis for the idea that "the nation is the first empire" and the saying "It took two hundred years to create Frenchmen."[32] So this produces two configurations, the state nation and the nation state, and two kinds of nationalism, which are now termed civic and ethnic, or republican and tribal nationalism.

The actual political formations, however, are not that different. Karl Renner and Otto Bauer viewed the nation as *Schicksalsgemeinschaft*, a community united by fate; whatever this fate may be—a common culture, a sequence of political events or both—state formation and republican institutions are an institutional stratum emerging from or superimposed on, but not annulling, underlying social formations. Civic nationalism overlays and coexists with ethnic nationalism. Ethnic identities, regardless of civic institutions, manifest at different social levels. There are outsider and insider minorities and outside borders and "inner frontiers" such as the colonial color bar and institutional racism. Contemporary studies of discrimination find institutionalized discrimination of minorities in admission to schools, jobs, housing, and so on, regardless whether nationalism is civic or ethnic.

Also in central and eastern Europe, historical processes and political factors—such as the disintegration of the Habsburg and Ottoman Empires and the demise of the USSR—created states for Poles, Hungarians, Czechs, Greeks, Romanians, Bulgarians, Serbs, Croats, and Lithuanians. Katunarić notes that "at the beginning of the nineteenth century there existed in Europe only eight nation states with more or less developed standard languages, a tradition of high culture, and established ruling classes: the English, French, Spanish (Castilian), Dutch, Portuguese, Danish, Swedish, and later Russian nation-states."[33] Most of these were state-nations that *over time created* linguistic and cultural unity rather than arising from them. So the distinction between civic and ethnic nationalism is pertinent but relative. Actual nations, notes Van de Putte, "are always situated somewhere on a continuum between the revolutionary and the Romantic nation. . . . The liberal nation state and its laws, therefore, are never entirely ethnically and culturally neutral. They are permeated by the ethos and the form of life of a particular majority. There is always a culture which is the culture of public life."[34] Besides, there are marked differences among civic nationalisms, for instance, between the French unitary state refusal to recognize cultural differences among citizens and the American Republic as a settler and slaveholding nation from the outset.

Civic and ethnic conceptions of nationhood influence policy and legislation, notably citizenship rights. Civic nationalism grants citizenship on the basis of residence (*jus solis*) and ethnic nationalism on the basis of ethnicity or blood ties (*jus sanguinis*). Civic and ethnic understandings of nationhood and citizenship matter in how the national social contract is understood, how migration is regulated, how minorities are treated and immigrants are received. They shape the terms on which the nation and ethnicity interact.

These differences also influence understandings of culture. Aram Yengoyan notes that it is French civilization (and seldom French culture) in contrast to German culture (and almost never, German civilization). A culture model is bounded, limited, not expansive, and hardly universalistic in scope; while the notion of civilization tends to stress an unbounded quality which the French have always asserted and valued. . . . Where universalism and unboundedness are rejected by German culture and thought for the sake of developing true German values, the French see themselves as the heir apparent to the true growth of civilization. . . . It is exactly on this point that German intellectual and cultural thought differs from that of its historical neighbors and (this) is evident in a range of writers and social theorists from Thomas Mann to Georg Simmel.[35]

I find this too schematic and generalizing (German idealism was quite expansive), and I'm not happy with the word "always" (intellectuals of the new Germany such as Habermas, Enzensberger and Ulrich Beck strike expansive cosmopolitan notes), but there is some truth to this especially before the war. Different understandings of culture and civilization inform politics of representation (which is taken up in chapter 6).

A report about the resignation of a chief executive at the firm Nike is headlined "Another outsider falls casualty to Nike's insider culture": "Nike executives, who are fond of starting meetings by playing videos of Olympic runners triumphantly crossing the finish line, say that it takes 20 years to fit in at the famously insular sneaker company."[36]

If insider cultures develop in corporations a few decades old, then nations that have been in existence for a hundred years or more and are often based on or include social formations that are much older still surely have insider cultures. So both ethnic and republican formations share tribal features, informal cultures tucked within formal institutions, with different rules and gradients of inclusion and exclusion. Business anthropology—with its etiquette guides to manners for businessmen operating across cultures—recognizes the club character of informal cultures.[37]

Ethnicity

So how does ethnicity fit in? Ethnicity derives from the Greek *éthnos*, an equivalent of the Latin-origin *nation* (from *natio*, birth) and the Germanic *Volk*. A study of word origins notes, "However, its use in the Septuagint (the early Greek translation of the Old Testament) to render the Hebrew word for 'gentile' led to its derived adjective *ethnikós*, and hence Latin *ethnicus*, meaning virtually 'heathen.' It was in this sense that English first acquired the word ('an ethnic and a pagan king,' Nicholas Udall, *Paraphrase of Erasmus*, 1545); indeed, early etymologists thought that the English *heathen* came from *ethnos*."[38] This was the original connotation of ethnicity in English.

In French, the term *ethnie* appeared in 1787 and likewise referred to "heathens" or non-Christians. By the mid-nineteenth century, considering that Judeo-Christianity was the only civilization worthy of the name, this encompassed all "savages."[39] From this time dates the colonial assumption that ethnicity (and "tribes") is a peculiar habit of lesser breeds, whereas nationhood is reserved to the civilized peoples. Part of this is the wider conjunction between modernity and nationalism. In the 1880s, at the time of the new imperialism, the terms "ethnography" and "ethnology," based on ethnos, were popularized through German social science. Ethnography carries a neutral meaning and a major anthropology journal is called *Ethnos*. Etymologically and in European usage ethnicity refers both to *éthnos* or people and to *ethnikós* or savage people. This distinction does not exist in Greek, old or current; it derives from Old Testament translations of Greek and ramifications of this translation in European languages.

In nineteenth-century Europe the question of "unrepresented peoples" was a major concern; the "national question" stood on a par with the "social question." For Marx and Engels it was subsidiary to the social question and the proletarian revolution to come. The Hungarians, Poles, and other unrepresented peoples, however, were never described as ethnic groups; they were referred to as peoples, nations, nationalities, and, in some places, minorities. This was the terminology of the Austrian school and writings such as Stalin's 1914 monograph *Marxism and the National Question*.[40] Within Europe the term "ethnicity" was used only in the course of the twentieth century but is now common. Thus, ethnicity as a term bears the stamp of a *period* (the nineteenth century onward), a *place* (colonial countries), and a *relationship* (a cultural and political hierarchy). Whether and on what terms it applies outside this relationship and to other groups should not be taken for granted. The distinction between nation and ethnicity, between *éthnos* and *ethnikós*, and the association between ethnicity and heathen/savage has gradually faded in the course of the twentieth century. Yet faint traces of the pejorative associations of ethnicity echo in the common view that ethnicity is somehow a lesser nationhood and ethnic nationalism or ethnonationalism is equivalent to minority nationalism or micronationalism. The English thesaurus that comes with the word processing program in which this text is written (Microsoft Word) gives "heathen" as a synonym for "ethnicity." Discussing African literature, Christopher Miller comments, "To think anthropologically is to validate *ethnicity* as a category, and this has become a problematic idea."[41]

Taken in this sense, ethnic politics is a politics of assertion on the part of "others" protesting their subordination or exclusion by the state or the nation, or competing with other ethnic groups. Many nationalisms that emerged after decolonization have since turned into forms of domination of internal "others." It is paradoxical and meaningful that the contemporary wave of ethnic politics comes at a time when the epoch of the nation is past its peak, a time of accelerated globalization and emerging postnationalism. The struggles of decolonization were part of a dialectics of empire and emancipation that was primarily played out between metropolitan and colonized nations.[42] Contemporary ethnic politics may be interpreted both as a continuation of old multiethnicity in a different setting and as the dialectics of empire and emancipation, now in a finer grain of history, descending from the national to group levels and yet part of a global dialectics of domination and emancipation. That, at least, is a broad sweep and optimistic take on ethnic politics.

Ethnicity can no longer be dismissed on the premises of modernization theory or Marxism for these paradigms themselves are in question. Neither can ethnicity be taken at face value because it is a container with uncertain contents, because it is fluid, protean, and hydra-headed, because doing so would yield an archipelago of particularisms, and because there is "life after ethnicity." If ethnicity in one sense represents a repudiation of a false universalism that paraded as a universal subject but was in reality exclusionary, coded, and stratified, what then emerges on the horizon beyond ethnicity? What are the points of reference for a new universalism that starts out from cultural pluralism? One route toward a new universalism is to take as one's point of departure the various arrangements between nation and ethnicity that have developed in the recent past—such as federalism and multiculturalism. A different route is to start out from the time before the nations and to treat nationhood as another ethnicity, which happens to be dominant during a particular period.

It is not clear whether ethnicity is in the nation or the nation is in ethnicity; it depends on how and in what time frame we approach the units. Ethnicity inhabits multiple time frames. In the West ethnicity is usually (or, rather, invariably) thought of as more recent than the nation because recent immigrants are viewed as "ethnic." Elsewhere it is often the other way round; the nation is recent and ethnicity old. Thus T. K. Oommen notes, "It is interesting to recall here the . . . answer Wali Khan, the doyen of Pashtun nationalism, gave in 1974 when questioned whether he was a Muslim, a Pakistani, or Pashtun first? He answered that he was a 'six-thousand-year-old Pashtun, a thousand-year-old Muslim and a 27-year-old Pakistani.'"[43]

According to the grand old man of Sindhi nationalism, G. M. Syed, a similar long memory applies to Sindhi identity: "Sindh has always been there, Pakistan is a passing show. Sindh is a fact, Pakistan is a fiction. . . . Sindhi language is 2000 years old, Urdu is only 250 years old."[44] As mentioned earlier, Sindh is the origin of the geographical term "Hindu" coined by Muslims. Research into the cultural heritage of Sindh and the Indus valley confirm these lineages.[45] Let's note that although these are counter-points to the western view, they are also primordialist, essentializing angles on ethnicity—which is problematized in the next chapter.

The notion of the ethnic origins of nations is problematic because the meaning of ethnicity changes over time and because ethnic identification often follows state or nation formation, rather than the other way round: "'Ethnicities' . . . are largely the product, rather than the foundation, of nation-states. . . . The ever more powerful structures of central state control—be they colonial or autochthonous, imperial or national—are what generate and motivate the new *need* for ethnic autonomy, and even, in many cases, the actual sense of ethnic identity on which the latter is predicated."[46] Instances where state formation preceded nation formation are numerous, particularly in the postcolonial world. Besides, many societies are multinational in composition. In such cases state-led efforts at national integration and development may provoke ethnic mobilization. This encompasses ethnic politics in the West such as emancipation movements of African Americans and Native Americans in the United States as well as regional autonomy movements in Europe.

It is a sound principle of poststructuralist methodology that identities are relational and constructed in relation to others rather than given. So if ethnic identity is relational, then how does ethnic identification come about? The theme of ethnicities-in-relation concerns an obvious point, that ethnicization is a social process, and a subtle point, that in many situations new subjects are termed "ethnic" whereas established subjects and the dominant group remain outside the field of vision. This refers again to the subtle difference between *éthnos* and *ethnikós*. Ella Shohat makes a point about American cinema that is of wider relevance:

> The . . . assumption that some films are "ethnic" whereas others are not is ultimately based on the view that certain groups are ethnic whereas others are not. The marginalization of "ethnicity" reflects the imaginary of the dominant group which envisions itself as the "universal" or the "essential" American nation, and thus somehow "beyond" or "above" ethnicity. The very word *ethnic*, then, reflects a peripheralizing strategy premised on an implicit contrast between "norm'" and "other," much as the term *minority* often carries with it an implication of minor, lesser, or subaltern.[47]

Inscribed then in the terminology of ethnicity is a coded relationship to power. Decoding this relationship must be the first step in the analysis. With regard to ethnic identity formation (ethnogenesis, ethnicization), an elementary starting point is that ethnicity is frequently imposed and that what often precedes it is a process of *othering* by a dominant group. Accordingly, ethnic identity may derive not from "roots" but from subordination imposed through social labeling, policies or legislation, which may subsequently be internalized. Hence it makes sense to consider first cultural strategies of domination. In the West, the study of *whiteness* should precede an analysis of ethnic movements because ethnic movements occur in a field that is *already* ethnically defined—though from the viewpoint of the dominant group this ethnic character is conventionally and conveniently perceived as national culture. Stuart Hall observes, "ethnicity in the form of a culturally constructed sense of Englishness and a particularly closed, exclusive and regressive form of English national identity, is one of the core characteristics of British racism today."[48] So the ethnic character of the center, the dominant group and cultural canon is also at issue.

This relates to the question of "whiteness as an absent centre,"[49] a center that is absent due to the denial of imperialism. A sizeable share of western imperialism and colonialism can be interpreted in terms of ethnic or racial strategies such as the White Man's Burden, *mission civilisatrice* and Manifest Destiny. Besides, there are specific episodes of racial or ethnic mobilization from above such as political anti-Semitism, Jim Crow, and Anglo-Saxonism. In the late nineteenth century Anglo-Saxonism served as a hegemonic ideology in Britain and globally. It was part of Manifest Destiny,[50] provided a vocabulary that linked leading strata in Britain and the U.S. and played a part in the hegemonic succession from the British Empire to the United States at the turn of the century.[51]

In colonial settler societies in the Americas, Africa, Australia, New Zealand, Israel, and Taiwan the relationship between nation and ethnicity is more obvious and salient than elsewhere. But it generally matters, also in contemporary multicultural societies, to *first* problematize the dominant cultural ethos and examine national hegemony as a constructed identity. In *The Wages of Whiteness*, David Roediger takes up the social construction of race and the "struggle for whiteness" by the Irish and other immigrants in the United States.[52]

In many instances ethnicity is first defined by the nation. Native Americans predate the Europeans, yet "it was the European who created the Indian."[53] The category "American Indian" owes its existence to European overseas expansion, the expanding western frontier and the policy of Indian Removal, and Native American nationalism developed later. Ethnicity then implies a relationship. The construction of ethnicity takes place through a mutual labeling process: "This labeling, the mutual process of identity construction, happens at ethnic boundaries, and both affects and is affected by the economic and political positions of groups."[54]

For a long time many western countries were "stable" in terms of ethnic relations. Ethnic identities were subsumed under the umbrella of the nation as regional identities, such as Ligurians in Liguria and Occitanians in Gascogne. Ethnicity occupied a marginal, often decorative status on the

periphery of the institutional and cultural mainstream. In the U.S., according to bell hooks, "The commodification of Otherness has been so successful because it is offered as a new delight, more intense, more satisfying
than normal ways of doing and feeling. Within commodity culture, ethnicity becomes spice, seasoning that can liven up the dull dish that is
mainstream white culture."[55] In the U.S. this is the familiar situation of a
stable core of WASP hegemony with a sprinkling of "ethnic neighborhoods" available for "slumming" and spicy variety. Thus "Little Italy" can
be consumed as a tourist commodity complete with local color, ethnic
atmosphere, and cuisine.[56] But due to demographic, economic, and cultural changes, this core-periphery relationship is no longer stable. The
passing of WASP hegemony[57] accounts for the ferocity of the battles over
political correctness, school curricula, identity politics, and the nation's
fragmentation or "Lebanonization." Here ethnicity, identity politics, and
multiculturalism are vocabularies for the renegotiation of hegemony.

In recent years the status distinction between nation and ethnicity has
been gradually fading; ethnicity is viewed more and more as a form of
"peoplehood" and the distinction between nation and ethnicity fades into
the background.[58] Thus media now refer to Protestants and Catholics in
Northern Ireland as "ethnic minorities" (until recently "sectarianism" was
the common terminology), a shift that reflects secularization and depoliti-
cization. "Ethnonationalism" merges both notions and denotes a kind of
second order nationalism. The distinction between nation and ethnicity is
fraying also due to criticisms of immigrants who resist being classified in
pejorative terms as "minorities" or "ethnics" and see no grounds why the
dominant center should not also be understood as another ethnicity. We
might term this sensibility the decolonization of ethnicity. Multicultural
societies are undergoing shifts of hegemony that affect the very terms of
analysis and change their meaning. Eliminating the status difference
between nation and ethnicity would create a level cultural playing field.
Probably this also reflects the diminishing status of nations in the context
of regionalization and globalization.

Originally ethnicity stands to nation as the lesser, minor, and other, and
as earlier. As such, nations and ethnicities have been interdependent;
nations create and sustain ethnicity when they need low-wage labor
reserves on their fringe. Ethnicity has become problematic also because
the distinction between nation and ethnicity is gradually losing its self-
evident character. Since the status of the nation is no longer sacrosanct and
many small nations have emerged, it is a small step to recognize ethnicity
as micro-nationalism, would-be nationalism, or nationalism-in-the-making.
According to Alberto Melucci, ethnic nationalism contains "a plurality of
meanings that cannot be reduced to a single core. It contains ethnic identity, which is a weapon of revenge against centuries of discrimination and

new forms of exploitation; it serves as an instrument for applying pressure in the political market; and it is a response to needs for personal and collective identity in highly complex societies."[59] This medley of meanings would be unimaginable until fairly recently. Not only, then, is ethnicity unstable in itself, continually metamorphosing along a broad continuum, but also its meaning is unstable and contextual. The question is whether we can detect patterns or trends in the changing meanings of ethnicity.

The solidarities that we describe as ethnic derive their meaning from their status in relation to the nation, and the architecture of the state shapes their status—which tends to be high in federal structures such as the German Federal Republic and low in centrist structures such as the French *état*. When nation and state change status in the vortex of a larger regionalism, such as the European Union, or are refigured by globalization, so does ethnicity. Ethnic identities are affected by variables that make them deeply local—historical legacies, socioeconomic change, political transformation, changing center-local relations—but local conditions are affected by macro dynamics such as the end of the Cold War, democratization, and the restructuring of states. The passing of the Cold War and the waning of the great political ideologies resulted in political and discursive realignments globally and locally. In Angola, Unita no longer follows the Cold War schema of anti-communism but has been organizing in the name of "authenticity" and along cultural, regional, and rural-urban lines. In post-apartheid South Africa, Inkatha also underwent a career shift. Ethnic association may also be viewed in terms of the absence or weakness of other bases of solidarity, in particular class and ideology.

The general trend toward democracy and electoral politics also affects ethnic and religious politics. Ethnic politics may represent a deepening of democracy if it concerns the mobilization of hitherto passive, alienated constituencies in response to regional uneven development or internal colonialism, for instance when indigenous peoples who were excluded assert their rights. Multiparty democracy may reinforce ethnicization and ethnicity may be manipulated to sabotage multiparty democracy, as in Kenya in recent years.

The era of the nation is past its peak and power and hegemony now play out at multiple levels. Postnationalism refers to the shift of allegiance from the nation to networks smaller or larger than the nation, generally because of diminishing returns from nationalism. "Informalization" is often interpreted as a retreat of the state due to globalization under the sign of neoliberalism and a general crisis of development. It is viewed as a decentering of the state or the center cannot hold, but in most instances it is more appropriate to view these changes in terms of the changing role and functions of states in the world economy. I discuss these changes in the closing chapter on global multiculture as a new, emerging formation.

Notes

1. Stannard 1994, 33; cf. Taylor 2001; discussed in Nederveen Pieterse 2002.
2. According to the 1991 census of India; Oommen 2004, 137.
3. Dick-Read 2005; Snow 1988.
4. Kazumichi 1996; Kaner 1996; Morris-Suzuki 1996; McCormack 1996b.
5. McCormack 1996a, 5.
6. Morris-Suzuki 1996, 86.
7. Morris-Suzuki 1996, 87–88.
8. Kohei 1996, 130.
9. Burgess 2004, 10.
10. McCormack 1996a, 11–12.
11. McCormack 1996b, 266.
12. McCormack 1996b, 283. The multiethnic character of Japan has been extensively discussed since the 1990s; for example, Yoshino 1995; Denoon et al., 1996; Weiner 1997; Lie 2001; Matsuda 2001; Sugimoto 2003; McLaughlan 2003; Burgess 2004; Roth 2005. Cf. *Japan Focus Newsletter* (http://www.japanfocus.org) under "Minorities" for relevant articles.
13. Jones 1999, 162.
14. Kaner 1996, 50.
15. Zhao 2006.
16. Cohen 2000.
17. Csete 2001; Dikötter 1992; Blue 1999.
18. Cf. Nederveen Pieterse 1989 (chapter on "Empire and Race").
19. Discussed in Nederveen Pieterse 1992.
20. Siddiqui 1997, xi–xii.
21. See Siddiqui et al. 1997.
22. Anzaldúa 1987. Cf. Ganster and Lorey 2005.
23. For instance, the Visit Stockholm online tour guide explains that "during the Viking period (ca. AD 750–1060) . . . in what was to become Sweden two 'tribes' or local 'nationalities,' 'Göter' and 'Svear' became the most influential and formed two 'states' with kings as leaders. Later in history these 'states' merged and formed Sweden. Even today we talk about 'Götaland' (the Land of Göter) and 'Svealand' (the Land of Svear)." Sweden, Sverige, means Svea Rike. And Götaland, Svealand and Norrland (east, west, etc.) are the units used in all weather forecasts (information from Jan Ekecrantz, Stockholm).
24. Mann 1986.
25. Discussed in Nederveen Pieterse 1992; cf. Fabian 1983.
26. King 2004, 79.
27. Linke 1999, 237.
28. Craig 1991, 22.
29. Van de Putte 2003, 66.
30. See Reynolds 2002
31. Cobban 1970, 119 and 121. Cf. Kymlicka 2004.
32. Discussed in Hechter 1975; Nederveen Pieterse 1989.
33. Katunarić 1997, 32.

34. Van de Putte 2003, 70, 71.

35. Yengoyan 1997, 796.

36. M. Barbaro and E. Dash, "Another outsider falls casualty to Nike's insider culture," *New York Times*, January 24, 2006, C4.

37. For example, Mole 1995; Whitney 1994.

38. Ayto 1990, 208.

39. Coquery-Vidrovitch 1994.

40. See Cahm and Fisera 1980; Cummins 1980.

41. Miller 1990, 31.

42. Nederveen Pieterse 1989.

43. Oommen 2004, 138.

44. Oommen 2004, 135.

45. See Siddiqui 1997, xi; Junejo and Bughio 1988.

46. Guideri and Pellizi 1988, 7–8.

47. Shohat 1991, 215.

48. Quoted in Parry 1991.

49. Pajaczkowska and Young 1992.

50. See Drinnon 1980.

51. Nederveen Pieterse 1989, ch. 12.

52. Roediger 1992; cf. Kovel 1970. A note on race: The common distinction between race and ethnicity is that race primarily refers to somatic differences whereas ethnicity refers to a combination of cultural (language, religion), place (region), and descent (claim to common descent) differences, which may or may not be accompanied by somatic differences. "Race" discourse spills over into culture because it is a cultural construction of alleged physical differences; and the "new racism" of the late twentieth century is cultural rather than biological. So the difference between race and ethnicity is a matter of degree rather than principle: the degree to which somatic attributes play a part in the social construction of cultural difference (cf. Nederveen Pieterse 1989, 1992).

53. Knight 1990, 75.

54. Leonardo 1984, 23.

55. hooks 1992, 21.

56. Leonardo 1984, 18.

57. Brookhiser 1991.

58. Paul Brass views the nation as a particular type of ethnic community: "an ethnic community politicized, with recognized group rights within the political system" (1991, 20).

59. Melucci 1989, 90.

2

❖

Deconstructing/ reconstructing ethnicity

> I have to forge every sentence in the teeth of irreducible and stubborn facts.
>
> —William James

The contemporary upsurge of ethnic and religious militancy and its often violent character gives rise to pervasive pessimism. Perplexity about its causes and intensity produces a sense of the irrelevance of beliefs in progress and universalism. Books such as Robert Kaplan's *The Ends of the Earth* and *The Coming Anarchy* and Daniel Patrick Moynihan's *Pandemonium* are expressions of this mood of pessimism. They tend to view ethnicity in primordial terms as ancient ethnic hatreds and archaic solidarities, a view that often comes with speculations about "primitive" human nature. In the process, ethnicity functions as a new imagery and code of racism: civilized peoples have nationalism whereas "others" indulge in ethnicity. Media representations of ethnic conflict—and of "fundamentalism" in another context—are replete with references to mass pathology and irrational crowd behavior. It is worth remembering that this kind of image has been projected onto collective action of virtually any sort whenever it threatened established order and vested interests.

In general perceptions ethnicity is often associated with conflict—violent, ruthless, and for stakes that, to outsiders, often seem remote or incomprehensible. What is at issue, according to Tom Nairn, is the "Ethnic Abyss"; according to Thomas Meyer it is "identity mania," and for the Sri Lankan political scientist Dayan Jayatilleka it is the "lunatic fringe."[1] On a different track, Amy Chua argues that globalization promotes free market capitalism and capitalism is dominated by "market-dominant minorities" that are "notoriously entrepreneurial" and elicit resentment and ethnic hatred.[2]

Yet there is another, everyday face of ethnicity—as in ethnic restaurants, ethnic cuisine, ethnic shopping malls, ethnic jokes, ethnic chic, ethnic fashion, ethnic models, ethnic décor, ethnic literature, ethnic bestsellers, ethnic music. In American supermarkets, an aisle is devoted to "ethnic products," and in Brazil shampoo for kinky hair is now advertised as *xampú étnico* (ethnic shampoo).[3] This is the light side of ethnicity, diversity as an expansion of consumer choice, ethnic appeal and atmosphere as a factor in tourism, and the political economy of ethno-marketing and diversity management. How do we rhyme these worlds, ethnic conflict that may culminate in violence and civil war, and everyday diversity and pluralism under the same umbrella of ethnicity?

First, these worlds are not so wide apart. Ethnic conflict is part of multiethnicity. Although practically all societies are multiethnic, few experience ethnic conflict, though the conflicts are conspicuous because they are often violent and some last a long time. To some extent the association of ethnicity with violent conflict is an optical illusion. Multiethnic peace is so common that it isn't worthy of media attention or social science analysis. If alongside ethnic conflicts we place multiethnic settlements, which are far larger in number and next to these multicultural societies as a similar situation by another name, usually located north of the equator and with a more recent history of migration, it yields a radically different map of ethnicity. The conflicts in multicultural societies are similar to ethnic conflicts in that both negotiate power and economic relations. Ashutosh Varshney argues that the actual problem is not ethnic conflict but violence. Many studies and ethnographies of ethnic conflict question the assumptions that identities are fixed, that ethnic hatred spreads easily, and that nationalist leaders have large numbers of followers.[4]

The central theme of this chapter is that most discussions of ethnicity are generalizing and homogenizing, as if there are only one or two types of ethnicity, standardizing ethnic experience in a way that is misleading. As Varshney observes, "We need variance as well as greater disaggregation in our analytic categories."[5] The focus on ethnic conflict also narrows perceptions of ethnicity to but one or two modes of ethnic experience. This treatment is organized around several general propositions.

Identity is best thought of as identification. Identity is too easily viewed as fixed and static; thinking of identity as *identification* brings out the agency in identity formation and is more insightful. The idea of identity not as given but as achieved goes back as far as the Renaissance.

Identification is ongoing and relational. Ethnic identification is a matter of ongoing relational positioning. Ethnic identification as ever changing relational positioning yields a continuum of forms of ethnicity that vary widely in terms of salience, intensity, and meaning.

We can distinguish several types of ethnicity: domination ethnicity, enclosure ethnicity, competition ethnicity, and optional ethnicity. Each stands in a different relationship to the nation. These varieties of ethnicity are interrelated, and one form of ethnicity tends to give rise to another.

Nationalism is a form of ethnicity. Nations arise from the multiethnic past as the institutionalization of a form of ethnic or interethnic dominance, whose ethnic character has often been lost or forgotten over time. Considering that the distinction between nation and ethnicity is tenuous and the term ethnicity implies a discourse of domination (as discussed in chapter 1), if the state takes the form of monocultural control, it reverts to domination ethnicity or ethnocracy.

Enclosure ethnicity comes in varieties of latent ethnicity, in which there is no salient relationship to a state, and cultural confinement that is enforced by a dominant ethnic group, as in the ghetto. In competition ethnicity the relationship to other ethnicities and the nation is contested; this form of ethnicity occupies the center stage in the vast literature on ethnic conflict. Finally, in optional ethnicity the relationship to other ethnicities and the nation becomes fluid and volitional and ethnicity becomes symbolic.

Ethnicity refers to emancipation as well as domination. It refers to the cultural politics of dominant *and* subaltern groups and often to both in different relationships. This combination isn't new. Nationalism has a similar double connotation with the Janus faces of an emancipatory meaning, as in national liberation and self-determination, and domination, as in chauvinism and jingoism. A familiar distinction runs between offensive, imperialist nationalism and defensive, anti-imperialist nationalism.[6]

The varieties of nationalism are part of common understanding; now we must come to terms with the varieties of ethnicity. This discussion is a deconstruction of ethnicity as a lumping concept in order to recover the agency in ethnicity. The chapter closes with a reflection on the endgames of ethnicity, or the paths of change of different types of ethnicity and the way each relates to ethnic conflict regulation.

Ethnic identity formation

The extremes on the conventional continuum of views in the debate on ethnicity are primordialism and instrumentalism. Primordialism is the essentialist view of ethnicity in which ethnic groups are taken as givens. In the classic tribal model, tribes are viewed as an archaic reality preceding and underlying modernity that resurfaces when modernization fails or cracks.[7] This kind of static perspective has been popular in media and for a long time in social science, for instance, in the concept of plural society (discussed in chapter 4). It produces a fundamentally pessimistic view of multiethnicity because primordial identities allow for little change. But this view ignores that "tribes" have usually been modern constructions or reconstructions through the intervention of colonialism, which froze the interplay of identities.[8]

The relative fixity of identities in Western Europe produced a static view of identity. Katherine Verdery notes, "The kind of self-consistent person who 'has' an 'identity' is a product of a specific historical process: the process of modern nation-state formation." A single consistent identity is a requirement for states: "One cannot keep track of people who are one thing at one point, another thing at another."[9] Yet, as anthropologists point out, these conditions don't exist in peripheral societies and generally in conditions where borders are unstable and contested, border crossing is frequent, so identities are shifting and multiple.[10]

In recent years the primordialist view has made place for the idea of the constructed nature of ethnicity.[11] In this view ethnicity is treated, like nationalism, as an imagined community and as politics. The question that arises then is *how* does construction take place and what are the political implications of this view? One option is to adopt a social movement perspective and to treat ethnic politics as a form of resource mobilization. Ethnic groups, then, are interest groups that use cultural capital as a mobilization resource. Attractive in this view is that it takes distance from essentializing identity claims; but if it is interpreted in a rational choice framework (which resources best generate desired outcomes), cultural meanings and symbolic resources are misrepresented as if they could be stripped from emotion and flattened to straightforward economic interests or political choices. Emotional attachment and belonging are part of ethnicity too (though not a necessary part).

The constructivist view on ethnicity is now commonplace, but work on *how* ethnicity construction takes place remains patchy. A classic approach is to explain ethnic identity formation in terms of elite competition. Thus Paul Brass argues, "The cultural forms, values, and practices of ethnic groups become political resources for elites in competition for political power and economic advantage." In this view, "ethnic communities are created and transformed by particular elites in modernizing and in postindustrial societies undergoing dramatic social change."[12] Most societies involve a hierarchy in place in the form of a *cultural division of labor* and alignments between political elites and social forces such as mass parties and religious authorities. Social and economic changes "may precipitate new center-locality conflicts in which issues of language and religion come into play again and provide bases for ethnic and political mobilization."[13]

The elite model of ethnicization, however, neglects the agency of subalterns and takes elites as givens rather than examining the process of contestation through which elites emerge. The implicit assumption is that elites manipulate and dupe subalterns, which is a variation on the theme of "false consciousness." However, this presents a passive view of subalterns and simplifies how subjectivities are formed. We shouldn't take elites for granted, but if we know the interests of elites in mobilizing ethnicity the question remains how we explain the interests of followers. In an authoritarian political culture elites may be able to influence followers, but authoritarianism cannot be assumed and neither can the ability of leaders to manipulate followers. The role of elites varies according to the form of ethnicity. Studying violence in rural Bosnia Herzegovina in the 1990s, anthropologist Mart Bax finds that not all conflicts were ethnic, but that local vendettas played a large part and that interpretations of ethnic cleansing "as the result of a political policy carefully orchestrated from above and systemically carried out . . . reflect an uncritical acceptance of a central or national leader perspective." Bax makes a case for studying influences "from above" and "from below" as interrelated and supplementary.[14] Indeed, viewing identity formation and elite formation *together* in the context of mobilization produces a richer perspective.

The complex role of elites comes across in an analysis of ethnic mobilization in "The development of political opposition in Taiwan, 1986–1989" by Fu-chang Wang.[15] Taking a social movement approach, Wang distinguishes two forms of ethnicity: ethnic competition and ethnic enclosure. The Taiwanese, who are assimilated into Taiwan's mainstream political culture dominated by the mainland Chinese, engage in ethnic competition and in the process experience discrimination on ethnic grounds. This makes ethnicity salient to them, so in effect they experience a double process of ethnic identity formation and assimilation. According to Wang, this is relevant for the start-up of ethnic mobilization, the phase of grievance formation. Next, political opposition in ethnic terms spread to the Taiwanese *enclosed* within the ethnic experience, who are mostly rural, less educated, and less mobile and for whom, therefore, ethnicity has not been salient ("fish don't talk about the water") but is *made* salient under the influence of the political protest actions initiated by the assimilating Taiwanese. This has been relevant to the diffusion stage of ethnic mobilization.

Hence this account presents *two* moments of ethnic identity formation: in the context of ethnic assimilation and competition and in the course of ethnic mobilization. The assimilated members, the initiators of the movement, according to Wang, tend to be moderates because for them ethnicity is an optional identity, whereas the non-assimilated members, once they have been recruited within the ethnic enclosure, tend to radicalize the movement. Accordingly, different elites are involved in ethnic mobilization: a bicultural

elite and an ethnic enclosure leadership that emerges in the course of ethnic mobilization. Hence the idea of elite *tout court* is too narrow and static
and discounts subaltern social movement leadership.

Varieties of ethnic experience

According to Milton Esman, "Several decades of observing and reflecting
on ethnic politics have persuaded me of the futility of searching for a general theory about the genesis of ethnic conflicts or for universal prescrip-
tions for managing or resolving them."[16] This weariness almost seems to
come with the terrain. I note that in explaining ethnicity one hurdle has
been passed—the hurdle of essentialism and primordialism, but another
remains—that of a homogenizing view of ethnicity, capturing it through
one lens, viewing it from one angle and then finding that the variety of
actual ethnic experiences escapes classification. The label ethnicity doesn't
capture the wide and fluid variety of notions and experiences. The static
nature of ethnicity talk is disabling. Ethnic identity runs across a wide
spectrum that ranges from objective markers of ethnicity to subjective
identifications of varying salience and intensity.[17] Following the idea of
ethnicization or ethnicity as process, I propose viewing ethnicity as a continuum. As a schematic approximation of the variety of ethnic experience
I propose four main types of ethnicity.

This kind of approach also has disadvantages. Taxonomy becomes easily preoccupied with terms and labels, boxes with selective fact finding
and anecdotal evidence to match the boxes. So this attempt at a better
approximation is an exercise that should not be pushed too far. Besides,
the very preoccupation with ethnicities draws attention away from non-
ethnic variables.

Terms often used in the sociology of ethnicity are the *persistence* and
resilience, survival and *revival* of ethnicity. This is deceptive because of its
essentialist logic, the assumption of continuity and sameness, suggesting
dichotomies of tradition and modernity, old and new, in the process con-
cealing the newness, modernity, and contemporary character of ethnic
responses. By implying that ethnic sentiments and identifications are
somehow primordial, this underplays how ethnicity changes and is not
simply the reassertion of an old identity but the production of a new one.

For instance, Anthony Smith seeks to explain "why ethnic groups survive."[18] He finds that "myths of election" are most strategic in reproducing
ethnicity; it is "chosen peoples" who survive. This is a legitimate focus and
characteristic of Smith's general interest in the nexus between ethnicity and
nationalism. But this outlook tends to reify ethnicity. Ethnicity, rather than
the changing structure of political and social opportunities, becomes the

independent variable. The conditions under which myths of election become salient are not specified, nor which myths of election become salient. While highlighting the continuity of ethnicity this argument overlooks the variable and changing nature of ethnic identity. Hence it is more significant to look at the *reconstruction* than the reproduction of ethnicity.

The notion of the ethnic origins of nations is erroneous not only because the meaning of ethnicity changes over time but also because ethnic identification often follows state or nation formation rather than the other way round. "'Ethnicities' . . . are largely the product, rather than the foundation, of nation-states. . . . The ever more powerful structures of central state control—be they colonial or autochthonous, imperial or national— are what generate and motivate the new *need* for ethnic autonomy, and even, in many cases, the actual sense of ethnic identity on which the latter is predicated."[19] Both perspectives are valid and we should not plead just one case: ethnicity is older than the nation *and* ethnicity is produced and reproduced by nation states (as discussed in chapter 1).

Ethnic identity is defined by a variety of markers. Paul Brass draws a distinction between *ethnic category*—defined by objective cultural markers such as language, dialect, dress, custom, religion, or somatic differences— and *ethnic community* or ethnicity proper, in which cultural markers consciously serve internal cohesion and differentiation from other groups. Brass defines ethnic category as "any group of people dissimilar from other peoples in terms of objective cultural criteria and containing within its membership, either in principle or in practice, the elements for a complete division of labor and for reproduction." He explains that "ethnicity is to ethnic category what class consciousness is to class." An ethnic community is an ethnic category that "has adopted one or more of its marks of cultural distinctness and used them as symbols both to create internal cohesion and to differentiate itself from other ethnic groups."[20]

The third notion is *ethnonationalism,* or the politicization of ethnic community. In this context a nation is a particular type of ethnic community: "an ethnic community politicized, with recognized group rights within the political system." As Brass notes, "Insofar as an ethnic group succeeds by its own efforts in achieving and maintaining group rights through political action and mobilization, it has gone beyond ethnicity to establish itself as a nationality."[21] The significant steps in the process of ethnicization, then, are ethnic identity formation or the step from cultural category to ethnic community, and ethnonationalism, or the ethnic community politicized.

These distinctions are useful but also problematic. If ethnicity refers to subjective consciousness, why call configurations that are only differentiated by objective cultural markers *ethnic* categories? Shouldn't these be simply termed *cultural* categories that can *become* ethnic following the process of ethnicization? Furthermore, *ethnic community* is a static and limited concept.

Community is a contested, homogenizing concept,[22] and there are more ways of experiencing ethnicity than through community. Indeed, ethnic identification may increase in the wake of the decline of ethnic communities (discussed below).

Brass distinguishes three sites of conflict—within ethnic groups, between groups, and in relation to the state. He rightly points out that most treatments of ethnicity focus on the second site of conflict and neglect the others, particularly conflict within groups, because of their homogenizing view of ethnicity. That which is to be demonstrated—ethnic identity formation or the degree of ethnicization—is taken as given. The negotiation of ethnicity in relation to other differences such as class, gender, age, place, ideology, is taken for granted. Yet by equating ethnicity with ethnic community, Brass too adopts a homogenizing approach to ethnicity. Rogers Brubaker makes a similar argument but simply draws a distinction between ethnic category and ethnic group.[23]

Ethnicity is an unstable category. As a constructed community, like the nation, its logic is that of imagination and imagination is a social practice. Ethnicity is plural with experiences ranging from the close comforts of enclosure ethnicity and the contradictory pressures of competition ethnicity to optional ethnicity. The objective markers that can form the basis of ethnic identification vary widely and according to circumstances. The circumstances under which objective cultural traits elicit subjective identification vary and are in part contradictory—the lessening of actual cultural differences can enhance cultural identification (such as when different groups are similar enough to compete for the same resources, discussed in chapter 4), or conversely, the increasing salience or hardening of cultural boundaries can foster cultural solidarity. These dynamics involve quite different experiences of ethnicity, though conventional wisdom groups them under the same umbrella, or allows only conventional classifications (such as regional autonomy movements, separatist movements and indigenous peoples). Thus it is appropriate to think of ethnicity in terms of a continuum of widely diverse experiences. The spectrum of ethnic identification ranges from ethnic fundamentalism to low-intensity or opportunity ethnicity, from ethnicity as a total identity to occasional, part-time ethnicity. Individuals and groups do not occupy a stable, fixed place on this continuum for their degree of identification varies according to the situation. In chapter 8 I call this "flexible acculturation."

Domination ethnicity: ethnocracy

One of the consequences of bracketing the distinction between nation and ethnicity is that we can speak of phenomena such as *ethnocracy*, which can be defined as the "monocultural control of the state apparatus."[24] In many societies the state is an instrument of domination by privileged ethnic groups who engage in a form of "cultural despotism." The modern state upholds a cultural division of labor that distributes valued jobs and economic development unevenly.[25] The ethnicization of the state is a familiar process. Nationality is often defined in terms of the majority ethnicity. The 1972 Bangladesh Constitution decreed that the citizens of Bangladesh shall be known as Bangalees, to the dismay of the Chamang peoples of the Chittagong Hill Tracts. Language policies are another indicator of ethnocracy. The 1956 Sinhala Only Act in Sri Lanka was one in a series of measures that marginalized Tamils and established a Sinhala Buddhist ethnocracy. Government hiring and contracts, the composition of the armed forces, media policies and the organization of public spaces are other indicators of ethnic bias.[26] Dawa Norbu observes,

> Since nationalism has a strong ethnic character . . . we must make a qualification of the careless characterization of the dominant ethnic groups' nationalism as "Arab" "British" "Chinese" "Indian," and so on. For the fact is that so-called Arab nationalism did not include the Berbers, Copts, Druse, Alawites, Assyrians, Kurds, and so on. The so-called Chinese nationalism was in fact Han nationalism which failed to involve the Tibetans, Turks, Mongols, Manchus and Muslims (Hui). The so-called Indian nationalism was in fact Hindu nationalism which failed to unite the Muslims, Nagas, Mizos, Adivasis, Santhals, Ghurkas, and so on. The so-called British nationalism or social imperialism in the nineteenth and early twentieth century excluded the Welsh, Irish and the Scots; its ethnic basis was Anglo-Saxon.[27]

We can distinguish majority and minority ethnocracies, stable and unstable ethnocracies, democratic and undemocratic ethnocracies. Apartheid in South Africa and its construction of racial and ethnic identities, ranging from occupational and political niches to Homelands, was a *Herrenvolk* democracy ruled by a minority. Israel has been characterized as an "ethnic democracy" that combines the ethnic dominance of Ashkenazi Jews with political and civil rights for Sephardim and Israeli Arabs.[28] The United States has been analyzed as a *Herrenvolk* democracy. Consider the difference between the American Declaration of Independence, which is universalist and inclusive in a patriarchal framework ("All men"), and the American Constitution, which is particularist and exclusive ("We the people").[29]

Many states practice some form of ethnic coalition government by ethnic juggling or more institutionalized arrangements (such as in Kenya, Zambia, Nigeria, Ghana, and Caribbean countries). One type of institutionalized arrangement is *consociationalism*, or government by a cartel of elites. The Netherlands during the era of pillarization (1917–1960s), Belgium (federalized in 1993), and Austria were classic instances of consociationalism, but now the main remaining instances are Lebanon (1943–75 and 1989–present) and, arguably, Canada since 1974.[30]

That minority ethnocracies tend to be insecure goes without saying, but a different problem is the insecure majority. In Sri Lanka at the time of independence in 1948, Sinhalese hegemony was established politically (ruling party) and symbolically (the lion on the flag) to make up for the privileged status Tamils had gained in education and the bureaucracy under British colonialism. Yet support for the Sri Lankan Tamils from the neighboring Indian state Tamil Nadu made the Sinhalese feel insecure. What ensued was a gradual, further ethnicization of the state—in government jobs and the armed forces, the victory of the chauvinist Sri Lanka Freedom Party, the Sinhala Only Act, ethnic riots instigated from above, and the role of ethno-merchants. Before independence the Tamil cultural identity movement, like the Sinhala cultural revival, was primarily anti-imperialist, but over time it evolved into an ethnonationalist movement and, ultimately, a movement with separatist tendencies.[31] Ethnocracy leads to the "securitization" of ethnic differences; expressions of cultural belonging and difference are seen as threats to the ruling elite and national security and this produces further polarization.

In India militancy in the Punjab and ethnonationalism in Kashmir have been fueled by the communalization of Indian politics. Leading parties, including Congress (I), played the communal card and mobilized majority Hindu identity as a prop for electoral support in unstable constituencies in North India.[32] In India ethnicity is conventionally termed communalism because the lines of cultural difference tend to be drawn in terms of religion rather than ethnic descent, though religion is often a stand-in for language and place of origin and thus for the same markers that underpin ethnicity. T. K. Oommen distinguishes five types of communalism in India: assimilationist, when a community tries to assimilate other communities into their fold, as in the case of Hindutva (or fundamentalist Hinduism); welfarist, when a community takes advantage of state provisions, as with Christians and Muslims; retreatist, when a community stays aloof from political involvement, as with Bahais and Christians; separatist, when a community seeks autonomy, as in Sikh claims to Khalistan; and secessionist, as in the case of Muslims in Kashmir.[33]

What happened in former Yugoslavia after the demise of Tito and the erosion of communism as hegemonic ideology was the gradual regionalization and ethnicization of politics and the ethnicization of the federal state and the armed forces by Serbian interests. The uncertainties of economic transition and ideological erosion made playing the ethnonationalist card politically attractive. The second Yugoslav state, like the first, was based on Serbian hegemony, but Serbs could be made to feel insecure and allegations of the subjugation of Serbs in Kosovo were politically useful.[34]

The general origins of ethnocracy are conquest and settler colonialism, a rank order between old and new immigrants, and postcolonial ethnic shuffles. According to Dawa Norbu, "Typically, in any contemporary multinational state, top posts in the following state agencies are reserved for the upper class or caste of the dominant ethnic group: (a) top bureaucratic and ministerial posts with crucial decision-making power; (b) top army posts; (c) top police posts; (d) and almost entire staffing of intelligence offices."[35]

Ethnocracies are gradually being undermined by demographic changes and globalization. South African apartheid is no more. Due to immigration, Israel has become a multicultural society. The Anglo-Protestant ascendancy in Northern Ireland is slowly inching toward power sharing with Catholics and Republicans. The hegemony of Amharas in Ethiopia has given way to ethnic federalism.[36] A Sikh is prime minister of India. An Aymara is president of Bolivia. A Muslim heads the Thai armed forces. Multicultural and ethnic coalition government is gradually becoming more common. Arguably the overall trend is toward multicultural settlements.

But ethnic and cultural conflicts are many; an overview is in Box 2.1. The overview is deliberately extensive (though not exhaustive) in order to illustrate the wide scope and variety of ethnic situations. Discussions of ethnicity often extrapolate from a handful of cases drawn from one region or concern only one type of ethnicity or stage of conflict. I only include ethnic conflicts because an overview of ethnic competition would be endless. I leave out instances where ethnic conflict has abated or has been settled (such as South Sudan).

Enclosure ethnicity

In class analysis the classic distinction runs between class position and class consciousness, class as condition and as mentality, objective and subjective class, class *an sich* and *für sich*. A parallel distinction runs between cultural category and ethnic group. In this view only an ethnic group is really "ethnicity." Similar distinctions run between dormant and salient ethnicity, generic and emergent ethnicity. As Pollock notes, there is a radical difference between *being* particular and *preaching* particularism.[37]

Wang, from whom I borrow the concept, refers to *enclosure ethnicity* with respect to the rural Taiwanese.[38] He doesn't develop it further, but it would seem that enclosure ethnicity can have several meanings. First, it can refer to a self-enclosed community—as in anthropology's "primitive isolates"—and their sense of peoplehood, their basic, unreflected identity. Because ethnicity makes sense only in a relational context, their identity would be "ethnic" in the eyes of outside beholders but not necessarily in their own eyes. We can term this latent or *dormant ethnicity*. Second, it can refer to a group whose

---

Box 2.1.   Configurations of ethnicity

Ethnocracies: Bangladesh (Bengali Muslims), Burma, Burundi (Tutsi), Cameroon, Chad, Egypt (Muslims, Copts), Eritrea, Fiji (Melanesians as quasi-majority), Indonesia (Javanese Muslims), Iraq (Shiites, Kurds, Sunnis), Japan, Malaysia (Malays, Chinese, Indian Tamils), Mauritania, the Philippines, Rwanda, Singapore (Chinese), Sri Lanka (Sinhalese, Tamils), Sudan (Muslims), Taiwan (mainland Chinese), Turkey (Sunnis, Kurds, Alevites), Uganda.

Minority ethnocracies: Bahrain (Sunni rulers, Shia majority), Jordan (Hashemite monarchy, Bedouins), Syria (Alevites).

Indigenous peoples: Americas (Native Americans, Inuit), Australia (Aborigines), Bangladesh (Chittagong), Burma, Laos and Thailand (hill tribes), Central Africa (Twa), Finland (Saami), India (Adivasis), Indonesia (Papuans), Japan (Ainu, Okinawa), Maghreb (Berbers), Malaysia (Orang Asli), New Zealand (Maoris), Philippines (Igorot), Russia (Siberia), South Africa and Botswana (San), Sri Lanka (Veddas).

Ethnic conflicts and autonomy movements: Algeria (Kabyle), Angola (Unita), Azerbaijan (ethnic Armenians in Nagorno-Karabakh), Bulgaria (ethnic Turks), Burundi (Hutu), Cameroon, Chad, China (Tibet, Xingjian, Hong Kong), Côte d'Ivoire, Crimea, Cyprus, Democratic Republic of Congo (Katanga, Shaba, North Kivu), Estonia (ethnic Russians), France (Basques, Brittany, Corsica), Georgia (Abkhazia), Ghana (north), Guyana, India (Kashmir, Assam, Northeast, Nagaland, Punjab), Indonesia (Aceh, Maluku, West Papua, Riau), Iran (Azeris, Kurds, Baluchis), Italy (North), Kenya (Luo, Kikuyu), Kosovo (Albanians), Kyrgystan (Islamic movement), Latvia (ethnic Russians), Liberia, Macedonia (Albanians), Moldova (Transnistria, ethnic Russians, Ukrainians), Morocco (Southwest Sahara), Nigeria (Muslim north, Ogoni, Ijaw, Bakassi peninsula), Pakistan (Sindh, Baluchistan, Pashtuntan, Islamic movements), Philippines (Moros), Russia (Chechnya, Dagestan, Ingushetia), Rwanda, Senegal (Casamance), Sierra Leone, Somalia (Ogaden, Somaliland), Spain (Basques, Catalonia, Galicia, Andalusia), Sudan (Darfur, Nuba Mountains), Tajikistan (Basmachis), Thailand (Muslim Malay South), Turkey (Kurds), Sri Lanka (Tamil Eelam, Muslims), Uganda (Acholi, LRM), Uzbekistan (Islamic movement), Zimbabwe.

Ethnic pluralism, ethnic coalition government: Botswana, Burkina-Faso, Ghana, Guinea-Bissau, Guyana, Jordan, Kenya, Mauritius, Namibia, Niger, Nigeria, South Africa, Surinam, Trinidad and Tobago, Zambia.

Consociationalism: Lebanon (1943–75, 1989-present), Canada (since 1974).

Ethnic federalism: Belgium, Canada, Ethiopia, Spain, Switzerland. Quasi-federalism: Finland, Great Britain, Italy, New Zealand, United States (Puerto Rico) (territorial autonomy, control over education, language).*

---

*Kymlicka 2004, 147.

enclosure is enforced and imposed by a dominant group—as in the case of indigenes in Bolivia and other Andean countries who in the wake of Spanish colonization and latifundio agriculture were gradually driven from the valleys higher into the mountains. Here is a sense of ethnicity that is held by both the dominant (who speak of *indíos*) and the dominated (Quecha, Aymara) and is profoundly shaped by the relation to the dominant group. Here enclosure itself is relational. A classic instance is the ghetto.

Enclosure ethnicity generally correlates with economic deprivation and low-class status. Hence it means low mobility, whereas competition ethnicity is associated with class mobility. As a practice it involves less cultural capital than competition ethnicity, which is essentially a bicultural discourse, and is less attractive to middle-class sensibilities than the outward-looking engagement of competition ethnicity. Once mobilized it tends to change into competition ethnicity over time; ethnic mobilization means engaging in ethnic competition and looking outward. Over time enclosure ethnicity is likely to transform into competition ethnicity. Due to modernization and globalization many "enclosures" are shrinking and are transformed into sites of cultural competition. The contemporary upsurge of indigenous peoples and ethnic movements is a manifestation of this momentum of uneven incorporation and represents attempts to negotiate autonomy or the terms of incorporation.

Enclosure ethnics, when politically fueled by class grievances, tend to be more radical than competition ethnics. Thus in Fiji the moderate bicultural customary elite of principal chiefs initiated the 1987 military coup and lower strata Fijians radicalized the intervention in the name of "Fiji for the Fijians."[39] We can differentiate between successful and unsuccessful assimilation and argue that unsuccessful assimilation fosters ethnic identification and can lead to ethnic mobilization to gain access to resources on a collective basis. Ethnic identification and mobilization, then, are strategies to achieve collectively what one could not achieve individually and in that respect they parallel class solidarities.

Enclosure ethnicity may lead to ethnonationalism and possibly separatism. Reviewing postcolonial societies, Mayall and Simpson find that ethnic mobilization turns into secessionism under the following conditions: if the ethnic groups have been treated differently within the same territory under colonial rule, if the postcolonial government imposes monocultural rule, and if there is support in the regional environment for the secessionists.[40] An inward-looking disposition may involve ethnic cleansing, homogenizing space and community, or delinking. This replicates the logic of ethnos but seeks to reproduce it on one's own terms. It follows a logic of opposition in which dominant ethnocentrism (nationalism) is both confronted by and mirrored in oppositional ethnocentrism (ethnic or micronationalism). In both perspectives nation and ethnicity are taken as destiny. A paradox of contemporary ethnonationalism is that it is usually sponsored by overseas diasporas and support networks,[41] some of whom may have implicitly given up on nationalism and have a postnationalist mentality at heart.

Competition ethnicity

The theory of ethnicization in terms of elite competition is more concerned with the how than the why of ethnic politics. Elites mobilize cultural identity as a resource in political competition, but *why* are certain cultural differences singled out? In his account of internal colonialism Michael Hechter notes, "The spatially uneven wave of modernization over state territory creates relatively advanced and less advanced groups."[42] The superordinate group seeks to stabilize its advantages by institutionalizing the stratification system in a cultural division of labor that consolidates cultural solidarities. In this argument, modernization (in the sense of economic development) and its uneven spread are woven *into* cultural differentiation.

This puts the modernization discussion on a different footing. The next question is, what is the effect of ongoing modernization? Whereas the postwar modernization literature posited a zero-sum relationship between "tradition" and "modernity," it is now widely recognized that "modernization intensifies communal conflict":

> The expansion of markets and improved communications increases contact and generates competition among communal groups. As people aspire to the same social and economic rewards, competition intensifies and communal solidarities become an important—often the most important—vehicle for mutual support and promotion, especially in urban areas. The expanding role of the state invites and even requires groups to mobilize for collective action to struggle for their share of the benefits available from government and for political access, cultural rights, and economic opportunities. . . . The competition generated by economic development thus politicizes ethnic pluralism and makes it even more salient than in earlier periods. According to this perspective, modernization does not erode communal solidarities, it modernizes them and converts them into more-effective instruments of group defence, promotion, and combat.[43]

This assessment is borne out in many places, such as Indonesia, India, and Québec.[44] Viewing ethnicization and ethnic competition as part of modernization is a drastic departure from the conventional modernization/nation building/assimilation perspective. Economic development and modernization may evoke ethnicization. Modernity and ethnicity coexist quite well. Development and economic growth do not eliminate but refigure ethnicity. Modernization and ethnicization intersect around the state, development resources and space. State formation, state centralization, nation building, cultural homogenization, and electoral politics in combination with regional uneven development, cultural bias in capital accumulation, and migration flows may unleash ethnic competition and rivalry.

Nation building often involves ethnonational elements such as the state-sponsored exclusion of minorities and foreigners or the privileging of an ethnic category. Atatürk's Turkey suppressed Armenians, Kurds, and Jews, expelled Greeks and many foreigners, and symbolically recentered the nation around Anatolia. Government policy in Malaysia favored the Bumiputra or "sons of the soil." Preferential treatment of Bumiputra over the ethnic Chinese and Indian Tamils was part of a state-led strategy of building an ethnonational bourgeoisie, which is now being phased out.[45] Fiji adopted the slogan "Fiji for the Fijians" during the 1987 military coup.[46] According to Rajni Kothari, in India ethnicity is part of the "dialectic of development." It "becomes a ground for reassessing the cultural, economic and political impacts of developmentalism. . . . Instead of disappearing, ethnic identities harden as a combination/convergence of three trends," namely, developmentalism as culture, as economics, and "in the role of electoral politics in dividing up the development cake."[47]

Ethnic competition for state power and resources is a key to ethnic group formation. "The state is itself the greatest prize and resource, over which groups engage in a continuing struggle in societies that have not developed stable relationships among the main institutions and centrally organized social forces."[48] But equally important is competition in relation to uneven development and space, though this is not a matter of simple deprivation. Political economy frequently cuts the other way and the economically prosperous areas seek secession or autonomy, as in the case of the Punjab (the wheat bowl of India), Kashmir (water, tourism), Biafra (oil), south Sudan (oil), Shaba (mining), Eritrea (infrastructure), the Basque country and Catalonia (industry), Slovenia and Croatia (industry), Québec and northern Italy.[49] But usually most significant is relative deprivation in terms of political control: "It is being shut out from political power which is decisive, rather than the presence, or absence, of economic resources in and of themselves."[50] So what matters is the interplay of state and development, power and profit.

In sub-Saharan Africa, Tim Shaw distinguishes different forms of ethnicity. Here ethnicity has changed form "from ethnic aggrandisement in the 1960s to ethnic fragmentation in the 1980s."[51] Focusing on the political economy of ethnicity Shaw compares two situations: sustained growth, as in Nigeria in the 1970s, and economic contraction, as in Ghana and Uganda and other Most Seriously Affected Countries. Sustained growth produces a mixed-sum situation in which patron-client relations work and ethnic identity is reinforced: "Factional ethnic politics are seen to work," there is a "'trickle down' of ethnic association." Negative growth produces a zero-sum situation in which patron-client networks break down and one would therefore expect class consciousness to develop. The contracting economies, however, tend to experience rural retreat: "a retreat from urban decline to rural survival in ethnic homelands." Thus Shaw distinguishes between an old and a new ethnicity: "In only the few expanding economies will the 'old' ethnicity of patronage remain a dominant factor, whereas in the many contracting countries, the 'new' ethnicity of survival may become prevalent."[52] So in both situations of growth and contraction, ethnicity is reinforced, ethnicization takes place, but they are different kinds of ethnicity, ranging from patronage politics to rural retreat. The relationship between development and ethnicity is complex. Ethnicity is a contingent category, and development and modernization are contingent processes and contested concepts as well. We can differentiate between economic growth and contraction, successful and failed, balanced and uneven development, center and local dynamics. Uneven modernization can be both a cause and effect of ethnicization. A cause because it generates group stratification; an effect because privileged groups seek to institutionalize their lead and discriminate against others, thus deepening cultural cleavages. Shifting center-local relations destabilize the cultural division of labor and in the process may both reinforce and refigure ethnic associations. In content and meaning, ethnicity changes character across this range of situations.

In former Yugoslavia, uneven modernization (more advanced in Croatia and Slovenia than in Serbia) and the authoritarian style of modernization during the Tito years are held responsible for setting the stage for ethnic conflicts through a process of "scapegoating."[53] Discourses of competition ethnicity are complex and varied. A radical position is to reject ethnicity altogether as a pejorative terminology. Or to turn the tables and declare *éthnos* a form of *ethnikós*—for from the viewpoint of bicultural others the nation is just another form of ethnicity that happens to be dominant.[54] When nation and ethnicity are equated, then, consequently both are bracketed and relativized. This is a matter of awareness of the way ethnicities-in-relation function, of the effects of the cultural division of labor and ethnicization in the stream of political and socioeconomic change, without essentializing and freezing ethnicities. Stuart Hall speaks of decolonizing ethnicity, recognizing difference and engaging in a politics of representation premised on the end of the essential black subject.[55] By the same token this also means questioning and bracketing British identity.

Competition ethnicity involves strengthening ethnic solidarity and cooperation. This can take a mild form of building cultural cohesion as in the Kwanzaa celebration in the U.S. It can take the form of political organization as in Muhammadya, the organization of urban Muslims established in 1914 in Yogyakarta, Indonesia, and black civil rights organizations in the

U.S. It can take an economic form, as in ethnic groups cooperating economically (chapter 3) or a legal form as in Native American nations cooperating in litigation. By looking inward, marrying inward, buying black, voting black, and celebrating blackness, people seek to build their collective resources in order to compete better. It can also take the form of self-enclosure, as a strategy of building collective self-definition and self-reliance, as in radical Afrocentrism and the Nation of Islam in the U.S.

Black intellectuals in the U.S. can take a position of double engagement and accept, in the words of Cornel West, the importance of "positive identity, self-affirmation, and holding at bay self-doubt and self-contempt and self-hatred" as "an indispensable element for people of African descent," as in the lineage of black nationalism that runs from Marcus Garvey to contemporary Afrocentrism. Yet they can reject the "black nationalist rhetoric that is still operating in a binary oppositional discourse,"[56] as in Louis Farrakhan's black/white discourse. The contrasting positions of West and Farrakhan illustrate the difference and tension between two forms of competition ethnicity—through engagement and through confrontation. In South Africa a parallel difference ran between the Pan African Congress (PAC) and Black Consciousness movement on the one hand, and the African National Congress (ANC) on the other. These characterizations are now passé because the Nation of Islam has evolved,[57] and since the ANC became the ruling party, different concerns, such as Black Economic Empowerment, have come to the fore.

Ethnic conflict easily becomes a heading of convenience under which diverse sentiments find shelter. Thus in "Sarajevo and some other cities, the Muslims were an elite more sophisticated and more affluent than their rural Serbian neighbors. The class antagonism of the Serbian peasants in Bosnia was easily converted into ethnic hostility by anti-Muslim propaganda from Belgrade." This comes across in Muslim women's testimonies of their rape by Serbs: "They kept pigs, they came down from the mountains, they stank . . . and now they are treating us this way!"[58] Considering that the majority of Muslims live in towns, the war in Bosnia has been interpreted as *urbicide*, a campaign of rural peasants laying siege to and bringing destruction and taking revenge on cities and their inhabitants.[59]

Optional ethnicity

> When shooting Westerns, use real Indians if possible; but if Indians are not available, use Hungarians.
>
> —Old Hollywood manual on lighting

Episodes of ethnocracy and ethnic conflict provide ethnicity with a certain reality and concreteness, a kind of practical objectivity. W. I. Thomas's theorem applies: If situations are believed to be real, they are real in their consequences. If this informs analysis the result is a kind of ethnic Realpolitik: ethnicity may have been constructed but now it is real. At this point constructivism becomes academic; in the end there is no noteworthy difference between a constructivist and an essentialist interpretation because the net social and political outcome is the same. So we are back to square one. The point of this section is to refute this idea. The point of constructivist analysis is to unpack ethnicity, to make its contingencies visible and to do so *through* the everyday realities of ethnic politics.

Ethnicity—like class, gender, occupation, religion—is a form of cultural capital that, to a degree, one can choose to foreground or keep in the background. Ethnicity as a resource is what the instrumentalist approach proposes. As a general position this is too shallow. Identity is more than a resource, it is not simply optional or volitional, yet choice does play a part. This refers not only to the *use* made of ethnic identity (which is not a given or constant factor) but also to ethnic identification itself. Identifying ethnic can be a way to connect and can serve as social capital, social glue, an economic gambit (discussed in the next chapter), a way to obtain state provisions, a political maneuver, or a cultural charm. Any identity comes in at least two forms: inward looking and outward looking. Isaac Deutscher described Spinoza, Heine, Marx, Rosa Luxemburg, Trotsky, and Freud as "non-Jewish Jews" who found the Jewish tradition too confining; they acknowledged their Jewish identity but looked outward.[60] The same applies to national identity. One can be an inward or outward looking Frenchman, and so on.

The fluidity and contingency of ethnic identification finds expression in several ways—in the selection of markers of identity; the salience, meaning, and application of markers; the definition of boundaries; and the meaning of identity, ambivalence, and multiple identity. This fluidity functions on two levels: as an attribute of *all* forms of ethnic identity and as constituting a way of experiencing ethnic identity itself, optional ethnicity. To a certain extent *all ethnic identity is optional* and occasional and not total, but where optionality is the salient feature it constitutes a type of ethnicity.

There is considerable variation over time and by situation to the objective markers of cultural difference that form the basis of ethnic identification. Which features of cultural difference are highlighted can vary greatly. Subjective ethnic identity likewise involves considerable variation in terms of which elements are foregrounded, their meaning and relevance. Although ethnicity is often associated with place or origin and claims to common descent, the actual variety of cultural markers is much wider and their salience changes over time. In Brass's elite model, "the choice of the leading symbol of differentiation depends upon the interests of the elite group that takes up the ethnic cause." In the case of a religious elite, religion will be the first and language the second symbol of differentiation. Next, an elite will try to promote multisymbol congruence through education and publishing religious pamphlets in the vernacular. Although the label remains the same, the actual nature of identity may shift. Thus, in Sri Lanka, Sinhalese identity used to be a matter of language first, religion second; but after independence and agitation by the Buddhist Sangha a new identity developed: "Where previously to be Sinhalese implied being Buddhist, now to be Buddhist implies being Sinhalese."[61] The new inflection changes the way group boundaries are drawn. Thomas Eriksen observes, "the compass of the 'We' category may expand and contract according to the situation. At general elections in Mauritius an individual may identify him or herself with the Hindu community at large; when looking for a job the extended kin group may be the relevant category, and when abroad he or she may actually take on an identity as simply Mauritian, even to the extent of feeling closer to Christian and Muslim Mauritians than to Hindus from India."[62]

The opportunistic character of the markers of ethnicity was apparent in former Yugoslavia: "Each side will alternately emphasize their common roots when it indeed suits its purposes. Before the war, for example, when the Serbs still hoped to keep Bosnia in Yugoslavia, the media frequently highlighted similarities with the Muslims, while Croats often stressed that Bosnia had been part of historical Croatia and that most Bosnian Muslims were originally of Croatian descent."[63] Albanians claim that many Serbs are "really" Albanians by origin. Serbs have labeled Croats "Catholic Serbs," and Croats have labeled Serbs "Orthodox Croats." Serbs claim that the Macedonians are southern Serbs, Bulgarians that they are western Bulgarians, and Greeks that they are northern Greeks.[64]

Some forms of ethnic identity represent not a hardening but a *weakening* of ethnic boundaries. In the United States, Alba finds that among white Americans objective ethnic markers and differences—of education, residence, occupation, marriage—have been steadily and irreversibly eroding, yet there has been a simultaneous *increase* in ethnic phenomena such as media broadcasts in ethnic mother tongues, ethnic studies courses at colleges and a growing social sensitivity to matters of ethnicity. But it is not the same "old" ethnicity. Ethnicity has become increasingly voluntary. It is no longer a working- and lower-class style. On the contrary, among third-generation immigrants the more highly educated "may be more likely to identify ethnically than those with less education."[65] Herbert Gans refers to this as symbolic ethnicity. "Symbolic ethnicity is concerned with the symbols of ethnic cultures rather than with the cultures themselves."[66] Also termed "twilight ethnicity" it finds expression in ethnic activities of an occasional character and of a kind that is acceptable in a multiethnic setting.

This indicates "the underlying transformation of ethnicity in the lives of white Americans." First, what has remained or resurfaced is ethnic identity, or the subjective importance of ethnic origins and affiliation. Second, for most white Americans ethnic identification has become volitional, situationally specific and shallow. Ethnic identification is most salient among Italians, Jews and Poles and least among people originating from northern and Western Europe. Third, ethnic identity is privatized—"a reduction of its expression to largely personal and family terms."[67] Fourth, among third-generation immigrants ethnicity has become a form of cultural capital and ethnic identity rises with educational level; hence the multiethnic chic. Fifth, in the new ethnic category of "European Americans" the nature of ethnic culture changes. Thus "the ancestors of people who wear the 'Kiss me, I'm Italian' T-shirt never thought of themselves as such—but as Sicilian, or Calabrian, or Neapolitan—and would be mystified by their 'Italian-American' children."[68] The Italian food served to visitors at home may be fashionable north Italian cuisine quite unfamiliar to their ancestors.

Part of ethnic opportunism is the flexibility and fluidity of labels. Whether social movements identify themselves as ethnonationalists or as indigenous peoples is a matter of political strategy. In Indonesia movements seeking autonomy in West Papua and Maluku present themselves as indigenous peoples rather than as national liberation movements, which is less threatening to the state and more likely to find international recognition and partnership in transnational support networks. Fretilin in East Timor consistently portrayed itself as a national liberation movement. Both types of movements strive for autonomy but on different terms.

Part of the medley of motives that underlie the politics of cultural difference is the political economy of ethnicity. As discussed in the next chapter, ethnic enterprise is as old as the world's trading diasporas. In its two main forms, trading minorities and ethnic enclaves, ethnic enterprise is an accumulation strategy in nodal cities and globalizing settings.[69] Ethnic associations offer mutual aid, savings clubs, community self-help, market niches. Ethnic association provides transnational networks that serve as information channels and supply lines, and cultural cohesion sustains trust and cooperation. The Jews in Europe, Chinese in Asia, Arabs, Armenians, Lebanese and Indians across the world are familiar examples. Joel Kotkin makes a strong case for "global tribes" as strategic actors in the global economy.[70]

In the era of the multiethnic chic, ethnicity can be commodified and identity turned into a mercantile ploy. A trader of mixed Native American descent active in the "Indian business" in the U.S. muses that "It would be real interesting if it turned out that all Indians are 'fake'" and observes, "The media began looking at the Indian fad about seven years ago. Dealers and collectors in New York went directly from the African fad to the Indian fad. And the funny thing is that African 'trade beads' are now passed off as Indian 'trade beads'." From an entrepreneurial viewpoint ethnicity can be a chameleon strategy: "The minds of the Indians operate so that they can be Indian when they want to, or white when it's profitable, or Chicano when it's necessary. They can do whatever does them the most good."[71]

Here too belongs marketing identity, as in the commercialization of race in Bahia, where the Afro-Brazilian character of the old city in Salvador has become a factor in tourist appeal.[72] Other instances are "Irish theme bars and the commodification of Irishness" and "Consuming Ireland: Lucky Charms Cereal, Irish Spring Soap and 1–800-Shamrock."[73] The counterpart of marketing identity is "shopping for identity."[74] Other variations on the commodification of identity are marketing places (such as New Orleans or Harlem),[75] countries (as in campaigns for "Amazing Thailand" and "Exotic Thailand") or identity displays (such as Mardi Gras and the Rio Carnival). With marketing places and authenticity comes impression management. A native of Rome notes that many pizza makers are Egyptians "because they look more Italian."

Migrants of mixed descent at the Burma, Thai, and Chinese borderlands avoid ethnic categorization by manipulating their identity in order to adapt to the changing political and socioeconomic environment. Given China's economic expansion, non-Chinese migrants benefit from flexibly adopting a "trans-localized Chinese identity." Thus identity is centered on social relations rather than ethnicity and is often "contradictory, multilayered and fluid."[76]

Hybrids of various stripes—half-castes, halfies, combis, creoles, métis, mestizos, mulattos, pardos, ladinos, cholos, edge walkers—can choose to identify with dominant ethnicity ("passing"), subaltern ethnicity ("roots"), with their in-betweenness as a bridging bicultural capital (rainbow identity), or with all these identities serially. Multiple identities are another expression of optional ethnicity. Another feature of optional ethnicity is ambivalence. In Asian American discussions of identity Lisa Lowe observes, on the one hand, "the desire for an identity represented by a fixed profile of ethnic traits, and at another, challenges to the very notions of identity and singularity which celebrate ethnicity as a fluctuating composition of differences, intersections, and incommensurabilities."[77]

Table 2.1 gives an overview of types of ethnicity. The dynamics of each type are deliberately formulated in probabilities (may, tend to) and not as necessary developments.

Table 2.1. Types of ethnicity

Types	Variants	Key words	Dynamics
Domination	Nationalism, ethnocracy	Monocultural regime, forced assimilation, ethnic cleansing	May engender enclosure and tends toward competition
Enclosure	Dormant, confinement, ghetto	Low mobility, monocultural	Tends toward competition
Competition	Patronage, survival, self-enclosure	Mobile, bicultural niche competition over state and development resources	Tends toward optional ethnicity
Optional	Symbolic, low-intensity ethnicity, hybrid	Multicultural, multiple identity, ambivalence, opportunism	Beyond or after ethnicity

Politics of ethnicity

Ethnicity is protean. Ethnicities are clusters of cultural difference, and there are as many ethnicities as there are boundaries that social formations generate and positions to take along them. How then, if ethnicity serves as a common currency of power, do we arrive at the routine representation of ethnicity as a social or political problem associated with irrationality, riots, bloodshed, terror? According to Tim Shaw, "Ethnicity is only unacceptable when it is used for reasons unacceptable to dominant social interests."[78] But this is too simple. Ethnicity may be unacceptable too because of its exclusivist particularism and its domination internally and of other groups.

In contrast to optional ethnicity, at the other extreme of the ethnic identity spectrum are the claims made in the language of blood, updated in the language of DNA. In the words of the Native American poet John Trudell, "genetic light, from the other side." Ethnic identification may be taken to the point of ethnic fundamentalism. Class and national mobilization refer to universalist ethics of egalitarianism and democracy as part of their horizon, but ethnic mobilization per se has a particularist agenda only. It may take the form of cultural polarization, posing an unbridgeable gap of cultural habitus, as in négritude and Afrocentrism.[79] The fundamental affinity between racism and racism-in-reverse is familiar. As long as antiracism follows the logic of binary opposition, the current is the same, only the polarity changes. For instance, as the great poet of négritude and later president of Senegal Léopold Senghor conceded, there was a definite family relationship between Nazi racism and négritude: "Unconsciously, by osmosis and reaction at the same time, we spoke like Hitler and the Colonialists, we advocated the virtues of the blood."[80]

To return to a point made at the beginning, ethnicity is a continuation of the dialectics of domination and emancipation in a finer print of history, finer that is than the conflict between nations.[81] In the grand sweep of history, nationalism is viewed as a hallmark of modernity and attributed a progressive place. Even though the ways it expresses itself have rarely been edifying it is by and large deemed to have an emancipatory momentum. The past 150 years or so have witnessed countless battles fought in the name of nations—wars of great power rivalry, empires expanding and contracting, battles of colonization and decolonization. The upside of the age of nationalism is the fall of empires, the demise of absolutism, and the onset of people's sovereignty, constitutions, universal suffrage, self-determination, decolonization, and civil rights. In fact, much of the contemporary lexicon of political accomplishment and civility is beholden to this era. If this is an "age of ethnicity," present times seem to subvert these accomplishments but also appear to be a continuation of the same kind of battles for power that once prevailed among nations, now unfolding as civil strife *within* nations or between groups straddling nations. Often these tensions and conflicts existed all along but were papered over by the overriding drama of interstate war, colonialism, decolonization, and the Cold War. For instance, there were frictions all along between the Kabyle Berbers and majority Algerians, but as long as the headlines focused on the Algerian war of independence with France they seemed a background issue. Only in the wake of independence did they spring to the foreground, to be eclipsed again by the conflict between secularists and Islamists (the Islamic Salvation Front [FIS] and "Arab Afghans"). In a sense, then, the shift from the age of nationalism to the age of ethnicity is the background becoming foreground and the foreground fading into the background—a shift in the scenery of history and a shift in collective optics. From a local viewpoint this shift may often be much less significant, because cultural differences mattered all along, than when viewed from a distant remove (except that macro dynamics also significantly alter local relations).

If, by analogy to the epoch of nationalism, we contemplate the emancipatory dimension of ethnic conflict and set aside the blind ferocity of enmity and conflict, because this was equally characteristic of class struggles and interstate wars, what are the emancipatory features of ethnic conflict? It's not that ethnic discourses can be regarded as emancipatory, for the most conspicuous feature of enclosure ethnicity is its unrelenting particularism and its social practice is that of domination within: "Although ethno-nationalist insurgent projects highlight, in a larger-than-life fashion, ethnic grievances and injustices, they can rarely offer democratically emancipatory solutions or alternatives."[82] Yet nationalism is steeped in particularist pathos too. The lexicon of nationalism holds *both* a record of political accomplishment and political vice—chauvinism, jingoism, patriotism the last refuge of a scoundrel, and national pride that has lost its sheen. Nevertheless, our vocabulary of political accomplishment is beholden to the same epoch of massacres and wars that have raged on a far more devastating scale than the contemporary ethnic conflicts. Essentially this is the point that the conflict transformation approach makes: Conflicts are social learning processes.[83]

What is the prognosis? Is a hundred years of nationalism, at its peak from 1840 to 1960,[84] to be followed by a hundred years or so of ethnicity? If interstate wars gave rise to some form of international settlement, precarious but less so than before, will the "age of ethnicity" over time likewise result in interethnic settlements? It is contrived and artificial to view this as different phases because ethnic strife both preceded and follows the era of the nation state; but we now focus on the latter. The outcomes of ethnic conflict vary from secession and the formation of new nations, to long periods of social disintegration and warlordism as in Somalia,

Table 2.2. Politics of ethnicity

Type of ethnicity	Domination	Emancipation
Domination (nationalism)	Monoculturalism, internal colonialism, oppressing minorities, xenophobia, regional hegemony	Self-determination, anti-imperialism , anti-racism
Enclosure	Insularity, cultural exclusivism, suppressing internal differences (gender, class)	Self-determination, autonomy, dignity
Competition	Suppressing internal differences while seeking advantage over other ethnic groups	Collective struggle for improvement
Optional	Alienation, inauthenticity, posturing, opportunism	Individual or collective agency, multiple identity, flexibility

Liberia, and Sierra Leone, to cantonization, federalism, or power sharing and intercultural cohabitation.

The rival particularisms of nation and ethnicity, *éthnos* and *ethnikós*, may not be edifying, but they are not symmetrical, for one is dominant and the other subaltern. Even so, also subaltern identity often functions as a form of domination in its own social domain in relation to the differences that crosscut ethnicity. As the Sri Lankan political scientist Jayadeva Uyangoda notes, "They are indeed mini ethnic state projects in which the oppressed minority yesterday wishes to be transformed to an oppressive, or at least majoritarian, majority tomorrow in its own homeland. The desire of the oppressed minority to establish its own liberation may not necessarily ensure the minorities within that 'liberated' minority framework the right to autonomy or even limited self-determination."[85]

Rather than adopting a wholesale, generalizing position, we should recognize the *moments* and features of emancipation and domination in *each* form of ethnicity. These are schematically charted in Table 2.2.

Ethnicity endgames

> Different identities breed cooperation more often than conflict. If that were not so humanity would long ago have left the world a smoking ruin.
>
> —John Lonsdale (2002)

Since ethnicity is a construction, can it be deconstructed? According to Michael Peter Smith,

If ethnicity is constructed and reconstructed by articulations arising from contemporary conditions and power relations among social groups and the interpretative meanings people give to them, rather than out of some timeless or primordial dimension of human existence, then creative leadership by political and cultural elites and public intellectuals, as well as the everyday interventions of ordinary people into the flow of racial and ethnic discourse, do matter, perhaps more than we are now prepared to imagine.[86]

This hope was contested by the late Nigerian sociologist Claude Ake: "Part of the appeal of this view may well be the fear and contempt of some of us for ethnic consciousness and the desire to wish it away. . . . For those who are threatened by ethnicity, the belief that it is constructed is more than wishful thinking. It is an important practical matter. For one thing, they use this belief to legitimize a concerted assault on political ethnicity for as they reason, if ethnicity is constructed, it is amenable to deconstruction and it is entirely legitimate to deconstruct it. Many of them have done just that often with crude measures of social engineering and outrageous brutality."[87] This polemic makes sense but also misreads constructivism— that ethnicities, like nations, are constructed is not to say that therefore they are not real; rather, it is to make a statement about the *character* of their reality, acknowledging that their reality is contingent and open-ended. Instead Ake argues that ethnicity is "perhaps better conceived as a dialectic between imagination and reality," but that is just what constructivism is about. Ethnicity is continually being deconstructed—as one mode of ethnic identity gives way to another, as ethnocracy unravels, as enclosure ethnicity fades into competition ethnicity, as ethnic conflict produces a settlement, and as ethnic identity becomes optional.

A criticism I received on this perspective from a colleague in Salvador, Bahia, is that it seems to restate Robert Park's race relations cycle of contact, conflict, accommodation, and assimilation. My approach differs from Park's in several ways. First, we need not assume a single script. Several perspectives can coexist just as diverse processes can coexist. We can experience lasting conflict, enduring pluralism and mixing all at the same time. The same groups, even the same individuals can experience all of these, even simultaneously, in relation to different groups and different individuals. Second, Park's view assumes the modernization paradigm, that with modernization ethnicity declines in significance; I hold the opposite view. Third, Park's view assumes a fixed center and mainstream; I don't assume a stable center but problematize the mainstream by questioning the difference between nation and ethnicity from the outset. Park's view is built around the teleology of the American melting pot. In Park's view racism appears as an accident on the way to the melting pot. In the U.S. in the face of lasting ethnic difference the race relations cycle has been abandoned for cultural pluralism: from the melting pot to the salad bowl. In my analytic there is no automaticity, no *necessary* sequence, merely a likely one and even for this *no time frame* is indicated. Competition ethnicity may well endure in a situation of ethnic gridlock as in Sri Lanka, Cyprus, and, until recently, Northern Ireland. Fourth, the unit of analysis is not "race" but ethnicity. Fifth, Park assumes the nation state as the unit within which these dynamics unfold, but in my view the dynamics are not necessarily endogenous but as much transnational. Several conflicts endure precisely because transnational forces play a major part and local pluralism is overdetermined by regional power balances and overseas diasporas, as in Sri Lanka, Cyprus, and Hindu-Muslim tensions in India, Kashmir, and Pakistan. By the same token, some conflicts are resolved because of changing transnational power balances, such as apartheid and the Northern Ireland conflict. U.S. interests in the Middle East and its strategic partnership with Israel play a major part in sustaining the Israeli-Palestinian conflict.

Nation and sovereignty are not simply the framework but part of the problem. The local minority may be a regional majority. Transnational influence on internal national conflicts has increased in contemporary globalization. Sustained ethnic conflict in most cases is a working out of transnational power relations in local and national arenas. Settling them usually involves renegotiating the relations between nations and the definition of sovereignty.

How does distinguishing types of ethnicity contribute to our understanding of ethnic conflict regulation? Forms of ethnic conflict regulation range from methods for managing differences (hegemonic control, third party arbitration, cantonization, federalization, power sharing) to eliminating differences (conversion, assimilation, partition or secession, population transfer, genocide).[88] Are different forms of ethnicity amenable to different modes of conflict regulation? The varieties of ethnicity do not neatly translate into distinct scenarios. The discursive and political strategies that are deployed refer more to changing opportunity structures and niches than to compelling dispositions that would be intrinsic to each type of ethnicity. With this proviso, endgames of different forms of ethnicity run as follows.

Is the world of ethnic politics merely an archipelago of particularisms? According to Chantal Mouffe, "The progressive character of a struggle does not depend on its place of origin but rather on its link with other struggles."[89] Competition ethnicity is in a better position to forge such links and engage in roundtable politics of rainbow, multi-issue coalitions than enclosure ethnicity, but enclosure ethnicity is open to coalition politics as well.

Enclosure ethnicity. The exclusivism of enclosure ethnicity can lead to ethnic cleansing and elicits the standard condemnation of ethnicity. But this too needs unpacking. Enclosure ethnicity is a consequence of or reaction to ethnocracy; enclosure ethnicity tends towards competition ethnicity and enclosure can be a competitive strategy too—delinking for the sake of relinking, as in the Nation of Islam. Self-enclosure as a strategy is reflexive and a form of competition. Thus the line between enclosure and competition is thin and cooperation between enclosure ethnics and competition ethnics is frequent. An example is Cornel West's participation in Farrakhan's Million Man March in Washington. West joined the march in the name of "black operational unity" and following the example of Martin Luther King: "Dr King, the integrationist, had no fear of a black united front and no hatred of black nationalists."[90] This echoes episodes of cooperation between King and Malcolm X and between the PAC and ANC in South Africa.

Competition ethnicity. The dynamics of competition ethnicity tend toward autonomy or separatism (in which case it may produce mini-ethnocracy), toward ethnocracy, if it succeeds (as in the 1987 coup in Fiji), or toward power sharing. If power sharing succeeds, ethnicity is likely to become increasingly optional over time. Present times show both worst and best case scenarios. The worst case scenario of ethnic politics is an unending chain gang of particularisms, a vendetta logic in which the sins of the fathers are endlessly revisited upon the sons. Ethnic cleansing in Bosnia, Kosovo, Rwanda, and Burundi are worst case scenarios; Sri Lanka, Cyprus, Palestine, and Kashmir are in a stalemate; and South Africa and potentially Northern Ireland are examples of power sharing.

In his discussion of Hindus and Muslims in India, Varshney argues that to keep ethnic conflict from turning violent the key point is interethnic engagement in civil society, both everyday and associational engagement.[91] Thus the degree of interethnic, intercultural engagement is an indicator of competition ethnicity, rather than turning violent, becoming bicultural and in the process less salient and exclusive and thus optional. I agree with this emphasis on interethnic engagement and I develop this perspective in the next chapter as an underestimated and under-researched strand in ethnic studies. Yet this also points to the limitations of interethnic engagement. Interethnic civic engagement was also common in former Yugoslavia and Rwanda. If interethnic engagement doesn't take an institutional form, interethnic relations can break down and yield to violence under the influence of changing circumstances. In the end, then, the only way to break the vicious cycle of ethnic exclusivism is not occasional but *institutionalized power sharing.* Since the state and development resources are the main bones of contention this is where sharing has to take place. State power needs to be shared in terms of decentralization or devolution, citizenship, government positions and contracts, language, education, the armed forces, and public symbolism, and development resources need to be shared across regions and in terms of civic representation and cultural accommodation.

The endgames of ethnicity are not determined by ethnic politics per se because there is no ethnic politics per se. Ethnic politics doesn't stand alone but is mixed in with other politics and shaped by political conjunctures. This is the elusiveness of ethnicity as well as a source of hope. I don't share the pessimism of many observers of ethnicity. The key problem is not ethnicity but nationalism; more precisely, the key problem is domination ethnicity. Do those who so readily condemn ethnicity also condemn nationalism? The single factor that is common to all varieties of ethnicity (besides ethnocracy) is that they contest some form of monocultural regime, while often the outcome of protest is to establish monocultural control in as large a domain as the dissidents can control.

The emancipatory moment of ethnic mobilization lies in the fact that ultimately ethnic conflict is an affirmation of difference in the name of sameness—sharing the same aims, claiming the same rights as dominant or rival ethnic groups. The same aims—self-determination, prosperity—which now manifest as conflict may, when the balance of interethnic power has crystallized at a point where mutual recognition becomes possible and the benefits of settlement outweigh those of continued conflict, translate into recognition of the same rights and a settlement on that basis. If this affirmation is implicit in enclosure ethnicity discourse, it is often explicit in competition ethnicity discourse.

This is not meant as an optimistic assessment or prognosis but as an acknowledgment of struggle as the furnace of history. Neither is it pessimistic. The pessimism that contemporary ethnic politics evokes is as misguided and stereotypical as the stereotypical representations of ethnicity themselves. If it has been possible to acknowledge the dialectics of conflict in relation to nation and to class, is it not possible and indeed plausible to extend this to ethnicity?

No single narrative exhausts the variety of ethnicity or defines the course of ethnic politics. The fluidity of cultural identifications is part of our times. Living with shifting boundaries means living with ethnicity. Meanwhile, "ethnicity" is a term charged with past prejudice. It would be analytically more productive to discard the term and replace it with cultural difference and replace ethnic politics with culturally articulated interest politics. On the other side of ethnicity are hybridity, heterogeneity, and difference. But life after ethnicity comes available only by living with ethnicity. For one cannot want the outcome without wanting the process.

Notes

1. Nairn, quoted in Pollock 2000, 623; Meyer 2001; Jayatilleka 1995, 154.
2. Chua 2003.

3. Sansone 2003, 1.

4. For example, Sadowski 1998; Duijzings 2000; Bax 2000; Varshney 2002; Gagnon 2004. On the fluidity of identity, see Hall 1996; Bauman 2002; Sánchez 2006.

5. Varshney 2002, 39.

6. Marx and Engels distinguished revolutionary and counterrevolutionary nations; Cummins 1980, 177.

7. For example, Isaacs 1975.

8. See Hobsbawm and Ranger 1983; Vail 1989; Lonsdale 2002.

9. Verdery 1994, 37.

10. For example, Duijzings 2000, 2004, and below.

11. For example, Sollors 1989; Roosens 1989; Varshney 2002.

12. Brass 1991, 15, 25.

13. Brass 1991, 275. Brass 2003 adopts a similar elite-driven approach.

14. Bax 2000, 28, 29. Note also Mkandawire's critique of elite assumptions in the rational choice approach (2002).

15. Wang 1992. This argument concerns relations between recent and earlier arrivals from mainland China and leaves the native Taiwanese out of the picture; see Yen Liang 1989.

16. Esman 1994, 203.

17. Another typology of varieties of ethnicity is Riggs 1994. I don't accept Portes's (2000) distinction between linear ethnicity and reactive ethnicity. There is no such thing as linear ethnicity; if it were linear it would be dormant ethnicity. Ethnicity is always relational and thus reactive or else would not be ethnicity. Ake's (1994) notion of political ethnicity isn't persuasive because ethnicity is generally "political."

18. A. D. Smith 1992.

19. Guideri and Pellizi 1988, 7–8.

20. Brass 1991, 19.

21. Brass 1991, 20, 23.

22. See, for example, Young 1990.

23. Brubaker 2004.

24. Mayall and Simpson 1992, 15. The term ethnocracy was first coined by Veiter (1977), quoted in Stavenhagen 1986, 83.

25. Hechter 1975.

26. A pertinent discussion is Norbu, "The monoethnic state and polyethnic system: the rise of ethnic nationalism" (1992, ch. 10).

27. Norbu 1992, 183.

28. Smooha and Hanf 1992.

29. Berghe 1978. Wider discussions are Ringer 1983 and Jennings 2000.

30. Smooha and Hanf 1992; Kellas 1991.

31. Wilson 2000.

32. Rupesinghe and Kothari 1989.

33. Oommen 1990.

34. Feffer 1992.

35. Norbu 1992, 190.

36. Paul 2000.

37. Pollock 2000, 620.
38. Wang 1992.
39. Norton 1993.
40. Mayall and Simpson 1992, 9.
41. Anderson 1992; Goonatilake 1995.
42. Hechter 1975, 9.
43. Esman and Rabinovich 1988, 15.
44. See Wertheim 1978; Kothari 1989; Esman 1994.
45. Lee 1990; Ibrahim 1989; Hefner 2001.
46. Premdas 1993.
47. Kothari 1989, 214, 217. According to Kothari, "Developmentalism, as culture, creates a universal spread of commercial values and conspicuous consumption based on western life styles and in particular on the hegemony of the 'Market.' . . . Unlike other models of universality in past civilizations, this particular model is so arrogant and ethnocentric that it has no in-built mechanism of self-correction in it. Ethnicity and recovery of ethnic spaces become the only correctives" (214).
48. Brass 1991, 275.
49. On northern Italy ("Padania"), see Cotesta 2005. Rich discussions of nationalisms within Spain are in Graham and Labanyi 1995.
50. Mayall and Simpson 1992, 19. Humphrey 1997 views ethnic conflict as conflict over state power on the model of civil war.
51. Shaw 1986, 590.
52. Shaw 1986, 598–99, 591, 602.
53. Flere 1992, 263; Nederveen Pieterse 1998b, 54.
54. Burdsey 2004 refers to bicultural identity as "dual ethnicity."
55. Hall 1992.
56. West 1992, 704.
57. Walker 2005.
58. Laber 1993, 6, 3.
59. Humphrey 1997.
60. Deutscher 1981.
61. Brass 1991, 30, 31.
62. Eriksen 1993, 30.
63. Bell-Fialkoff 1993, 121.
64. Duijzings 2000.
65. Alba 1990, 16, 29.
66. Alba 1990, 306; Gans 1979; Waters 1996.
67. Alba 1990, 292, 300.
68. Delbanco 1992, 84.
69. Waldinger et al. 1990; Light and Bonacich 1988.
70. Kotkin 1992.
71. Steiner 1976, 209, 211. On the "Indian business," see Meyer and Royer 2001.
72. Sansone 2003, 72.
73. McGovern 2002; Negra 2001.
74. See Halter 2000.
75. Gotham 2002; Hoffman 2003.

76. Toyota 2003, 317, 307.

77. Lowe 1991, 27.

78. Shaw 1986, 597. "Ethnicity is only characterized as a 'problem' by the bourgeoisie when it ceases to be functional. . . . In short, ethnicity only becomes a problem when (i) ethnic groups turn the tables on each other in terms of access to the state; or (ii) ethnic politics degenerates from a form of political support into a basis for political secession."

79. Asante 1988.

80. Quoted in Hymans 1971, 71.

81. On dialectics of empire and emancipation, see Nederveen Pieterse 1989, ch. 15.

82. Uyangoda 2005, 967.

83. Lederach 1995.

84. Harris 1990.

85. Uyangoda 2005, 967.

86. M. P. Smith 1992, 526.

87. Ake 1994, 53.

88. McGarry and O'Leary 1993, 4.

89. Quoted in Mercer 1992, 429.

90. West 1996, 98.

91. Varshney 2002.

3

❖

Social capital and migration
Beyond ethnic economies

How does social capital relate to cultural difference? Considering the importance of crosscultural trade and economic relations, historically and now,[1] one would expect this to be a salient issue, but it hardly figures in the literature.

The conventional assumption is that social capital is culturally bounded. In most literature this is precisely taken as the strength (particularist loyalties lower transaction cost, etc.) and the weakness of social capital (group exclusiveness). There are two major strands in the literature. In one, cultural difference fades into the background and informal social relations and group bonds are at the foreground; this is the course taken in the work of James Coleman and Robert Putnam. In the other strand, culture (usually reified as "ethnicity") is both a resource and boundary of social capital. Here I focus on the latter terrain. In a sense this line of inquiry appears as an extended commentary on "ethnicity" as the pattern of a particular type of social relations, much of which is modeled on the role of the Jews in commerce. This was the subject of classic studies, Simmel's essay on *The Stranger* and Sombart's sequel study of *The Jews in Modern Capitalism*. An implication of these studies was that ethnic social capital is a premodern hangover in modern times.

Immigrant enterprise is now widely considered as a factor of economic dynamism in many countries. A matter of keen debate in the U.S. and Canada is whether immigrant enterprises are more significant employment creators than domestic enterprises. Headlines such as "Millions of immigrants needed to sustain economies" are increasingly common in Canada, Germany, Italy, and other countries.[2] The backdrop is graying labor markets in OECD countries. In addition, specific immigrant groups make special contributions such as Indian software programmers and Chinese engineers and programmers in Silicon Valley, and are actively sought after. At the same time that countries relax rules to facilitate the deportation of undocumented immigrants, they relax immigration laws to facilitate bringing in desired migrant entrepreneurs and to attract dotcom enterprises and programmers.[3]

In this context several stereotypes of immigrant enterprise are gradually being left behind. A recent study of Tunisian immigrants in France shows that, unlike in the 1970s, immigrants are now more often self-employed, community ethics give way to economic pragmatism, and commercial organization and transnational networks are emerging. This also applies to Asian and Turkish immigrants in France, and there are similar findings in Germany.[4]

The economic significance of international migration is large and growing. Migrants' remittances to their countries of origin are $150 billion a year, and informal remittances are estimated at another $300 billion, far in excess of foreign aid (ca. $50 billion in 2005) and as a source of revenue for developing countries second only to foreign direct investment.[5] Overseas diasporas are also sources of foreign investment, as in the case of China.[6]

Meanwhile, in most research the attention remains focused on the *ethnic* character of enterprise. This chapter argues that *ethnic economy* is more often a misnomer than accurate. Cultural capital matters alongside social capital but viewing it as "ethnic" in character is not helpful and likely to be misleading. The second general point is that immigrant economies are often embedded within crosscultural economies. I consider whether *immigrant economy* would be a more insightful terminology but find similar problems. I find that drawing a distinction between monocultural and *multicultural social capital* is most productive.

In relation to social capital a key distinction runs between *causes* of social capital (norms and values or "habits of the heart," and social networks) and *outcomes*, such as lower transaction costs.[7] Among causes, a distinction runs between strong and weak social ties. Further distinctions run between *bonding* social capital (strong ties among close relations), *bridging* social capital (weak ties among people from diverse backgrounds but similar socioeconomic status), and *linking* social capital (or "friends in high places"). Considerations of cultural difference or ethnicity apply across these different dimensions of social capital and take on cultural hues, that is, each apply within and across cultural settings. The question of cultural difference and social capital arises in three different contexts: immigration and migration, transnational enterprise, and ethnically diverse societies. In this treatment the emphasis is on migration and immigrant enterprise.

A related question is how is cultural difference conceptualized? Is *ethnicity* adequate or burdened by time? Much literature and reporting on ethnicity is fraught with friction, tension, and antagonism. Media report on ethnicity mainly when it generates conflict in line with the principle "when it bleeds it leads," but what of the situations when ethnicity doesn't involve conflict or when conflict is minor?

This chapter opens by probing the notion of social capital. The next section deals with the problematization of ethnic economies and ethnicity, continuing the conversation of the previous chapters. This leads to shifting the focus to crosscultural enterprise. Because a historical dimension is often missing in this line of research and focusing on the present confines analysis, I also consider immigrant economies in a historical setting. This yields several types of crosscultural economies that can be linked to varieties of social capital. The closing section considers policy ramifications of the shift in orientation from ethnic to crosscultural enterprise.

Social capital

The theme of social capital emerges on the heels of human capital. Just when the importance of capabilities, capacitation, and enablement is recognized, the attention shifts—"It's not what you know, it's who you know!"[8] Also on the horizon is cultural capital, and other newcomers are natural and moral capital. A background consideration (discussed below) is that none of these would add up to much without economic resources. And so the debate runs the course of several forms of capital—economic, physical, financial, human, cultural, social, moral, political, natural—and eventually comes back full circle, to economic capital. Presumably the question is what we learn during the journey.

Social capital is usually defined as the capacity of individuals to gain access to scarce resources by virtue of their membership of social networks and institutions. Putnam gives a wide definition of social capital as "features of social organization such as networks, norms and social trust that facilitate coordination and cooperation for mutual benefit."[9]

Social capital is a notion of the times and "the latest conceptual fad across the social sciences."[10] A hybrid notion, social capital mixes angles that used to be wide apart. It brings the *social* into economics and, by the same token, looks at the social from an economic point of view. Its social angle on the market comes at the price of a market angle on the social. One is not sure whether just to scratch one's head or pull out one's hair. The appeal of social capital can be read both as an agenda in its own right and as a sign of the times.[11] The significance and appeal of social capital is that it serves as a bridge among sociology, economics, and politics, as a linking concept that bridges diverse fields and invites interdisciplinary research. In the process it presents several problems.

World Bank language refers to social capital as "the glue that holds society together." Social, all right, but capital? This is a very particular way of looking at social relations. The "social" of course figures in many approaches, such as network analysis (anthropology), social distance, chains of interdependence (sociology), and reciprocity; trust, solidarity, and belonging are other ways of looking at social relations.

The terminology itself is heavy luggage. The backdrop of capitalism becomes foreground in that social capital refers to social relations and institutions that are being viewed as instrumental within a capitalist framework, so social relations and networks become "capital," assets that can be employed for income generation. For Bourdieu this was part of a social technology of domination, another glance at how the elite runs things and a French equivalent of the "old boy network."[12] With Coleman it is part of a rational choice approach to collective action and a functionalist perspective in which social relations are defined as exchange relations.[13] Robert Putnam establishes a link among social capital, civic democracy, and public and economic performance. In the wake of Putnam's work, social capital and democracy has become a well-established theme.[14] It suggests a causal link between social connectedness, social trust, civic engagement, and civic democracy,[15] and a further link to economic prosperity.

"Capital" in human, cultural, social, and natural capital holds a promise of measurability, which is a highly strategic attribute in market-driven times. Rational choice and functionalism contribute to an analytical approach that can be readily transformed into a policy package. No wonder that for some time social capital has been à la mode and in the spotlight of funding agencies. Yet social capital is a slippery concept that ranges from cultural attitudes and social practices to public policy, politics, and economic development. Attending a World Bank conference on social capital, Desmond McNeill jots down the following stray remarks: "Social capital is a battering ram to get social issues into development." But according to an economist, "This is pure smoke." Alternatively, it is "anthropological wine in economic bottles."[16] These sprawling observations illustrate the perplexity surrounding the concept.

Social capital would make it possible to link concerns such as civil society (along with social cohesion and participation), democracy, and good governance with economic growth and development. A booming literature, particularly in economics and political science, scans the contours of social capital to examine whether it meets the requirements of clear definition, measurability and applicability and can serve as an instrument of analysis and policy. Much current literature is concerned with conceptual clarification and is of a modeling nature, like rival exercises in reductionism. The objective is to uncover and, next, to instrumentalize social capital as the newest variable of productivity and development policy. "If you can't count it, it doesn't count." Whatever can be turned into an indicator is welcome in an age of managerialism. For now, we bracket this problematic and turn to the question how cultural difference is conceptualized in this setting.

Ethnic economies?

The common point of departure is the notion of ethnic economies.[17] In economic sociology it is defined as follows: "An ethnic economy consists of the ethnic self-employed and employers, and their co-ethnic employees" and "An ethnic economy exists whenever any immigrant or ethnic minority maintains a private economic sector in which it has a controlling ownership stake."[18] The assumption is that particularistic loyalties involve and engender trust and thus lower transaction cost. Jewish diamond traders in New York and Antwerp passing one another diamonds for inspection on trust, without written contracts, are classic examples. The general argument is that social control is greater and the enforcement cost of noncompliance with business expectations is lower within ethnic settings.

At this point let us pause and consider the term ethnicity. "Ethnicity" in "ethnic economy" performs a double duty. It is defined as a social science concept (as above) while it borrows the aura of "ethnicity" from general usage. One problem is that these two uses, the definition and the image of ethnicity, cannot be kept neatly apart.

What precisely is *ethnic* in ethnic neighborhood, ethnic food, or ethnic economy? The term "ethnicity" expresses a relationship; it denotes foreignness, but a particular kind of foreignness. It seems that some national origins are foreign whereas others are also ethnic. Ethnicity denotes difference and cultural distance from the mainstream. For instance, in researching migrants in Brussels and Belgium, Favell distinguishes between two kinds of migrants, in his words: European (professional, elite) and non-European or "'ethnic' (i.e., crudely speaking, post-colonial and third world) immigrants."[19] So some nationalities are more ethnic than others.[20]

In the United States the language is ambiguous; the idea of "white ethnics" has gained currency (in the slipstream of ethnic chic), yet Canadians, Brits, Australians, and Germans are rarely referred to as "ethnic." German, British, Irish, or Scandinavian food in the U.S. may be foreign but not necessarily ethnic, presumably because these cultural influences had been integrated into the mainstream in an earlier phase. Yet this also applies to Native and African Americans, though these are still regarded as ethnic. Ethnicity is a marker of cultural distance, but not every cultural distance qualifies. A people's or country's location in the hierarchy of power also matters.

In the U.S., Dominicans, Salvadorans, Cubans, Koreans, Ethiopians, and so on are considered as "ethnicities," but in fact this refers not to ethnicity but to *national origin*. This means that "ethnicity" serves as a descriptor of a relationship between cultures, a parameter of cultural difference and distance, which doesn't necessarily tell us much about the group itself. Within the host country, the nationality may be viewed as an ethnic group or minority, but this doesn't necessarily match relations within the country of origin. *Within* each of the nationalities mentioned there are multiple cultural groups and subcultures identified by region, language, religion, and sect, which in some contexts are called ethnic groups. In Manchester, Pakistanis are viewed as an ethnic group, but they hail from quite different regions in Pakistan.[21] Cubans from Cuba are quite different from the "Miami Cubans,"[22] and among the latter Cuban Jews are different again.

Let's consider the example of Ghanaians. Ethnic groups among Ghanaians include Asante, Fante, Brong, Kwahu, and Adansi, which belong to the broader Akan ethnic group, and other groups are Ga, Adangbe, Ewe, and Dagban. These groups are reproduced in the migrant communities overseas where usually ethnic associations have been formed. Ethnic associations "provide social and moral support, especially in time of bereavement and fatal sickness, much more than any tangible economic and social value for the establishment of business, hence their limited membership base and level of participation."[23] Ethnic associations exist alongside other networks such as national associations, churches, old boy networks, professional associations, class-based networks, and women's clubs. Although there are some ethnic patterns and clusters in migration, migrant communities are ethnically mixed.[24] Accordingly, ethnic association is only a narrow basis for social capital. Ghanaian researcher George Amponsem comments on its implications for business:

> Due to intense competition, playing one's membership of a particular ethnic group too high leads to the risk of business being branded as an "ethnic shop" by the immigrant community at large and, therefore, risks exclusion and patronage from other members in the community. Rather, membership or affiliation with Ghanaian (national) associations such as the Ghanaian National Association of Hamburg, Sikaman Association in Amsterdam, and Association of Ghanaians in Toronto, even though difficult to organize in bigger cities like London and New York, are more neutral and preferable to ethnic ones.[25]

Thus what from a Canadian, American, German, or Dutch point of view is an "ethnic shop," from a Ghanaian point of view is precisely *not* an ethnic shop. It wouldn't make sense as, and could not afford to be, an ethnic shop. By labeling it thus and assuming social capital to be based on "ethnicity" we have precisely missed the point.

This is probably generally valid. Lebanese businessmen in West Africa, North America, or Australia hail from different regions and denominations within Lebanon. Although they belong to a nationality different from that of the host country, their social and economic cooperation need not be among Lebanese and still less likely on an "ethnic" basis.[26] Although Jews are generally considered an "ethnic group," Israel is now a multicultural society. Korean grocery stores in the U.S. rank as ethnic shops in media and literature, but their social cooperation need not be on an ethnic basis since they come from different regions in South Korea. Only occasionally are we told of a *regional* or specific identification besides the national one, for instance, Palestinians owning stores in the San Francisco Bay Area are mostly Christians from the Ramallah area.[27] Similarly, Iranians in Los Angeles break down into at least four different groups: Jews, Bahais, Muslims, and Armenians. This has been interpreted as "internal ethnicity in the ethnic economy"; thus what seems to be an ethnic economy upon closer inspection turns out to be four ethnic economies.[28]

The foundations of ethnicity may include region, language, alleged common descent, or religion, and these can crosscut one another (same language, different religion, etc.). Take the case of religion. Instances where religion and ethnicity (i.e., region, language, alleged common descent) coincide, such as Sikhs, Parsis, Ismailis, and Jews, are rare by comparison to crosscultural religions. Besides, these groups are not homogeneous either: not all Sikhs, Parsis, Ismailis, or Jews follow the religion or the same variant (as in Orthodox, Hasidic, and Reform Judaism). The "world religions" are typically crosscultural and so are their adherents, in their countries of origin as well as in immigration countries. A Shiva temple in India or Nepal is a meeting place for Saivaite Hindus from different parts of India or Nepal. The four hundred Hindu temples in the U.S. have typically been built by Hindus from different regions of India—Gujaratis, Bengalis, and Tamils working together.[29]

Metropolitan Phoenix, Arizona, counts six mosques that are places of worship for Saudis, Sudanese, Pakistanis, Lebanese, Maghribians, and so on. The largest mosque is located in Tempe. Next to the mosque complex are a Lebanese restaurant (named Carthage), a barbershop, a bazaar with a *halal* butcher, and other trades, a combination of services that reflects the communal character of Islam.[30] The center also serves as a crosscultural meeting place. The social capital that is invested in and arises from this complex is typically crosscultural, as a reflection of Islam as a crosscultural religion. Thus it refers not to ethnic social capital but to rainbow social and cultural capital. Mosques in Europe and other places of Muslim diaspora function in the same way as crosscultural meeting places. Smaller mosques cater to Sunni Muslims of specific national origins, notably for language reasons (e.g., mosques in Amsterdam neighborhoods for Moroccans, Surinamese, or Turks, but rarely for all). Even then they are not necessarily "ethnic" because Moroccans from different parts of Morocco may frequent the mosque.[31]

The Detroit suburb of Dearborn, Michigan, known as the Ford Motor Company headquarters, now ranks as a center of "Arab America" where 275,000 Middle Easterners have settled, the largest concentration of Arab Americans in the country. Middle Eastern immigration started with Lebanese early in the century and has since brought immigrants from every country across the Middle East. Although no more than half of these are Muslims, a new mosque complex, billed as the largest mosque in the country, is being built, spread over ten acres. Services at the existing mosque "draw a diverse crowd of devotees from throughout the area, including many Americans whose ancestors emigrated from Europe or Africa long ago and who have since converted to Islam."[32] In such crosscultural and crossnational conglomerations as East Dearborn, "ethnic economy" becomes useless as an analytic and is clearly too narrow; a different conceptualization is needed.

It follows that we need to question and open up the notion ethnic economy itself.[33] It's true of course that ethnic groups have been formidable social, cultural, and economic forces past and present, but "ethnos" simply means people and so does "ethnicity" when stripped of its older connotations (discussed in chapter 1) and there are many different peoples within a people.[34] In reality there are no neat boundaries between ethnic groups; the boundaries are typically fuzzy and permeable.[35] Thus many immigrant entrepreneurs who are labeled ethnic are in reality hyphenated and mixed, and on this ground alone ethnic economies tend to be hyphenated economies. The ethnic economy approach, like most approaches that deal with ethnicity, ignores the hybrids, the in-betweens. Furthermore, an "ethnic economy" is not necessarily an economy with a degree of interconnectedness or integration but just as likely a random set of businesses. It may be a different case if we consider ethnically diverse societies (i.e., diverse not because of recent immigration). Here ethnicity and ethnic social capital *may* be relevant terms with the proviso that there are many different varieties of ethnicity here too (as discussed in chapter 2). Of course, crosscultural relations count here as well.[36]

In his fine study of transnational informal enterprise of Ghanaians worldwide George Amponsem rejects the term ethnic economy and opts for *embeddedness* instead.[37] He argues that what distinguishes "'ethnic' from 'non-ethnic' enterprise is the degree of embeddedness of organizational strategies in informal personal networks, trust and social relations.

This study has shown that Ghanaian immigrant business strategies and practices are highly organized along crosscutting and cross-community ties, social trust and informal relations." What sets them apart from mainstream firms is that the latter are organized "along formal and contractual relations." "Given that the differences are contextualised and analysed in the dualist model rather than the interface process, the difference is conceptualised as 'ethnic' and 'non-ethnic' enterprises. The ethnic economy discourse is therefore another dualist dichotomy of 'otherness' in strategy and practice."[38]

If we consider that what matters is a *difference of degree*, between the prevalence of formal and informal, contractual and noncontractual relations in business, the discussion is set on a different footing. Formal and contractual enterprise also involves informal relations and implicit understandings, that is, it is embedded in cultural and social practices but embedded in different ways.[39] In the background looms the paradigm of modernity and Parsons's pattern variables. The point of social capital, trust, institutional density, and related notions is to open up this framework to examine the underlying social relations that make business tick.[40] Yet embeddedness is too vague a notion and not distinctive if we consider, following Polanyi, that *all* market relations are socially (and culturally) embedded.

Would it be more insightful if instead of ethnic economy we would say *immigrant enterprise*? This leads to several other problems. Does it concern first- or second-generation immigrants? There is cultural segmentation among immigrants, too. They relate to widely different economic specializations, and immigrant enterprise comes in many varieties, as the discussion below suggests. An alternative is that, instead of referring to ethnicity, we distinguish between (mono) culturally embedded and crosscultural social capital.

Crosscultural enterprise

A general consideration is that immigrant economies in order to function need to build ties with other communities and cultural groups. By labeling immigrant enterprise "ethnic" and by focusing on its informal and grassroots character we set it apart. The major drawback of "ethnic economy" discourse is the suggestion and assumption of ethnic boundaries. Ghanaian informal enterprise reaching across the world—Düsseldorf, London, Amsterdam, Vancouver, Tokyo, and so on—involves many non-Ghanaians, formally and informally. Informal business relations are not confined within ethnic boundaries. Amponsem describes the social relations of Ghanaian traders in Bangkok as follows:

Successfully living in an isolated Bangkok hotel for four weeks, without family and with limited contact with the foreign social environment, is only made possible for the trader through the social interaction and the family atmosphere created together with other traders and migrants—a "little local community". It is usually a scene of sharing and interaction reminiscent of a social gathering of "communities" as Ghanaian traders from different parts of the world meet their counterparts from Nigeria, South Africa, Zaire, Mali and Guinea, for example, at the lobby of the Top High Hotel in the Pratunam area in Bangkok.[41]

If Dearborn as "Arab America" and Jackson Heights in Queens, New York, for South Asians are spectacular examples of crosscultural agglomerations, the principle of crosscultural relations *across* immigrant groups holds much wider. It applies to the overseas Chinese and Chinatowns where immigrants from different regions often mingle.[42] It applies to settings such as Amsterdam Southeast, where Surinamese, Antilleans, Moroccans, and Ghanaians, Ethiopians, and other Africans each tend to have their own circles but also mingle.[43] Or to the mixed Latino presence in Mount Pleasant in Washington, D.C., Jackson Heights in Queens, Spanish Harlem in New York, and East Los Angeles, and to Dubai, where 85 percent of the population is foreign born.

Labor, training, customers, supplies, credit and possibly real estate, accountants, and solicitors necessarily bring immigrant enterprises into contact with many other networks. Neighborhood and social life are other factors. All this tends to be concealed from view if the heading is "ethnic economy" and so these links are under-researched. Meanwhile, it is also true that when it comes to issues that represent deeper forms of integration, such as unionization and health insurance, immigrant groups often appear to be insular, as found for instance in California.[44]

Labor is a keynote in the definition of ethnic economy. "The ethnic economy is ethnic because its personnel are co-ethnics."[45] This is a narrow criterion, but even by this criterion ethnic economies may be a shrinking phenomenon. With growing migration in conjunction with a hierarchy among emigration countries, crosscultural employment has long been on the increase. Thus Japanese restaurants with Korean waiters are common, and examples along these lines are abundant.[46]

Job seekers in the culturally segmented labor market of Toronto use both ethnic and interethnic circuits, which fulfill different roles. Using interethnic ties helps people gain access to diverse resources beyond their homogeneous networks. Access to social capital beyond the ethnic group's boundary principally benefits members of the ethnic group who are concentrated in lower paying jobs, whereas for members of mainstream, high-status ethnic groups, using intra-ethnic ties is associated with higher income. Research indicates that the advantage of using interethnic ties is conditional on the socioeconomic status of job seekers and job contacts: if the contact is with higher-status ethnic groups, the use of inter-ethnic ties is more rewarding than are ties with members of lower-status groups.[47]

Los Angeles ranks as "the sweatshop capital of the United States."[48] Here, according to a *Los Angeles Times* poll, "minority-owned firms tend to hire within their own ethnic group," but actually the patterns diverge. Businesses owned by Latinos in Los Angeles County describe their work force as three-quarters Latino; 41 percent of black businesses report a mostly black work force, and a third of Asian firms employed mostly Asian workers and almost as many had a mostly Latino work force.[49] The latter pattern of crosscultural (or interethnic) employment, such as Asian garment manufacturers in California employing Mexicans, is confirmed by further research.[50]

The distinction between exploitative and non-exploitative trust[51] does not likely coincide with the line separating crosscultural and same-culture employment. Is trust less exploitative when employer and employee share the same national origin? That would overestimate the homogeneity of national origins; among South Asians, caste crosscuts national and regional identities; class, region, and religion also come in.

In East San Jose, the Latino shopping center Tropicana has in recent years seen an increase of immigrant Vietnamese business owners who now own nearly one third of the shops. In a new shopping center across the road, El Mercado, a deliberate attempt is being made to blend Mexican and Asian cultures. Art is used as a tool to blend the communities (for instance with an exhibit on marketplaces from Mexico, Vietnam, Nigeria, and Portugal). A Vietnamese architect comments, "We need to create a myth, the kind of myth that highlights our relationships and the good things between the communities."[52] Crosscultural commerce is a growing trend and an emerging theme. Part of this is the rise of ethno-marketing as a function of growing multiculturalism across the world.[53] For commerce in crosscultural settings the importance of crosscultural skills such as language is obvious.[54]

Research on ethnicity and ethnic economies has generally concentrated on the *inward* character of ethnicity to the neglect of relations with the outside world. But how do immigrants relate to the wider economy and society? They function commercially and as entrepreneurs by acting as go-betweens or by integrating. Armenian businessmen in Europe and North America, Lebanese contractors and shopkeepers in West Africa, Chinese *tokos* in the Caribbean, Chinese businesses in Hungary and Spain, Surinamese stores in the Netherlands, Korean grocery stores in the U.S., Palestinian stores in California, Indian corner dairies in New Zealand—all deal with suppliers, customers, and employees of different ethnicities, whether local or of other immigrant communities. Operating in an inter-cultural space affects the consciousness and identity, habitus and business practices of immigrants, as research among Colombian businessmen in the Netherlands shows.[55]

In Germany, Turkish businesses employing more than ten people increased to almost five thousand in 1998; Turkish businesses include not only retail and restaurants (61 percent) but also service, manufacturing, and construction sectors (27 percent). A Turkish enterprise that began as a travel agent for guest workers has become Germany's eighth largest travel agent with an annual revenue of 914 million marks.[56] In these cases family or coethnic labor and credit may often play a part but by no means across the board. The trend in immigrant economies is toward greater use of bank credit.[57] Muslims require interest-free loans for business and mort-gages, which puts them in touch with the crosscultural circuit of *hawal* bankers or alternative institutions.[58]

Immigrant enterprise, then, is a wheel within a larger set of wheels. Cul-tural social capital functions and over time can only function as part of crosscultural social capital. Immigrant business includes several varieties:

1. Immigrant business catering to same nationality immigrants. *Not* the same ethnicity because that would be too small a market.
2. Immigrant business catering to other immigrants. A Dominican gro-cery in California selling Mexican products to Salvadoran customers. A Turkish carpet shop selling Belgian factory carpets to Moroccans in the Netherlands.
3. Immigrant business serving a niche market. For instance, a French hairdresser, Italian pizzeria, Chinese restaurant, Korean contractor in New York. In this case ownership, management, labor, supply, and credit may or may not follow immigrant or national origin connec-tions. Within this pattern, there are many variations. One variation is an immigrant business acting as intermediary between immigrants and locals, for instance, in labor recruitment, contracting, ethno-marketing, or crime.[59]
4. Immigrant businesses from diverse origins clustered together, either by tradition or by design, as in the recent trend of *ethnic shopping malls* from Toronto to Amsterdam.[60] (Note again that "ethnic" here has the popular meaning of non-western and doesn't refer to a sin-gle ethnicity but on the contrary to the combination of cultural groups.)
5. Immigrant business catering to local customers. In other words, a business that has entered the mainstream; although different in na-tional origin it is not necessarily different in business practices.
6. A second- or third-generation immigrant business. Now the business

may either continue to occupy a niche market using national origin for sign value (the Jewish Deli in New York) or national origin may fade into the background. In terms of business practices and ownership (e.g., a joint venture with nationals or being traded on the stock exchange) it may become indistinguishable from local enterprise. A Chinese-owned garage in Jakarta may differ from other garages only in ownership or management.

This is what a short-term typology yields. The picture changes further if we consider the *longue durée*.

In the *longue durée*

The crosscultural dimension acquires greater depth the longer the time period we consider. That change across generations makes a huge difference in immigrant careers is well known. Yet most current research does not involve intergenerational data and yields narrower conclusions than if we would widen the perspective over long time spans by taking into account historical research.[61] Immigrant economies are widespread and as old as the trading diasporas and the combination of commerce and migration. The major varieties of immigrant economies distinguished in the literature are minority or immigrant enterprise, trading or middleman minorities, and enclave economies.

Minority enterprise and commerce is the general category and a common phenomenon, as the study of economic history of virtually any region shows. Enclave economies or immigrant business catering to customers of the same ethnicity only or mainly, is probably relatively rare and limited; trading or middleman minorities are much more common. The Jews in Europe are the classic example. The collaboration between the Chinese and the Spanish in the Philippines, between the Chinese and the Dutch in the East Indies, between Chettiars from Madras and the British in Burma, and between Ismailis from Gujarat and the British in East Africa are other examples. Closer examination shows that before the minority was recruited in a particular function and assumed middleman status in the interstices of colonialism or empire, it was usually already present and active in the region. Dobbin's account of the role of the Chinese in Manila begins like this: "The Spanish expedition which arrived at Manila in 1570 found four Chinese junks in the harbour. Manila, the Spaniards reported, 'was large and carried on an extensive trade. In the town lived forty married Chinese and twenty Japanese.'"[62] The Spanish built on the Chinese junk trade between Manila and Fujian province and wove this regional commercial network into their own growing intercontinental galleon trade.

A similar pattern applies to the Parsis who were such important brokers for the British in their commerce and empire building in India. Before being enlisted into collaboration by the British they were already active as a commercial minority in the region. The presence of Parsis on India's West Coast goes back to the ninth and tenth centuries when due to Arab competition in the Persian Gulf they moved the center of their activities eastward. "Thus the Parsis should not be seen as a refugee community settling down in India as agriculturalists and weavers, woken to commercial life by the European East India Companies, but rather as having much earlier developed a new trading diaspora between the Arab-dominated Middle East and Hindu India."[63]

Immigrant economies are embedded in intercultural economies. For immigrant enterprise to be successful, entrepreneurs must be at least bicultural. The Chinese diaspora in Southeast Asia and the Pacific has prospered thanks to its capacity to integrate and build relations with the environment, in language, cultural savvy, and through weaving relations of reciprocity and trust. Thus over time mestizo groups developed, such as the Chinese Mestizos of the Philippines (later the Catholic Chinese Mestizos) and the Peranakan Chinese in Java and Malaysia and their conversion to Islam (*peranakan* means "child of the country").[64] This doesn't match Furnivall's classic description of colonial plural society in Java and Burma according to which different ethnic groups met and mingled only in the marketplace. Conversion and intermarriage don't take place in the marketplace. Chinese Mestizos in the Philippines are nowadays deeply integrated and typically interact with other businessmen not on an ethnic footing but as members of the business community in settings such as Lions and Rotary Clubs.[65] At times Peranakan Chinese integrated in multiple circuits at the same time, for instance in the multicultural East Indies: Christian, Muslim and Javanese.[66] It doesn't match either Amy Chua's account of the Chinese in Southeast Asia as market-dominant minorities that evoke hatred and resentment—which does happen but pertains mainly to a wealthy segment of the ethnic Chinese.[67]

The literature distinguishes *political incorporation* of immigrants, such as strangers in the Buganda kingdom in East Africa who attach themselves as clients to district chiefs or to their subjects, delivering tribute in kind or labor, and *cultural incorporation*, the adoption of language, customs, dress, mode of livelihood, fictive kinship, and religious practices, such as strangers in Central Africa.[68] The relationship between colonialism and trading minorities can be considered a specific type of political economic incorporation of immigrants.

An asset of the Chinese diaspora has been their readiness to integrate with native society and adopt the local language and religion. This also applies to migration within China.[69] The capacity and willingness for intercultural adaptation stem from prior experience with other trading diasporas:[70] "A large number of Chinese settlers were converted to Islam. Having come largely from Fujian, they not only found it advantageous to adopt the predominant religion of the Javanese port towns, but in fact were familiar with the role of Islam in Fujian's trade. In Quanzhou, Fujian's most important seaport by the late thirteenth century, both trade and administration were dominated by foreign Muslims and an Islamic diaspora promoted trade with the rest of Asia."[71]

This suggests that intercultural enterprise is often part of a *chain of diasporas*, each imparting skills, networks, and models of crosscultural intercourse. As mentioned above, the classic middleman role in colonialism is often a specification of earlier commercial activity. Phoenicians in Carthage and Barcelona, Jews and Greeks from ancient times onward, Arabs, Hadramis, Persians, Parsis, and Armenians partly in their footsteps and Chinese, Indian, and Malay diasporas in their turn, thus form an interlinked series that stretches back deep in time and wide across space. Thus for centuries Christian Armenians were the *trait d'union* in the silk trade between the Safavids in Persia and the Levant.[72] Arab and Hadrami trade diasporas in Asia and Africa also integrated and intermarried with local society.[73] This brief gloss leaves out many other trading diasporas and networks; witness the history of crosscultural long-distance trade.[74] How deep in time several of these networks run is suggested by the traces of trade found between ancient Egypt and the Harappa culture of Mohenjodaro and of trade with the Romans found in Cochin on India's west coast.

A fundamental reason why diasporas have played throughout history and continue to play such a key role in crossborder trade is that "contract enforcement is more problematic across national boundaries than it is domestically." Ethnic networks offer social control that makes up for the lack of legal recourse, which is particularly important in crossborder trade. As Dani Rodrik notes, "The role played by ethnic networks in fostering cross-border trade and investment linkages (for example, among the Chinese in Southeast Asia) suggests the importance of group ties in facilitating economic exchange. But such ties are hard to set up across national borders in the absence of fortuitous ethnic and other social linkages."[75] In times of accelerated globalization diaspora links take on added importance.

Chain and network migration are familiar themes. In addition, a multicultural history serves as a skill and cultural capital among immigrant groups. In explaining the powerful influence of Middle Eastern entrepreneurs in various industries in California, built over a short period of time, Kotkin notes that "particularly Jews, Arab Christians and Armenians, have a long history of being minorities in great polyglot cities of the Old World: Beirut, Tehran, Jerusalem, Cairo or Damascus."[76]

Coming back to Fujian (old Fukien), it is not among China's poorest regions but is a land-poor region that developed an emigration culture that goes centuries back in time. Fujian is now estimated to send around one hundred thousand emigrants abroad every year.[77] The case of human smuggling that had tragic consequences in Dover, England, in the summer of 2000 concerns Fujian migrants, and so do several other episodes of illegal Chinese migration into Europe and North America.

Ulrich Beck speaks of "place polygamy," and Pico Iyer charts the lives of global souls.[78] Crossborder and transnational social relations are growing in density and importance, and these increasingly complex relations can only be understood by recognizing multiple identity. For instance, the identities of settler and sojourner are not mutually exclusive (a point made in an account of the trans-Pacific character of the Chinese presence in San Francisco).[79] Akio Morita, the late Sony chairman, argued that "insiderism" is a necessity for multinational corporations: multinationals can only be successful if they become insiders in the host economies and societies, so they must "look in both directions."[80] Migration history suggests that "insiderism" is common and has deep roots in time. What is now called *glocalization*—after another Japanese expression—has been the common practice in the historical chains of trading diasporas.

Rainbow economies

Whereas the *ethnic enclave economy* approach emphasizes clustering in *space*, the ethnic economy approach emphasizes difference and bonding along lines of *culture*.[81] When research in this field takes into account cultural difference, it speaks of "ethnicity." The hurdle of ethnicity entails an overriding preoccupation with the difference between mainstream and "other" identities to the neglect of crosscutting relations. In effect this involves a twofold reification: cultural difference is reified as "ethnicity" and ethnicity is reified as "ethnic economy." If we look closer, there are ample instances of intercultural economic activity and ample literature as well.[82] Yet by and large this remains under-theorized and under-represented, so these instances rarely reach the threshold of awareness in research or policy.

This review of various settings and types of immigrant economic activity past and present draws attention to their crosscultural or multiethnic character. Reviewing the arguments presented and focusing on the key hurdle of ethnicity, the concept *ethnic economy* involves the following problems:

1. "Ethnic" as an ethno-centric term (merely denoting distance from European or western culture) must be distinguished from "ethnic" as an account of cultural embeddedness. However, since "ethnic" is

often used loosely in many different senses (i.e., emic and etic, or by outsider and insider standards), it may not be feasible to maintain such a distinction.

2. Using "coethnic labor" as the criterion to define ethnic economy is vague (how do we know whether labor is actually coethnic or merely from the same national origin?). Besides, it is narrow: customers, credit, suppliers, services, ownership, and location are other relevant criteria.

3. If it is possible to verify whether what seems "ethnic" really is ethnic, or culturally embedded, its significance should not be taken for granted at the risk of stereotyping. Therefore, a more effective and neutral distinction is that between monocultural and crosscultural social capital.[83] Considering that cultural and group boundaries are typically fuzzy and fluid, this distinction should not be given exaggerated weight.

4. Culturally embedded norms and social networks may indeed be significant, but immigrant economies also require crosscultural social capital to function.

Twinning social capital and cultural difference yields the following distinctions:

- Bonding social capital or close ties—which may be culturally embedded;
- Bridging social capital, or loose ties at the same socioeconomic level—which may be culturally embedded and/or crosscultural;
- Linking social capital, or ties with others at a higher socioeconomic level—which may be culturally embedded and/or crosscultural.

Thus "ethnicity" as suggested by the ethnic economy terminology may be relevant with regard to bonding social capital but not necessarily with regard to bridging or linking social capital. A précis is in Table 3.1.

Table 3.1. Social capital and cultural difference

Types	*Meanings*	*Cultural variations*
Bonding	Strong ties among close relations	Possibly culturally embedded ("ethnic")
Bridging	Weak ties among people from diverse backgrounds but similar socioeconomic status	Culturally embedded or crosscultural (ethnic or interethnic)
Linking	"Friends in high places"	Culturally embedded or crosscultural

What emerges from this inquiry is that beyond "ethnic economies" are rainbow economies. This can be summed up in two points. Cultural difference does inform social capital but ethnicity is not helpful as a terminology and analytic. The "ethnic economy" concept must be rejected because what matters generally is not ethnicity but nationality or varieties of national origin. Moreover, in immigrant enterprise social capital is not merely internal to the immigrant community but spills over cultural boundaries. Immigrant economies are often blended or rainbow economies that rely on crosscultural resources and social networks. Thus, for bonding social capital to deliver requires bridging social capital. A third variable, linking social capital, relates particularly to home country resources.

What matters is neither the situation of full separation behind cultural boundaries ("ethnic economy" and multiculturalism as a static mosaic of ghettos) nor the situation of full assimilation (cultural boundaries don't matter), but the in-between zone that Alejandro Portes refers to as "segmented assimilation."[84] Most research on social capital tacitly assumes or overtly focuses on cultural boundaries. It would be appropriate for research to pay as much attention to bridging social capital, in the sense of loose relations *across* cultural boundaries, as to bonding social capital within cultural boundaries. An implication for policy is not to rely merely on ethnic or immigrant social capital but to take into account and enable crosscultural relations, that is, not simply within but between immigrant groups and between immigrants and others.

Political economies of multiculturalism

If the intellectual importance of social capital is to bridge social science disciplines (sociology, political science, economics), its policy significance is to link civic cooperation (sociology), democratic governance (political science), and economic growth (economics). Thus Putnam's study of administrative reform in Italy points to the importance of civic traditions and local democracy for administrative and economic performance. Similar implications follow from studies of institutional density in geography, of industrial clustering and districts as exercises in collective learning, government enablement and intersectoral partnerships of local government, firms and NGOs.[85] These lines of research involve interesting takes on social capital. The recognition of good governance as a social capital asset holds policy implications beyond the stipulations of the World Bank and Washington policy discourse. It suggests that local democracy is not merely desirable on political or moral grounds but also economically productive; social capital can serve as a bridge among social cooperation, progressive politics, and forward-looking economics. However, this uplifting story falters when it comes to ethnic diversity. A World Bank report notes, "Recent research has found that ethnically fragmented countries tend to have slower growth, lower levels of schooling, more assassinations, less financial depth, and higher deficits." Current research is concerned with examining "how political institutions can be reformed to secure the benefits of ethnic social capital while diffusing the costs."[86] It would be interesting to examine crosscultural social capital also in these settings.[87]

A point often made and a fundamental consideration for policy is that social capital without resources is a cul de sac. At the time, when social capital was becoming a fad in addressing urban poverty in the U.S., its downside was also becoming apparent: "There is considerable social capital in ghetto areas, but the assets obtainable through it seldom enable participants to rise above their poverty. . . . the call for higher social capital as the solution to inner city problems misdiagnoses the problem and can lead to both a waste of resources and new frustrations. It is not the lack of social capital but the lack of economic resources—beginning with decent jobs—that underlies the plight of impoverished urban groups."[88] This raises the question whether, indeed, social capital is capital.[89] At any rate, the importance of resources varies according to circumstances. Research bears out that "the relative importance of investments in physical capital and schooling appears to vary with the extent of social development. In particular, schooling is important at low levels of social development, but physical capital becomes more important at higher levels."[90]

This must be factored into understanding different immigrant economies. East Asian immigrants in North America are backed by the financial hinterland of the Tiger economies; immigrants from the Middle East can tap into oil revenues or remittances of relatives working in the oil economies. Backed by financial capital from overseas, relayed by regional banks, they can buy into prosperous markets. In free enterprise capitalism, without government support for job creation, these groups can create their own jobs by buying stores or businesses. The link between capital and migration is clearly on the map in relation to Chinese and Taiwanese immigrants.[91] In Los Angeles alone, the home of the largest Korean population in the US, there are seven Korean-American banks.[92] Start-up capital is a component that African immigrants lack; relative poverty in much of sub-Saharan Africa does not provide them with a deep financial hinterland to fall back on. The same applies to many Latin Americans and Southeast Asians.[93] For African Americans too there is no financial depth backing them.

A further consideration, as Anirudh Krishna points out, is that neither social capital nor economic resources may deliver in the absence of *capable agency* (or human capital). So another pertinent resource is education, which is more advanced in some regions than in others. South Asians can bank on a good education. Indian immigrants in Britain and North America have been able to enter the professions early on, in particular, medicine, education, and software creation.[94] Immigrants' differential economic and social performance is also a function of differential country resources and their class status in the country of origin.

Affirmative action and multiculturalism policies usually focus on supporting immigrant communities or on relations between immigrants and the host community.[95] The present argument suggests a further angle, namely, reckoning with crosscultural relations not only between immigrants and locals but also among and across different immigrant groups. In urban policy, taking into account and under some circumstances fostering such crosscultural relations may be a consideration.

What is underway implicitly in areas such as planning "ethnic shopping malls" may become an explicit policy consideration. There are ample situations where such an approach is being implemented.[96] An example is the development of a local exchange trading system (LETS) of local inhabitants and asylum seekers in Woudrichem, a small Dutch town. The system involves asylum seekers providing services (haircuts, food preparation, household and garden work, party catering, or drawing lessons) and Dutch locals offering goods (used bicycles, computers, videos, etc.) and services (cab rides, language and orientation). Since asylum seekers may stay long periods but do not have work permits, this system integrates them into the local economy and community without payment of money. An economist from Rwanda administers the system. A café night every two weeks serves to facilitate contacts. This initiative involves the generation and deployment of crosscultural social capital, both among asylum seekers (from many different parts of the world) and between asylum seekers and locals.[97]

Policy, national or local, can make up for specific social capital shortfalls. Thus, under some circumstances, especially targeted start-up credit facilities could be provided to immigrant entrepreneurs who don't come from rich hinterlands, that is, who are short of linking capital. Using a grand term, we could call this a policy of "crosscultural democratization" and a step from multiculturalism to interculturalism. The forms this rainbow social policy might take would differ on a case-by-case basis.

Notes

1. See Griffin 2000.
2. A. Wordsworth, "Millions of immigrants needed to sustain economies," *National Post* (Canada), March 22, 2000. "Europe's immigrant entrepreneurs are creating thriving businesses—and thousands of jobs," *Business Week*, February 28, 2000. A headline notes, "Today's refugees are Europe's future assets" (P. Preston, *Guardian Weekly*, April 18, 1999). "Immigrants create wealth," according to Luke

Johnson. "They add critical ingredients to the mix that generates progress. They tend to take risks" (*Sunday Telegraph*, February 6, 2000). Immigrants are credited with other effects as well: "Keeping the hive humming. Immigrants may prevent the economy from overheating" (*Business Week*, April 24, 2000).

3. This applies to the UK, Germany, and Australia (M. Saunders, "Sweeteners for business migrants," *Australian*, November 24, 1999) and Israel (G. Hoffman, "The dot.com pioneers," *Jerusalem Post*, April 23, 2000). "Last week a scheme began under which foreign entrepreneurs can move to Britain with nothing to declare but a good business plan—previously they had to bring £200,000 ($290,000)" ("Immigration: after the flood," *Economist*, September 9–15, 2000). The context is boosting e-commerce (cf. A. Parker, "Rules on entrepreneurs to be relaxed," *Financial Times*, July 25, 2000; G. P. Zachary, "People who need people: with skilled workers in high demand, employers are hunting them down—no matter where they live," *Wall Street Journal*, September 25, 2000). On Germany, see, for example, P. Finn, "The immigration imbroglio," *International Herald Tribune*, November 24, 2000; on Switzerland, see Piguet 1999.

4. Boubakri 1999; Özcan et al. 2000; Pécuod 2004.

5. *Migration in an interconnected world* 2005, Annex II.

6. Crawford notes that between 1979 and 1993 countries dominated by overseas Chinese (Hong Kong, Singapore, Taiwan, Macau, and Thailand) accounted for 81 percent of enterprises with operations in China and 84.6 percent of foreign investment (2000, 82).

7. Newton 1999.

8. Barr and Toye 2000.

9. Putnam 1993, 67.

10. Fine 2001.

11. This chapter derives from a large research project on social capital, and the present treatment is just brief. For critical reflections on social capital, see McNeill 1996; Woolcock 1998; Fedderke et al. 1999.

12. Bourdieu 1976. Smart 1993 criticizes Bourdieu for using inconsistent definitions of different kinds of capital.

13. Coleman 1988.

14. Putnam 1993; for example, van Deth et al. 1999.

15. Rose et al. 1997, 87.

16. McNeill 2003.

17. For example, Light et al. 1988; Waldinger 1990 and 1992; Light and Gold 1999; Haberfellner et al. 1999; Haberfellner 2000; Schmidt 2000.

18. Light et al. 1994, 647, 648.

19. Favell 2001, 3.

20. In popular usage a French restaurant in Bonn is foreign but not ethnic. Is a Japanese restaurant overseas qualified as an ethnic restaurant? The French Quarter in Tunis is foreign but not ethnic, whereas the Maltese quarter and other neighborhoods of minorities are ethnic. See AlSayyad and Roy 2006, 15. By way of experiment, consider *which* foods are included in an American supermarket aisle under the heading "Ethnic Foods."

21. Werbner 2001.

22. Portes 1987.

23. Amponsem 1996, 161–62.

24. Amponsem 1996, 161; cf. Owusu 2000.

25. Amponsem 1996, 162–63.

26. Cf. Hourani and Shehadi 1993.

27. Kotkin 1992, 236.

28. Light et al. 1993 and 1994.

29. Tambiah 2000, 181.

30. Cf. Satha-Anand 1998.

31. Nederveen Pieterse 1997.

32. Gary Lee, "Not your father's Detroit," *Washington Post*, January 9, 2000.

33. Criticisms of the ethnic economy approach are growing. Noting several problems in the sociology of the ethnic economy, Cobas 1989 mentions a contradiction between the stranger hypothesis and the protected market hypothesis. According to Timm 2000, the notion suffers from culturalism and ethnicism, while MNghi Ha 2000 draws attention to the underestimation of hybridity. Cf. Werbner 2000.

34. For example, Leonardo 1984; Kotkin 1992.

35. Lowe 1991; MNghi Ha 2000; Nederveen Pieterse 2003; Sansone 2003.

36. A study in South Africa observes, "The communities of urban men consisted of colleagues, neighbors, and *shebeen* friends and were multiethnic" (Pinglé 2000, 33).

37. Many others also refer to embeddedness in this context, for example, Portes and Sensenbrenner 1993; Portes 1994, 1995; Rath 2000; Schmidt 2000.

38. Amponsem 1996, 213.

39. Cf. Schmidt 2000.

40. Cf. Portes and Sensenbrenner 1993.

41. Amponsem 1996, 95. Transnational informal enterprise is not necessarily crosscultural as, for example, Portes 2000 describes.

42. For example, Liu 1998; Lin 1998; Minghuan 2000.

43. Sansone 1992; Hannerz 1992; Nimako 1999.

44. Milkman 2000; Cleeland 2000.

45. Light et al. 1994, 649. Light et al. 1999 adopt the term "immigrant economy" instead of ethnic economy if there is "non-ethnic labor"; in other words, labor is the key criterion.

46. On the steep rise of "ethnic restaurants" in western countries because of migration, see Warde 2000.

47. Ooka and Wellman 1999.

48. Bonacich et al. 2000.

49. L. Romney, "Minority-owned firms tend to hire within their own ethnic group," *Los Angeles Times*, September 18, 1999.

50. Light et al. 1999.

51. Eisenberg 1999.

52. C. S. Melendez, "Vietnamese, Mexican émigrés find common ground at checkout stand," *San Jose Mercury-News*, January 14, 2000.

53. See, for example, M. Halter, "Chasing the rainbow: now that marketers realize people come in other shades besides white, ethnic background is a sizzling commodity," *San Francisco Chronicle*, December 10, 2000.

54. For example, a report on the Adams-Morgan neighborhood, which is close to Mount Pleasant in Washington, D.C., notes the importance of Spanish language in fast food restaurants. D. Fears, "The language of money: business finds it takes Spanish to translate chicken into cash," *Washington Post*, April 25, 2000.

55. Cotthem 1999.

56. K. Richter, "Secret of success for many Turks in Germany lies in start-ups," *Wall Street Journal*, July 13, 1999.

57. A survey of Latina business in Orange County, California, shows that "few borrowed money from banks to start businesses, but the percentage of those with bank credit has grown" (J. Norman, "Diverse industries covered in Latina business survey," *Orange County Register*, September 26, 2000). Boubakri 1999 shows the same for immigrant enterprise in France. Others report the lack of access to bank credit for fast growing immigrant enterprises (e.g., E. Aguilera, "Minority owned firms lack in backing," *Orange County Register*, September 25, 2000; cf. Fisman 2000).

58. *Hawal* banking is a financial infrastructure using informal networks among Muslims worldwide. Reports on *hawal* banking circuits in Washington, D.C., are Y. Noguchi ("Matching faith and finance: alternatives to loans cater to area Muslims," *Washington Post*, October 28, 1999) and, in the Netherlands, M. van den Eerenbeemt ("De ondergrondse naar de Prinsengracht," *De Volkskrant*, March 25, 2000).

59. For example, the Mexican owner of a grocery in a small Tennessee town "became something of a fixer, a multipurpose intermediary between the Hispanic and Anglo communities. He helped white farmers and plant managers find workers. He took Mexicans to used-car dealers and landlords and vouched for their reliability. He was an informal interpreter for the police and the courts." He also provided illegal workers with counterfeit documents. K. Sack, "Under the counter, grocer provided workers," *New York Times*, January 14, 2002.

60. Choenni 2000.

61. Cf. Nederveen Pieterse 2003, ch. 2.

62. Dobbin 1996, 21.

63. Dobbin 1996, 79.

64. Wertheim 1964, 1978.

65. Oral information from Peter Chua, Santa Barbara, California.

66. Taylor 1986; Oei 2000.

67. Chua's 2003 pessimistic account of Chinese minorities in the Philippines generalizes on the basis of rich segments of this population. An alternative account is Ramsay 2001; a critique is Nederveen Pieterse 2004, ch. 7.

68. See Obbo 1979, Wilson 1979, and Shack 1979 on varieties of incorporation of strangers in sub-Saharan Africa.

69. Dobbin 1996, 64; Seagrave 1996; Kwok Bun 2000. "They [the south Fujianese] were prepared to merge with the social and economic networks of the host city and in Shanghai, for example, many Fujianese were regarded as having 'become local people', enabling them to penetrate local networks in most business circles" (Dobbin 1996, 64–65).

70. Cf. Tambiah's (2000) fascinating account of the intergenerational Man lineage of Chinese.

71. Dobbin 1996, 47–48.

72. Matthee 2000. On Hadramis, see, for example, Jonge 2004.

73. See Bajunid 2004.

74. Curtin 1984; Stearns 2001; Hoerder 2002.

75. Rodrik 2005, 203.

76. Joel Kotkin, "The new ethnic entrepreneurs," *Los Angeles Times*, September 12, 1999.

77. Deutsche Presse-Agentur, "Mysterious Chinese immigrants baffle the Spaniards," *Hindustan Times*, July 30, 2000.

78. Beck 2000; Iyer 2000.

79. Chen 2000.

80. Ohmae 1992.

81. The *ethnic enclave economy* is a precursor of the ethnic economy approach; see Light et al. 1993; Werbner 2001.

82. Scanning some five hundred articles in social science journals under the keyword "interethnic," I find that articles primarily refer to either conflict or marriage, yet employment and enterprise are also amply represented.

83. I deliberately refrain from defining "culture" in this discussion (cf. Nederveen Pieterse 2003 and chapter 9 this volume). At a subtler level of analysis, the distinction between mono- and crosscultural enterprise and social capital is up for discussion. Cultural differences run, of course, also among nationals, for example, by region. Ethnomarketing and import and export trade are crosscultural as well; witness literature on "international manners" in business and the varieties of capitalism thesis (Nederveen Pieterse 2004, ch. 11).

84. Portes 1996.

85. See Amin and Thrift 1993; Ottati 1994; Brown et al. 1999.

86. World Bank 1998, 18. Note the choice of words of ethnically "fragmented" rather than ethnically "diverse" societies.

87. Nederveen Pieterse asks, "Under what conditions do we get widening circles of social capital?" and argues that government can play a facilitating role in the form of managed pluralism (2001, ch. 8). Cf. Midgley 1995; Gold and Light 2000.

88. Portes and Landolt 1996, 20, 21.

89. Robinson et al. 2002.

90. Temple et al. 1996, 41.

91. Tseng 1994, 2000.

92. M. Andrejczak, "In L.A. Korean area, 7 banks are too many," *American Banker*, September 20, 1999.

93. This may explain reports that new immigrants in Canada and the U.S. are not doing as well economically as previous waves—they may have less access to financial resources in the country of origin (e.g., "Today's immigrants worse off," *Globe and Mail*, March 22, 2000)—and why Indonesian immigrants in the U.S. lag behind other Asian immigrants (Antara News Agency, "Indonesian immigrants in US lag behind others," September 21, 1999).

94. Krishna 2001. Thus in Britain, South Asians, "although they represent just under 3 per cent of the population . . . provide about 16 per cent of the total number of GPs, nearly 20 per cent of hospital doctors, and about 12 per cent of phar-

macists. They own just over 50 per cent of the 'cash and carry' shops and just over 55 per cent of the independent retail trade" (Parekh 1997, 65).

95. The informal economy is generally "a bastard sphere of social integration" (Rath 1999) and not a high priority policy area.

96. Cf. d'Andrea et al. 1998.

97. P. de Graaf, "Zeventig druppels voor een PC," *De Volkskrant*, March 7, 2000. E. van Wageningen, "Voor een handvol druppels," *Metro*, July 25, 2000. Cf. Amin 2002.

4

❖

Many doors to multiculturalism

Multiculturalism is a moving target. The term refers to both an ongoing cultural flux and a variety of institutional arrangements. Multiculturalism is typically criticized from diverse points of view—conservative ("too much") as well as progressive ("too little"). Stakeholders resent being either ignored or stereotyped. As an institutional arrangement, multiculturalism is both a target of criticism and a reform platform. There are many doors and many faces to multiculturalism, and at times it isn't clear which multiculturalism is at issue.

Multiculturalism is multifaceted, for it reflects the many streams, past and present, that it is on the receiving end of. We need a wide-angle, kaleidoscopic approach, a complex, rich take on multiculturalism as a configuration of trends and a contested notion. Multiculturalism represents a reworking of local, national, regional, and global identities and hierarchies. To develop a multiperspective view, this discussion probes several vortices around which multiculturalism takes shape—cultural flux, citizenship, everyday experience, the politics of recognition, and class.

Conventional discussions of multiculturalism suffer from methodological presentism: Most discussions view multiculturalism as a recent phenomenon. Second, multiculturalism discussions are marked by methodological and policy nationalism. The nation state is usually taken for granted and not problematized. Third, discussions of multiculturalism tend to trail behind the facts on the ground.

There are nearly 200 million international migrants in 2005, well beyond the population of the world's fifth largest country (Brazil with 180 million). International migrants make up more than 10 percent of the population in seventy countries. Between 1990 and 2000 immigrants accounted for 89 percent of the population growth in Europe. Between 1995 and 2000, had it not been for immigrants, Europe's population would have declined by 4.4 million.[1] When it comes to soccer, multiculturalism is suddenly a good idea: France has more blacks in its national soccer team (13 of the 23 players in 2006) than in its 577 member National Assembly (10, none from the French mainland).[2] Germans know that in their old age they will be taken care of in old-age homes and hospitals by care givers and nurses from Poland, the Philippines, or other countries. These circumstances rarely factor into the discussions that, often prompted by newsworthy incidents, reiterate the policy choices of integration and assimilation.

Much theorizing about multiculturalism is theorizing about multiculturalism in the West. The literature straddles sociology, geography, cultural studies, and anthropology, but political theory plays a major part, mostly focused on the relationship between multiculturalism and the state, with the U.S., UK, and Canada as leading cases. This primarily concerns the relationship between multiculturalism and liberal democracy, rather than, say, the welfare state, which would imply a political economy perspective. This relationship is discussed in normative, legal, and policy terms. Multiculturalism discourse is largely monolingual, English, and multiculturalism theory is largely Atlantic in its conceptions and situatedness, assuming "Euro-American value terms and working conditions."[3] Several studies seek to establish a connection between multiculturalism and globalization, but their perspective is often regional rather than global.[4]

The literature on multiethnicity stretches wider than the multiculturalism discussion but there is a large gap between these literatures. In broad stroke, multiethnicity pertains to the global South and multiculturalism to the North. The split is relative because there is a growing overlap between these themes. Although multiethnicity, ethnonationalism, and secession remain the common headings in the global South, multiculturalism is an emerging discourse in Malaysia, Singapore, Japan, China, Brazil, Mexico, and South Africa, and also in Turkey and Eastern Europe, because of increasing migration, the influence of human rights approaches, and other globalization effects. Scholars of multiculturalism show growing interest in multiethnicity in the global South, yet the overall discussion, certainly in theory, retains an Atlantic flavor.[5] Among the studies that bridge these approaches and break with presentism are studies of indigenous peoples.[6]

The hiatus between multiculturalism and multiethnicity is understandable, for they concern not just different parts of the world but different histories. Multiculturalism in the West is largely the outcome of recent migrations: postcolonial and labor migrations, family reunification and asylum seekers. Multiethnicity in the global South usually refers to older migrations and the long-term cohabitation of peoples because of conquest, colonialism, and postcolonial state formation, often in combination with recent migrations and refugees.

Multiethnicity is an ordinary condition throughout the world (as discussed in chapter 1), though there is wide variation in what kind of differences are recognized and in what terms (as discussed in chapter 2). Thus *multiethnicity* is the *condition*—a normal condition throughout the world, though at times ethnic diversity is not recognized—and *multiculturalism* is a normative and institutional *policy* framework that regulates multiethnicity in relation to the state and in terms of citizenship. In everyday use, multiculturalism also loosely refers to existing cultural diversity, so at times the two discourses fold into one another. Institutions accommodating ethnic diversity are not new; they existed in empires with different citizenship statuses and institutions such as the Muslim dhimmi and the Ottoman millet system that granted group rights on the basis of religion (chapter 7). The historically novel contribution of multiculturalism is to recognize and valorize cultural diversity.

Time

This book takes a historical comparative approach to multiculturalism, the kind of approach that was pioneered by Ibn Khaldun in the fourteenth century. The historical approach means viewing multiethnicity in the *longue durée*. The comparative approach assumes that multiethnicity in the global South is as relevant as multiculturalism north of the equator, and that their interrelations matter as well.

It seems that to each mode of understanding there is a time frame, as if understanding itself has temporal rhythms, as making sense at certain cognitive wavelengths and bandwidths, from the viewpoint of a particular epoch. Michel Foucault referred to such bandwidths as *epistèmes* and others refer to collective *imaginaires*.[7] The meaning and sense of time varies across history and by culture. Multiculturalism implies multiple temporalities intersecting, *tiempos mixtos*. A simple example is the different days of prayer—Friday, Saturday, and Sunday—and different cultural holidays that enter into the mix of everyday multiculturalism.[8]

Everyday life is embedded in a time frame of two to three generations. Perceptions of social and political processes are measured against ordinary life expectations. Problems that remain unsettled beyond this are often felt to be particularly vexing and there is an emotional reluctance to invest in problems that offer no prospect of reasonable change within one's life time. This is not merely the urge for the quick fix, though that plays a part, but an emotional reservation to invest energy in what seems to be insoluble within one's life time as if doing so poses a burden that is heavier than one should carry. This is the moral economy of not worrying about problems beyond one's life world.

The time frame of politics ranges from a year to an election cycle. The time horizon of business studies parallels the business cycle and draws lessons from previous cycles. The time frame of policy sciences—economics, political science, public administration, conflict studies, development studies— typically ranges from several years to a generation or two. Political theory considers questions at hand in light of institutional frameworks, standards of moral obligation, and ethical principles. The time frame of law is likewise layered, preoccupied with questions at hand against the backdrop of legal principle and precedent and the future implications of setting legal precedent. Social science is multilevel and proceeds at operational, political, and structural levels. Policy-oriented social science provides tools for short- to medium-term problem solving and managerial knowledge for policy makers, operatives, and activists. Social science that is concerned with structural problems places itself in the framework of long-term institutional and structural processes in historical, theoretical, or critical modes. In social science, "theory" usually means "modernity" (and variations such as new modernity and postmodernism), industrialism (post-industrialism), capitalism (stages and varieties of capitalism), the state, democracy, civil society (the public sphere), and so forth. These levels pose different limitations on addressing questions of ethnicity and multiculturalism. The operational time frame of policy approaches is often too short and inadequate. Anna Simones observes,

> It is only *through time* that structures of state prove trustworthy. Or to turn this around, only once state structures prove (largely) solvent, (largely) stable, and (largely) responsible over generations is the state likely to be credibly viewed as *the* guarantor of security by large enough numbers of its citizens.[9]

The structural approach is inadequate if it presumes structures that are Eurocentric (such as the modern world-system), of limited relevance (such as modernity), or theoretical and value assumptions that are belied by the questions of ethnicity and multiculturalism, which are modern too, but modern in ways that exceed conventional understandings of modernity.

Most perspectives on ethnicity and multiculturalism take a snapshot of the present, nested in a time frame of two or three decades, the usual time frame of research and policy, in which prevailing discourses and representations of diversity shape and reflect the terms of cohabitation. Situate this in a time frame of fifty years backward and, if possible, fifty years forward in time and the influence of discourse retreats, discourse changes and agency and institutional and structural variables come to the foreground. Extend the time frame further, five hundred years back and five hundred years forward, and discourses and representations of diversity become merely local chatter. Thus understandings of ethnicity and multiculturalism are a function of time frames. In this light it is understandable, for instance, that the *conflict resolution* approach, which is short term, has been followed by the *conflict prevention* approach, with a wider time frame, and by the *conflict transformation* approach, which emphasizes social learning and adopts a time frame that extends into the future.

So what?

Cultural diversity exists as just-so cultural difference, matter of fact, and cultural difference that elicits emotion and carries a value. The latter concerns social science; this involves a boundary with an inside and an outside, a cultural center that evaluates and a periphery that is evaluated—in other words, a gradient of power. Discursive power lies with the center. The center establishes the boundary, the ranking discourse that frames the meaning of difference.

The discourse of the periphery is rarely recorded. Many studies record the stereotypes and discrimination of Roma in Eastern Europe,[10] but how many discuss how Gypsies view Europeans? Many studies discuss how South Africans view the San, but how many consider how the San view South Africans? Or how Okinawans and Ainu view the Japanese, how Kurds and Armenians view Turks, how Turkish immigrants view the Germans? Anthropology in reverse, from the periphery to the metropolis, from the ladder of power *upward*, occurs but is rare. Views at the bottom of the ladder have less power to organize space, but they have power to inspire agency and resistance. "The silence of the native" is fictional; of course subalterns speak, but often they aren't heard. The hidden texts of resistance and subversion are recorded only if they sway the relations of power, usually after the fact. Cases in point are the car burnings in the French banlieues and the July 7 bombings in London, both in 2005 (discussed in chapter 8).

The views of the periphery are rarely recorded unless the periphery is also a center in relation to another periphery. Japan has long been a periphery in relation to China (except during the first half of the twentieth century) but a center in relation to Okinawa and the Ainu. Nomadic and seafaring peoples such as the Huns, Mongols, Tatars, and Vikings left fewer traces than the settled, agrarian cultures that erected public works, architecture, and monuments, as have industrial societies. Oral cultures leave fewer imprints than those that express themselves in written texts. Less is known of the African empires of Ghana, Songhai and Mali, though they made profound impressions on travelers at the time, because they left little in the way of architecture and writing. So our perspectives are already skewed at the source; they privilege views from the center, the language and values of the center, even if we would wish otherwise.

But the relationship between center and periphery is not stable over time. Conquest, technology and demography change the equation. Weapons change the balance of power between peoples; transport technologies alter trade routes and reroute commerce; mining and extraction generate resources; technologies affect productivity and modes of production, the meaning of space and distance, the scope for control and agency. Accordingly, center-periphery relations are often concerned with attempts to negotiate these variables.

Centers are also ranked internally. There are minorities within and without, internal and external frontiers. A civilization or empire entails a code of conduct, standards of civility, and codes of honor and etiquette, such as noblesse oblige and gentlemen's standards. There is a club inside the club, a club nested within the insider club, and so forth, like a set of Russian dolls. Hence hierarchy is always a gradient, not a binary. The question in the vast sway of time and space is where do ethnicity and multiethnicity fit in? Table 4.1 uses the example of the relationship between Europe and its others over time to illustrate changing center-periphery relations and perspectives over time. There are several reasons to bring this up. First, it shows that the *criteria* of differentiation change radically over time—in this case they range from culture and religion (particularly salient until the seventeenth century) and race, power, and development to Europe as a marker, citizenship, and again culture. Second, what is often viewed as a binary divide between self and other (notably in structuralist accounts) is really a series of *gradients* on either end of the continuum. Third, external and internal differences intertwine and interact, and the external differences need not be the most important.

The changing meanings of ethnicity are a prism for viewing collective itineraries in which the changing status of the nation, the changing architecture of states and economies, processes of social composition and recomposition, international realignments, and the dynamics of globalization are refracted.

Different differences

Multiculturalism in the sense of ongoing cultural cohabitation and flux is matter of fact and matter of course, a just-so circumstance. Haven't we all been multiethnic all along? Aren't our history, heritage, and philosophy steeped in multicultural experience? In the words of Louis Tobback, Mayor of Louvain, "We are all a strange mix."[11] Julia Kristeva takes this a step further: "Nous sommes étrangers à nous-mêmes." So does Rimbaud:

Table 4.1. Europe and its others over time

Time	Boundaries	External	Internal differences
BCE	Culture	Language (barbaroi)	Free men, slaves, helots, gender
CE—present	Religion	Pagans, non-believers, Muslims, and other religions	Heathens, heretics, witchcraft; Christian denominations
1790—1940	Race	Race, language	Class, status, minorities, ranking among and within European countries
1800—1970	Imperialism, colonialism	Civilization and savagery, evolution; colonizer and colonized; Orientalism, Eurocentrism	"Backward areas" in Europe (e.g., Celtic fringe, "urban jungle")
1950—present	Development	Developed and developing countries, north and south	Uneven development in Europe and in countries (deindustrializing regions)
1900—present	Europe	European civilization	Europe of multiple speeds; tension between deepening and widening EU identity, boundaries
1960—present	Culture	Ethnicity	Multiculturalism; lifestyle, sexual preference, age; hybrids
1980—present	Citizenship	Illegal migrants, asylum seekers	Citizens, denizens

Source: Adapted from Nederveen Pieterse 2000.

"JE est un autre." And Paul Ricoeur: "The self is another." Multicultural-ism in this sense has ever been and will ever be like history itself—multi-ethnicity runs through the lines of the faces of history. Diversity is part of the flow of history.

Besides, cultural difference is but one difference among many—like hot and cold, wet and dry, dead and alive, metaphysical, or transcendental difference. Cultural difference matters, but when it comes to ecology for a small planet, does it matter? What difference does cultural difference make in relation to our common human vulnerability? What difference does it make when it comes to astronomy and cosmology?

Arguably, cultural difference in itself does not invite judgment unless it is articulated with class, mobilization and conflict, or confronted with rigid group boundaries. Culture is an arena of hegemonic struggle and cultural difference is a medium of hegemonic struggle. Is this necessarily and intrinsically so, or is it so as a function of circumstances and forces that lie outside cultural difference per se?

Difference, including cultural difference, is an inspiration, a source of beauty and pleasure, too. This is, of course, the cute and politically correct angle on multiculturalism, celebrating difference and intercultural mingling and jostling—confetti culture and multiculturalism lite. We experience it in food and art, music and healing, and advertising and consumption, as well as in the rainbow worlds of Coca-Cola and the United Colors of Benetton. Here differences are opportunities for play—play mainly in the sense of consumer choice. This is the corporate and harmony model of multicultur-alism. We cross boundaries often enough: Forget boundaries! Border cross-ing ("there are no frontiers") is another advertising slogan. The consumer world is temptingly presented as a domain of unlimited choice and unlim-ited mobility—cultural, geographical, social, opening doors to different lifestyles—which is a major part of consumer allure and thrill.

One set of politically correct friends would dismiss this for it's "only culture," whereas we live the realities of, so to speak, "only capitalism." The world of consumption, however, is real too. Who needs Baudrillard? The depths of history manifest in the surfaces and cracks of everyday life. Even so, the postmodern Tinkerbelle take on cultural difference as *jouis-sance*, on the one hand, and the political economy of *jouissance* and the uneven distribution of pleasure and survival, on the other, don't make for an easy mix. The film *Mardi Gras: Made in China* (David Redmon, 2005) juxtaposes images of intoxicated revelers in the New Orleans carnival throwing beads in voyeuristic rituals and of the factory in southern China where down narrow paths filled with dangerous machines teenage girls produce the beads. To what extent does the consumer promise of mobility owe its allure and status value to its dark side and the relative immobility of others?

Recognition, it is argued, is a politics of difference. Just what is the meaning of "difference" in this context? The conventional explanation for ethnic friction and conflict is that it is caused by difference. But that is only a half-truth at best.

In describing the growing rivalry between the Javanese and Chinese in colonial Java before World War II, W. F. Wertheim noted that this became an issue only when the differences between the groups sufficiently *narrowed* so Javanese Muslims were able to compete for the same resources and opportunities that the Chinese held. The Dutch colonial administration had long cooperated with the Chinese as a trading minority who therefore occupied niches in commerce and enterprise; only when the Javanese Muslims had urbanized and acquired enough education were they in a position to begin to present a challenge to the Chinese minority.[12]

So what is at issue is not difference per se, but the *narrowing of difference* sufficiently to create the conditions for competition but insufficiently for cultural difference to fade from view. What is at issue is the zone *in-between* complete difference (otherness, alterity) and complete similarity in socioeconomic profile, opportunities and cultural capital (assimilation). Conflict, then, is a function not of difference tout court but rather of growing likeness. Competition between ethnic groups is a matter of changing expectations and opportunity structures that involve bicultural capital (as discussed in chapter 2).

Existing boundaries also change when groups vie for political recognition in a legal sense, for instance gays or disabled people. Here foregrounding or highlighting difference—for example, seeking recognition for deafness as a language—is a way to claim equal rights in the form of access or entitlement. Difference is emphasized, but the reason *why* it is emphasized is to enable effective equal rights and equal treatment. Thus difference and identity politics serves as a key to sameness.

Difference can arise or become salient due to political manipulation or intervention too, for instance when the British in late-nineteenth-century Northern Ireland played the "Orange card" (playing on Protestants' fears of Ireland's Catholic majority and fostering an insecure minority complex). Then differences between communities become politically salient and charged and existing group boundaries change meaning and function, in this case, initially due to outside intervention. The way "tribes" came about or, rather, changed meaning due to colonial interventions in Africa is similar.

Another line of thought holds that cultural differences arise from traditional differences between communities. But there is a profound distinction between the typically fuzzy, permeable boundaries of traditional communities and the enumerated, statistically circumscribed and strictly drawn boundaries of modern times. Thus the British Raj in India introduced sharp lines of demarcation between Muslims and Hindus, which had never been part of old-style communities, along with different voting rights and educational systems.[13]

These considerations yield at least four different meanings of difference:

1. Difference growing in salience because or as a byproduct of growing similarity.
2. Difference foregrounded as a way to achieve equal rights.
3. Difference foregrounded due to changing political conditions.
4. Difference arising from the shift from old communities to modern communities.
5. And finally, *vive la différence*.

It follows that "difference" carries different meanings and cannot be taken at face value. Besides, difference is experienced in many ways, such as polarized and dialogical, static and fluid, deep and shallow. In this light the distinction between identity politics and interest politics may not be as large as is often made out to be.[14] There is a close link between representation and redistribution. Identity politics may be regarded as interest politics in the era of the cultural turn.

Everyday multiculturalism

> When people talk about the failure of the cultural melting pot, it might be because they cannot appreciate the popular culture melting pot.
>
> —Gautam Malkani, "Mixing and Matching," *Financial Times*

In everyday experience, *le quotidien*, what we find is in the eye of the beholder. No generalization, no matter its finesse, can encompass the range and complexity of ordinary experience where cultural variety manifests in myriad ways. According to a dim view, this is a terrain of strife and anxiety, guilt and pain, carefully calibrated give and take, chambers of historical torment, domains of hierarchy and hierarchy-within-hierarchy, like sets of Russian dolls. Depending on the time, country, city, neighborhood, and observer, everyday multiculturalism varies and changes like the colors of a rainbow. Whether the venue is Toronto or Oldham, England; Lhasa or Harare; Kaduna or Kabul; Granada or Saloniki; New York or Nuevo Laredo makes a world of difference.

By another view, *actual* multiculture, street-level cultural diversity, is miles ahead of multiculturalism—and represents circumstances that policy is yet to address. Anthropologists and sociologists caution that group boundaries are contingent and provisional and culture is open-ended.

And not just cultural boundaries matter, contingent as they are, but also the in-betweens who are in the cracks of boundaries no matter how defined, the hybrids who are "neither and both."

A constructivist approach to identity and group boundaries is now commonplace in social science. Accordingly, some treat identity as if it is optional, a matter of individual choice and agency. But this raises the question whether the outcome is being mixed up with the process. Another question is what are the grounds for dialogue between those for whom identity is optional (a matter of identification) and those for whom identity is destiny (a matter of fate, imposed by force of circumstance or from individual disposition). These questions are taken up in the next chapter.

Multiculturalism and class

According to Louis Tobback, speaking about multiculturalism as an institutional and political arrangement, "It's a matter of money. How much change can a democratic public swallow?" He notes that when it comes to Japanese immigrants in Belgium, cultural difference suddenly turns out not to make much difference. In other words, behind cultural difference lurk class and status.

Multiculturalism if it comes about through immigration means letting people into the social contract—or else risk creating an underclass. Accordingly what matters is to examine the various social contracts that exist in nations and compare them in terms of political economy, for instance, welfare states (such as Belgium, the Netherlands, Germany, Scandinavia), free enterprise and residual welfare or workfare states (the U.S.), countries in-between (such as Canada, Australia, the UK), and developing countries (with neither welfare nor workfare). In each setting, cultural difference carries quite different ramifications.

In free enterprise economies the social contract is "thinner" than in welfare societies, social provisions are fewer, so admission to the social contract carries less weight. A residence permit and citizenship essentially mean a green card and the right to work. By comparison to that of Europe, American multiculturalism is both more open (the U.S. is an immigration society) and more conservative in an economic sense (Wal-Mart capitalism) and, in some ways, a cultural sense. In the South of the United States cultural difference and minority status have long served as part of a low-wage regime, as under the Jim Crow laws. Since the 1980s the southern model of plantation capitalism has increasingly become the national standard of high exploitation capitalism or neoliberal capitalism, which I refer to as "Dixie capitalism,"[15] or the political economy of Jim Crow. Migrant labor has long been part of this, as in the postwar Bracero program.

In the recent American immigration crisis several streams come together: capitalism that depends on migrant labor (entire sectors such as agriculture, food processing, construction, hotels and restaurants depend on migrant labor), cultural chauvinism (as in the Minutemen guarding the U.S.-Mexico border) and state regulation (large numbers of undocumented migrants pose social, economic, and security problems). Regulating migrant labor by making it legal would increase wages relative to what they are now (for migrant workers and employers) and decrease wage rates for American unskilled labor (though most studies argue that this effect is negligible); not regulating it would criminalize twelve million undocumented immigrants and those who employ them. An alternative is to increase the minimum wage (which was raised in 2007 after it hadn't been raised for twenty years), which means changing the rules of high exploitation capitalism.[16]

Free enterprise economies are hospitable to those who come with high-level skills (such as engineers and programmers from Asia) and capital, but for those without skills and without a financial hinterland to draw on it may be a rough existence. The state is a night-watchman law-and-order state, welfare entitlements are residual, and access is restricted. In cultural terms the United States has been characterized as "multicultural unilateralism":

> Europe is rightly envious of America's multicultural society. . . . But the American multicultural model also generates an illusion. . . . It is always an American version of otherness that is encountered in the United States. You will not necessarily learn anything about the culture and history of Vietnam by working alongside a Vietnamese doctor in the teaching hospital at Stanford. . . . Foreign films account for less than 1 percent of the American film market, and the figures are similarly low for books and news from abroad. The impressive integrative power of American society seems to generate a kind of obliviousness to the world, a multicultural unilateralism.[17]

In social market economies in which citizenship means entitlement to welfare benefits, cultural difference may recede over time and multiculturalism may fade into background as productive capabilities and welfare entitlements become foreground. However, access to these polities is conditional. Social democracy is in principle an exclusionary social contract bounded by the nation state and historically guarded by chauvinism, both the general "chauvinism of prosperity" and the specific chauvinism of protecting the labor market against the intrusion of foreign workers. A current circumstance is the "graying of Europe" and the need to sustain and rejuvenate the labor force. Demand for skilled labor from abroad—in Germany, Italy, the Netherlands—meets with the old restrictions of the social contract. In Germany the proposal to bring in software programers from India elicited the slogan "Kinder, nicht Inder" (children, not Indians), as if education could fill the gap in time. Keeping the old social contract of the enclosed welfare state is no longer a viable option on account of technological, structural and institutional changes, summed up under the headings of post-Fordism and flexible accumulation, and on account of the relative erosion of national borders. Against this backdrop three forward options arise. Keep and rebuild the welfare state on a national basis with voting rights for immigrants, rebuild the welfare state on a European Union basis through a strong social charter, or combine this with global reform and transnational social policy.[18]

There is a growing awareness in Europe that migration is the expression of profound global inequality and that the problems of migration must be ultimately addressed at the source, through development cooperation, and some would argue, eventually a global social policy. In the U.S. the general outlook is to view the world as a chaotic, dangerous place, a rough neighborhood run by armed thugs that must be controlled by military power. Through their career as a superpower, Americans have been socialized in a conservative worldview that requires and legitimates a strong security state, a worldview that is optimistic about the U.S. and pessimistic about the world. In this setting migration is seen as a force that either aids or weakens the American position in terms of global competitiveness.

Redistribution may be more important than recognition but is conditioned by recognition. Recognition is part of the threshold of access: difference is the door to equality in the sense of equal rights and the door to redistribution and access to resources. From the viewpoint of political economy there is much more to multiculturalism than ethno-marketing, ethno-management, and ethnic economies. Rather, what are at issue are *intercultural* or rainbow economies and cultural diversity as a stimulus to economic innovation and growth (as discussed in chapter 3). In this view, cultural diversity is not an obstacle but an asset to be nurtured, a harbinger of world culture and the political economy of world culture (discussed in chapter 8). Handled effectively and with forward policies, diversity can foster economic growth. What matters is not merely the contribution of immigrants in terms of skills but also the interface between immigrant economies and national economies and among immigrants of different national origins.

Multiculturalism and citizenship

Most literature treats multiculturalism as a negotiation of cultural differences in relation to liberal democracy. Discussions are conducted in philosophical terms of identity and recognition; in ethical terms of solidarity and hospitality; in legal terms of citizenship rights and duties; in economic

terms of labor market conditions and welfare entitlements, in cultural
terms of language, lifestyle, customs, frictions, and representations; and in
sociological terms of identity politics. In many discussions the same questions keep coming up—redistribution or recognition, assimilation or integration? Is multiculturalism good for women? Profound as these questions
are, they typically address the problems in a limited horizon. The time
frame of multiculturalism studies is typically short and the regional scope
limited. According to van Brakel,

> The influential theorists tend to rigidify the issue into one monolithic thing.
> Multiculturalism is *one* thing, *one* problem, for which *one* ideal universal the-
> ory (or universal rejection) has to be found. If alternative theories are recog-
> nized, then they are alternative *universal* theories, which simply clash with
> their competitors. . . . Moreover, there is a tendency in this literature to go
> over the same examples (such as the Amish in the U.S. or the *affaire du foulard*
> in France), again and again, and make quick statements like "in a liberal state
> Sikhs should be allowed to wear a headdress in school or in the police force,
> but not a dagger." Questions such as "which Sikhs?" or "which liberal state?"
> are not raised.[19]

This monolithic approach to multiculturalism applies to proponents
and critics alike.

In many multiculturalism discussions the center barely moves. The literature deliberates on what terms newcomers should be let into the nation
state (immigration law, citizenship), the society (social cohesion), the
economy (the labor market), the social contract (welfare entitlements),
cities (urban policy) and the cultural ambience (adding variety but frag-
menting culture). Attention usually focuses on the newcomers, on
whether, for how long and on what terms they should be allowed to stay,
what entry and citizenship tests are required, whether they should integrate or assimilate. The destination society is considered in terms of its
laws, policies and political and cultural climate, which is a discussion of a
different order because it concerns established institutional orders. Germany, the Netherlands, Sweden and other countries have introduced
compulsory integration courses for immigrants with language and civics
programs. In Germany the citizenship course concludes with an exam
with questions so difficult that few Germans would be able to answer
them and a failure rate of over 90 percent. Questioning the newcomers is
commonplace in stereotypes, ethnic jokes, hostile attitudes and restrictive
policies as part of "normal adjustment." Questioning the center, however,
is easily taken as an insult to the collective ethos. When the Parekh Report
on multiethnicity in Britain came out in 2000 with detailed investigations
and extensive policy recommendations, the media immediately zeroed in

on a single passage that problematized "Britishness," and this skirmish took most of the oxygen out of the issues that the report raised.

> Britishness, as much as Englishness, has systematic, largely unspoken racial connotations. Whiteness nowhere features as an explicit condition of being British, but it is widely understood that Englishness, and therefore by extension Britishness, is racially coded.[20]

This is an ordinary point in social science where the debate has long moved on from examining race and ethnicity to posing dominant identities, such as whiteness, as a problem, but in public discourse this line of questioning is still heretical. Discussing multiculturalism is fine, but don't mess with Englishness or Britishness.

The unwillingness of the center to see itself with clarity is a matter of political and emotional blocks. Problematizing "them," not "us" is a variation on blaming the victim. The center blames others, turns the tables, at times passive aggressive, at times aggressive. Newcomers are welcome if they conform; others are okay if they meet our expectations, in other words, stripped of their otherness. A prevalent attitude is reluctant liberalism; another variant is imperialist liberalism (discussed in chapter 8). Yet as Pierre van den Berghe cautions, "It takes two to assimilate."[21]

Multiculturalism often stirs up cultural strata such as regional identities that predate the nation state. Hence negotiations in relation to the nation state are partial. They don't do justice to the complex layers of actual population flows and cultural traffic and by privileging the nation state as the arbiter uphold the myth of the (enduring, homogeneous) nation state. This underestimates the scope and significance of what is at stake in multiculturalism. Postnationalism (prompted by globalization, diasporas, and macro-regionalism) also builds on pre-national trends. Multiethnicity is regional before it is national.

In institutional terms multiculturalism is a reworking of power relations in relation to nation states (or multinational states). Here the bottom line is the redefinition of citizenship and multiculturalism is first a matter of legal status and citizenship rights. That this isn't necessarily so is illustrated in Germany, where minorities were typically referred to as *Ausländer* (foreigners), racism translated as *Ausländerfeindlichkeit*, and multiculturalism used to be viewed as a cultural rather than a political-legal matter, because until recently in Germany citizenship was defined on the basis of ethnicity,[22] unlike in most western societies, where citizenship is granted on the basis of residence (republican citizenship).

As a negotiation of citizenship rights, multiculturalism represents an accommodation with liberalism and the liberal state. Hence normative political theory plays a prominent role in multiculturalism discussions, notably in the work of Parekh, Kymlicka, and Iris Young, along with immigration law and legal experts. The general backdrop to political understandings of multiculturalism is the liberal state. Notions of institutional multiculturalism generally assume common citizenship and a commitment to individual rights (with countries that grant citizenship on the basis of ethnicity as exceptions). In this sense they are all liberal multiculturalism: liberalism *plus* recognition of cultural differences. Liberalism has always dealt with pluralism of interests, which in multiculturalism is stretched to include cultural pluralism.[23] A further assumption is a secure polity that is able to guarantee and enforce citizenship rights.

One question is how individual rights and collective rights interrelate. Equality and difference is an old question, also in relation to gender and Catholic emancipation. In institutional multiculturalism the allocation of group rights freezes group boundaries. At best this addresses issues of domination (such as majority oppression, racism, and discrimination), but it does not address domination-within-domination (such as clientelism and sexism within culturally demarcated groups). There is, then, a recurrent tension between institutional multiculturalism and group boundaries, whose shifting or fluid character is hard to map and translate into policy; this is taken up further in the next chapter.

The conventional setting of normative political theory and law is the global North. The field tends to be defined as a matter of state-minority relations and the treatment is often decontextualized from history, political economy and class. The legacy of colonialism and postcolonial luggage travels along in the cargo section. At issue is the definition of a problem (cultural diversity) and next, managing the problem (integration or assimilation). At times the question is reduced to a legal and administrative problem, as in the question of undocumented aliens. The approach is law- and rule-oriented and as such represents multiculturalism from above.

Normative political theory tends to take states for granted as the setting in which to settle immigration issues, which is understandable from a political viewpoint. From a historical point of view, however, the relationship is contingent. We can look at migration not merely in terms of costs and benefits to the nation state, but also the other way around and ask what use are nation states to the comings and goings of migrants?[24]

The nation state is embedded in the matrix of global history.[25] The modern state, based on the principle of territorial sovereignty, took shape in the Treaty of Westphalen that ended the Thirty Years' War. As Seymen Atasoy notes, forces outside Europe contributed to this development: "The defeat of the hegemonial attempt of the Habsburgs and the development of the Westphalian system were made possible by Ottoman pressure."[26] Thus forces outside Europe enabled the modern state system. Second, its application in Europe was differentiated; the German princedoms were excluded from the arrangement (as discussed in chapter 1) with momentous ramifications for European history. Third, the principle of popular sovereignty that emerged following the French Revolution also owed to influences outside Europe. As C. L. R. James observed, the wealth accumulated by the merchants in Bordeaux and Nantes contributed to and precipitated the French Revolution.[27] Fourth, the history of liberalism is embedded in the history of western expansion and the triangular trade and is a history of exclusions within and outside the West too.[28] Thus liberalism, as Parekh argues, is not merely the solution to diversity but also part of the problem.[29]

Border controls and passports developed much later.[30] The nation state system experienced its peak between 1840 and 1960. Although nation states remain vitally important, since the 1960s the momentum of regionalism—in various forms from free trade zones to the European Union—has gradually begun to overtake that of nation states. This changes the setting in which multiculturalism unfolds. The Schengen and Dublin accords in the European Union affect immigration, which is renamed migration in official policy documents.

Whither multiculturalism?

In this kind of question the time is the future and the units of analysis are usually states. In political theory this involves renegotiating liberalism; in policy it means the adjustment of legal systems and legal practices, as in the changing body of immigration law. The underlying approaches to culture and difference range widely from static and conservative views (cultures are givens, boundaries are natural and fixed) to fluid (culture is liquid, boundaries are contingent). The shape of the future matches the future shape of legitimating discourses and, accordingly, of policies and legal and administrative arrangements. These are shaped by cultural and economic changes and political struggles, the future course of which we cannot anticipate.

What is missing from this line of inquiry? Can the question of the future course of multiculturalism be answered solely in terms of the experiences and itineraries of states? Absent in this line of questioning are world history and the global setting. The global setting is one of complex and dramatic North-South differences and vortices of change. Uneven development and transnationalism are two faces of the same coin, and migration and multiculturalism are part of a *global* politics of difference, recognition and struggle. In this setting multiculturalism in one country is at the downstream of global political economy and politics. We no longer inhabit a compartmentalized world in which cultural belonging, social solidarity and political responsibility can be neatly compartmentalized. Multiculturalism, then, is also a particular mode and stage of reworking global relations of power and a historically pregnant notion (a discussion taken up in chapter 8).

This treatment seeks to bring history back into the discussion of multiculturalism. History is steeped in intercultural traffic and mingling. Social life has been multiethnic all along, not least in recent history ("We are here because you were there"). Now geography is more compressed and in many places once distant differences have become neighborhood affairs, which involve a new politics of place. Another aim is to highlight diversity *within* multiculturalism. Multiculturalism is as diverse as the spectrum of political economies and capitalisms, states and institutional and legal provisions. The meanings of cultural difference are as diverse as the meaning of difference itself. The next chapter takes this up by juxtaposing the discourses of ethnicity and multiculturalism.

Notes

1. *Migration in an interconnected world* 2005, 83–85.
2. K. Bennhold, "For French blacks, a face on TV news is only a start," *New York Times*, August 14, 2006, B2.
3. Van Brakel 2003, 147.
4. For example, Kivisto 2002.
5. Treatments of multiculturalism beyond the Atlantic world include Parekh 2000; Cornwell and Stoddard 2001; and Hefner 2001 on Southeast Asia. Relevant too are comparative studies of ethnicity and ethnic conflict such as Shibutani and Kwan 1965; Boucher, Landis, and Clark 1987; Guideri and Pellizi 1988; David and Kadirgamar 1989; Rupesinghe and Tishkov 1996; Turton 1997; and Wimmer et al. 2004.
6. For example, Oommen 2004; Young 2004.
7. Maffesoli 1993.
8. Whitrow 1988 and Laguerre 2003.
9. Anna Simons, quoted in Rothchild 2004, 241–42.
10. Fraser 1995.
11. Addressing a conference "Whither Multiculturalism?" in Louvain, Belgium, October 1999.
12. Wertheim 1964.
13. Kaviraj 1991.
14. For example, Kaviraj 1996.
15. Nederveen Pieterse 2004, ch. 1.
16. Cf. Borjas 2005.
17. Peter Schneider, "Across a great divide," *New York Times*, March 13, 2004.
18. Discussed in Nederveen Pieterse 1999.
19. Van Brakel 2003, 146–47.
20. Parekh Report 2000, 38. Cf. Kivisto 2002, 154.
21. Quoted in Ramsay 2001, 55.

22. Parekh 2001, 3; Roth 2002; Nathans 2004.
23. Kukathas 1998.
24. This angle is developed in Nederveen Pieterse 2002 and 2003, ch. 2.
25. Cf. Calhoun 1994; Nairn and James 2005.
26. Atasoy 1999, 260.
27. James 1938.
28. See Mehta 1999.
29. See Parekh 2000.
30. Torpey 1999.

5

❖

Politics of boundaries

Ethnicities and multiculturalisms

How far have ethnic studies advanced past the finding that ethnicity is constructed, not primordial? While the "decolonization of ethnicity" is still underway, at times the stream of ethnic studies seems to add up to little more than a series of vignettes. Ethnicity is still talked about in a generalizing fashion, as if in each contribution the sociology of ethnicity has to be reinvented again. Chapter 2 unpacks ethnicity by means of a typology and taxonomy of ethnicities and thus tries to bring finesse and method into the sociology of ethnicity. The aim of this chapter is to twin the ethnicity discussion with the discussion on multiculturalism, combining and contrasting discourses of ethnicity and multiculturalism. Ethnicity is a vocabulary for various notions of group boundaries, and multiculturalism, likewise, negotiates group boundaries. Ethnicities arise from different ways of drawing group boundaries; diverse notions of multiculturalism are also based on different ways of drawing group boundaries. Both ethnicity and multiculturalism address the underlying theme of the politics of group boundaries. Group boundaries, a perennial theme in anthropology and social science, now come back in various guises, such as the "spatial turn" that takes us beyond fashionable notions of nomadism, border studies, reterritorialization, and so forth.[1]

This discussion resumes the conversation of chapter 2 and problematizes ethnicity and ethnic conflict. Next I consider each of the four major varieties of ethnicity from the point of view of domination and emancipation. Notions of identity, difference, and intergroup relations interact to produce diverse angles on how group boundaries come about and decompose. In the closing section I consider how ethnicities relate to multiculturalisms and merge the two discourses.

Ethnicity as curse or as emancipation

Let us consider two diametrically opposite positions in relation to ethnicity—the disease model and the emancipation model. One is familiar, the other less so, but both are readily understandable. According to David Lake, *"To use a pessimistic but apt metaphor, ethnic conflict may be less like a common cold and more like AIDS—difficult to catch, but devastating once infected."*[2]

Here the focus is on ethnic *conflict*, the metaphor is that of *disease*, and the implied process is one of inevitable disaster. This is a familiar doomsday scenario of ethnic politics. The sequel argument is that there are hundreds of peoples in the world and about as many conflicts and civil wars to come. In this view, common in media representations and somber social science accounts, ethnicity is an evil politics stalking the Enlightenment world of growing modernization.[3] A radically different view holds that *"recognizing rather than denying ethnicity holds the key to democratizing the state and development."*[4]

In this view, ethnic politics is an emancipatory politics. Ethnicity is grassroots politics and a vehicle of vernacular democratization. The emphasis is on the state and development politics and recognizing ethnicity is viewed as a means toward democratization. This revisionist position relates to wider concerns such as the reconciliation between traditional and modern institutions, whether modernization is indigenous or imported, and so on.[5]

There are other views, including the position that the importance of ethnicity is being exaggerated,[6] but from the viewpoint of analyzing cultural politics these two diametrically opposite views, ethnicity as curse or as emancipation, are probably the most significant positions. Much is at stake in these perspectives. The former implies a blank check for external intervention in local conflicts while its rationale is profoundly pessimistic, that is, conflict management without hope. Its pessimistic perspective— sometimes nicknamed "Kaplanism" after the neoconservative journalist Robert Kaplan—justifies authoritarian interventions in the name of humanitarianism, which are in effect based on ethnocentrism.[7] The second perspective opens the way to vernacular empowerment and endogenous politics but in the process raises several problems.

These views leave us between a rock and a hard place. Both perspectives are generalizing. The former does not problematize nation state politics, does not problematize the domination that has usually given rise to ethnic mobilization in the first place. It presents conventional politics, which is part of the problem, as the solution and thus in the name of conflict resolution offers more of the same. It addresses symptoms, not causes. At best it promises containment of the disease, not therapy. The second view does address state domination but does not reckon with the problem of domination-within-domination. Since the problem of state domination is familiar enough and widely discussed, it is the second problem of domination-within-domination on which we need to focus. This means a double take or multifocus look at ethnicity. That ethnic politics shows features of both domination and emancipation at the same time has been argued before (chapter 2); now we go further into specifics. If imposing conditions on state action (as in various frameworks for collective rights and multiculturalism) is a matter of course, should ethnic groups have carte blanche? While political discourse devotes much attention to the state, the politics of ethnicity is not talked about as much.[8]

In relation to African politics, at times state and ethnic politics are combined. In one view, African polities have increasingly become kleptocracies, ethnicity is decentralized kleptocracy, and ethnic conflict often serves as a way to settle Mafia-like struggles. A markedly different view holds that *Africa Works* and works precisely through neotraditional institutions of redistribution via ethnic and kinship networks.[9] In seeking to account for rebel movements in Africa, Thandika Mkandawire criticizes these views ("much of this writing takes historical continuity and cultural relativism to absurd extremes") and related approaches: "The problems start from the view that by enumerating the uses to which war may be put by individuals (economic gain, psychic relief, 'Rambo demonstration effect,' escape from rural boredom, etc.), one can establish the rational nature of the pursuit of particular wars." Mkandawire also rejects the rational choice approach of Paul Collier and other World Bank economists, noting that "the argument is not falsifiable and has little empirical or moral sense. Rationality is emptied of any social and empirical meaning."[10]

Mkandawire locates the source of postcolonial African rebel movements in urban crises in combination with decades of structural adjustment and economic crisis and differentiates between stationary and roving rebels. Most rebel movements have been of the roving type due to their urban origins, ideological fuzziness, disconnect with rural agendas, and the ethnic fragmentation of the African countryside. The stationary rebels are regionalist and secessionist movements—and here varieties of ethnicity can be a valid framework. Note that here we move from a generalizing to a specific, empirical framework.

These issues can be addressed from various points of view. The angle taken here is that of reflexivity and collective learning. The point of collective learning as a perspective is not to suggest some ideal standard, model, or end state, but to focus on the ongoing process and to view it as a social learning process, the objective of which is learning itself rather than some kind of ideal or "end of history" settlement.[11] Since learning is contextual, the question is which approaches are most conducive to collective learning in particular contexts. If we seek collective reflexivity in relation to the state and the public sphere (as in notions such as reflexive modernity), what about reflexivity at the level of ethnic and religious groups? Can we then view ethnic politics as exercises in collective learning, in multiple directions—within and between ethnic groups, in their interaction with other social forces, the state and institutional change, and, ultimately, at the international level? This suggests reflexive ethnicity and in fact multiculturalism can be viewed as precisely a politics of reflexive ethnicity.

Reflexive ethnicity and parallel universes

The first consideration is to problematize ethnicity itself. Is the terminology of ethnicity appropriate at all? Does it belong to an era that is past? Does terminology matter? Are we moving about the twenty-first century burdened with nineteenth-century terminology? Is discourse a sign of the times or a badge of identity, a passport or green card to labor in discursive worlds? In that case, which one to chose, and perhaps more important, how do they interrelate? To *which* ethnicity do the two arguments spelled out above apply? Do we inhabit parallel universes in which what is a problem in one setting pops up as a solution in another?

In academic discourse, in anthropology and sociology, perspectives on ethnicity have in recent years been increasingly problematizing and open-ended.[12] Ethnicity fades into race, nationalism, multiculturalism, identity politics, and community. Its significance and dynamics are conjunctural, contingent. Early discussions of ethnicity in comparative politics and political science followed the modernization paradigm in which all differences would lead to national integration and nation building. Since the 1970s the awareness grew that modernization may well increase the salience of ethnicity and by the 1990s the focus shifted to ethnic conflict. In most of these discussions ethnicity is presented as an independent variable. Yet according to Rupert Taylor, what ultimately remains unresolved is where ethnicity comes from and what it actually is.[13]

There is no need to rehearse the large literature on this score except to make some key points, further to chapter 2. First, there is no point or advantage to naturalizing, essentializing or reifying ethnicity. There is nothing "natural" about ethnicity. Ethnicity need not be considered as a primary affiliation with given territorial or other claims.[14] Second, the term "ethnicity" recalls the colonial era and the prejudices of colonial anthropology. One option is to discard the term and opt for the plain language of *cultural difference* instead (as I suggest in chapter 2). Despite the constructivist turn, "ethnicity" still bears the stamp of essentialist thinking; even so, it works as a way to connect with the literature and besides, "culture" invites problems too. It might be preferable to speak of cultural politics or culturally inflected politics, in contrast to class, interest, and ideological politics, for all "ethnicity" ultimately comes down to some form of cultural difference—such as national origin, nationalism, language, religion, region, community, kinship, clan, and caste—all of which, including "race," are themselves cultural constructs. However, similar problems as in relation to ethnicity apply to "culture," which cannot be settled here.[15] A neat distinction between interest politics and cultural or ethnic politics is not tenable either because interest too is culturally constructed, mediated, and articulated (as in class consciousness), so ultimately these distinctions do not hold; which is not to suggest that class dissolves into culture but merely that it cannot exist outside culture.

Although the "thingness" of ethnicity is bracketed and questioned in social science and considered unresolved in political science, in policy discourse, for instance, in the context of humanitarian intervention, fixed assumptions and closed, narrow understandings of ethnicity often prevail.[16] "Managing ethnic conflict" has become another cottage industry. But what, in fact, are "ethnic conflicts"?

- Hypothesis: *When politics is up front, we speak of political conflict. When politics is opaque, we speak of ethnic conflict.* Did we refer to conflicts in Kosovo and East Timor as ethnic conflicts? They are generally perceived as questions of nationalism in which ethnic groups play some part. What about Sierra Leone, Liberia? Political conflict refers to conflict among interest groups; these may be partly defined in cultural terms, but that does not necessarily alter the basic make-up of the situation. The visibility and transparency of "politics," however, is also a function of social distance and political conditions, including channels of information. Up close or as locals we would know the political interests that are at stake. Yet locals may be hoodwinked too, for instance, through the monopolization of media. Thus the conflict in Rwanda was a political conflict among rival regional interest groups that largely involved Hutus, but for political reasons it was presented in Rwandese state-sponsored media as an *ethnic* conflict.[17] In Afghanistan in the 1990s, "it was not 'ethnicities' that made war but political organizations with ideological objectives."[18] Let's note the gradual changes in perceptions of distant conflicts when through continued reporting and analysis the conflicts become less distant. Conflicts in Sierra Leone in the 1990s were originally presented and perceived as ethnic or tribal fury, but gradually the stakeholders' interests became more visible: control over diamond mining and trade, warlords and gang warfare, small-arms traffic, and support for warring factions in neighboring countries.[19]

- Hypothesis: *Majority politics are designated "political" and minority politics are termed "ethnic," that is, ethnicity is minority nationalism.* The war waged by the Tamil insurgents in Sri Lanka is perceived as an ethnic or ethno-nationalist struggle, whereas majority Sinhala politics is tacitly treated as ordinary national politics. Yet if we step into the thick of the situation we may find majority Sinhala politics every bit as "ethnic" and steeped in prejudice and cultural bias as Tamil politics.[20] This illustrates the tenuous and biased distinction between nationalism and ethnicity, which privileges and naturalizes majority interests and politics and looks askance at minority politics, as a bias inherent in the terminology of ethnicity.

- Hypothesis: *Nationalism refers to urban nationalism, whereas rural nationalism is often termed ethnicity.* According to Ramet, the "nationalist movement which made rapid gains after the death of Yugoslav President Josip Broz Tito in May 1980, and which came into its own in 1987, relies above all on rural support and is, in essence, a profoundly rural phenomenon. To say this is also to suggest that Milosevic's ascent to power represented the victory of the Serbian countryside over the city." She distinguishes between urban nationalism and rural nationalism, which is "more ethnic." Among all of former Yugoslavia's provinces Serbia has by far the greatest percentage of the population engaged in agriculture (27.6 percent).[21] The conflict in Bosnia has been termed *urbicide* or the revenge of the predominantly rural Bosnian Serbs against predominantly urban Bosnian Moslems.[22]

- Thesis: *Ethnicity is relational.* Chinese food eaten by Chinese in a Chinese restaurant overseas is food (a particular kind of food, a regional food, etc.); the same food eaten by non-Chinese in the same restaurant becomes "ethnic food."

These points suggest, first, that "ethnicity" fades and *interest* comes to the foreground as a function of growing knowledge of the situation, that is, what may underlie the distinction is the difference between local optics and long-distance optics. Second, the term "ethnicity" may be a function of majority-minority relations. Third, "ethnicity" may be a function of perceived rural-urban differences. Fourth, "ethnicity" is relational and contextual. In Dwyer's words, "Ethnicity is a product of contact, not of isolation."[23] Since ethnicity is relational it necessitates the scrutiny of relationships, and since social relations change over time different types of ethnicity emerge.

Ethnicities

Reflexivity begins by opening up ethnicity, unpacking its "thingness," viewing ethnicity as process and showing diversity underneath the label. Ethnicity can be unpacked by distinguishing four types which may be viewed as snapshots of ethnicity as a moving target; I briefly sum up the discussion of chapter 2.

Domination ethnicity. Considering that the term "ethnicity" itself is a discourse of domination and the distinction between nation and ethnicity is tenuous, if nationalism takes the form of monocultural control, it may be considered a form of ethnicity or ethnocracy. Ethnic mobilization is often a reaction to the imposition of a monocultural regime and discriminatory treatment or regional uneven development.

Enclosure ethnicity. This exists in varieties of dormant ethnicity and cultural confinement, which share a restriction of mobility and space. This may be an existing (dormant ethnicity) or involuntary condition (imposed). Dormant or latent ethnicity exists in an isolated group or where intergroup contacts have little salience, as in the case of the "primitive isolates" of anthropology. Cultural confinement occurs as a consequence of conquest (Amerindians in the Andes driven up the mountains by the encroaching Hispanic conquests and latifundios) or external imposition (the Jews confined to ghettos, the segregation of African Americans under the Jim Crow laws, the Bantustans in apartheid South Africa).

Competition ethnicity. This involves competition with the state or other cultural formations in relation to state power, resources, and development. This is the major problem zone of ethnic relations. One strategy of building group strength is dissociation, self-chosen segregation, or inward-looking ethnicity. Delinking can be a strategy of competition or preparation for competition. A mild variety is "buy black, vote black," and a stronger version is the Nation of Islam.

Optional ethnicity. Low-intensity ethnicity is light, volitional, and fluid, as in the case of ethnic entrepreneurs, symbolic ethnicity, ethnic chic, and "shopping for identity."

The question that arises next is how these varieties relate to one another, how one mode shifts to another or the dynamics of ethnicity. A simple account is that nationalism awakens dormant ethnicity and imposes "minority" status or enclosure ethnicity, and over time enclosure ethnicity tends toward competition ethnicity. Competition ethnicity, in turn, over time tends toward the widening of choices of cultural affiliation because competition itself generates the accumulation of crosscultural capital, which may eventually lead to optional ethnicity.

What is the status of this sequence? Is it a likely or a necessary process, that is, is teleology involved? Even if this sequence is widely observed, it does not mean it is universal. Under which conditions does this process apply? How long does it take to unfold and what determines its pace? Is there only forward or also backward movement? Experience and research suggest that these dynamics occur, but the instances where they do *not* occur, even though they may be relatively few, are precisely those that call for explanation. For instance, Sinhala Buddhist chauvinism in Sri Lanka has maintained its hold over a long period and continues to inform government policies and popular attitudes, thus reproducing the conditions in which Tamil nationalism persists and is nourished by long-distance nationalism, resulting in a situation of ethnic gridlock. With these provisos, these dynamics have heuristic value, also in showing up counter instances. (For an overview, I refer to Table 2.1.)

Domination-within-domination

If we assume that cultural differences are not problematic per se, then the main factor that makes cultural differences salient and problematic is if and how they intersect with power relations. This too needs to be considered in process form. Each variety of ethnicity then represents features of both domination and emancipation in different relational contexts. Thus the classic problem of domination-within-domination takes different forms across the varieties of ethnicity sketched above:

1. Nationalism may be emancipatory in relation to colonialism and external domination but turns into domination when it takes the form of internal colonialism, xenophobia, and chauvinism, imposes a monocultural regime, and practices suppression and discrimination of minorities and deliberate uneven development across regions. An example is Kemalism in Turkey: emancipatory in relation to foreign powers and repressive in relation to minorities such as Armenians, Kurds, Alevites, and foreigners, especially during the early period of nation building.
2. In dormant ethnicity, cultural difference is latent and not a political factor. Cultural confinement often involves a chain effect in which the dominated reproduce domination in their own circles. Group membership is involuntary, internal differences are suppressed, group boundaries are rigid, individual choice is restricted, and "passing" into another group is prohibited or discouraged. Similar constraints apply when self-segregation is a competition strategy.[24]
3. Competition ethnicity stretches across a range of culturally inflected politics that is too wide for comfortable generalizations. Unity is strength and therefore there may be a tendency toward suppressing internal differences. Competition means seeking advantage in rela-

tion to other ethnic groups, which may lead to playing up differences. In recent work, Samuel Huntington redefines WASP identity as, in effect, a competition ethnicity that should compete by imposing rules on newcomers, such as English as the national language.[25] The vast legacy of "ethnic jokes" is a mild reminder of this pattern. However, interethnic cooperation and rainbow coalitions can also be a competition strategy, such as the coalition of Jews and blacks in American politics during the 1960s.

4. Optional ethnicity may be emancipatory by widening mobility and identity options, in effect, opening the way to post-ethnicity. In optional ethnicity, domination may relate to the self rather than others. Thus "passing" or adopting chameleon identities for the sake of mobility or gain can lead to alienation. An example is the practice of skin bleaching, widespread in South Asia, the Middle East, parts of Africa, Latin America, and the Caribbean and among immigrants in the West. Such politics of complexion includes "passing" in the United States, "browning" in Jamaica, and the saying "money whitens" in Brazil.

Table 2.2 gives a précis of the ambivalent politics of ethnicity on the argument that to each variety of ethnicity there is a dimension of domination and of emancipation in different relational settings.

Since ethnicity is relational it involves relations among ethnic groups which are each not merely different but also different types of ethnicity. They are not merely different ethnic groups but different ethnic *strata* occupying different class positions. An example is the distinction between "race" and "ethnicity" in the U.S., which Mary Waters draws as follows: "European ethnic groups are generally composed of voluntary migrants and their descendants who chose to come to the United States. Those defined racially, such as blacks, Native Americans, Mexicans in the South-West, and Puerto Ricans, have generally been incorporated into the United States historically through conquest or the forced migration of slaves."[26]

Considering that mobility is a function of power, dominant groups and individuals are per definition more mobile than subalterns; they can choose to identify ethnic or post-ethnic, to identify "white," to shop for identity, to identify as liberal or humanist, or to step outside the framework altogether and identify as world citizen. For "white ethnics," then, according to Waters, "ethnicity itself takes on certain individual and positive connotations. The process and content of symbolic ethnicity then make it increasingly difficult for white ethnics to sympathize with, or understand, the experience of a non-symbolic ethnicity, the experience of racial minorities in the United States."[27]

Another way of phrasing this is that since ethnicity is relational it implies multiculture of one sort or another. Ethnicity and multiculturalism, then, are two ways of describing the same situation.[28] Next, since ethnicity is always plural and implies ethnicities (for no ethnicity exists alone), to ethnicity there is always a reflexive moment (the one exception is dormant ethnicity, which is pre-ethnicity or the absence of ethnic consciousness). Ethnic consciousness implies awareness of other ethnicities. In a similar vein, multiculturalism implies *multiculturalisms* in that different groups hold different views on the nature of their interrelations, which brings us to the question of multiculturalisms.

Multiculturalisms

To contextualize multiculturalism, let's first consider what it is not and what kind of thinking preceded it. Earlier views essentialized cultural difference. To give one example, in the Romantic take on nations of Herder and de Maistre, each nation and people possesses its own genius and soul. In this view, the units of cultural difference are peoples; difference is typically expressed in language and other components of folk culture, and if boundaries do not naturally exist, state policy should strive to make them coincide.

But what if different peoples do coexist within the same polity because of migration, conquest, colonialism, or decolonization? Classic responses have been to institute status differentials (such as slavery, caste, and the medieval estates), to provide autonomy within an overarching tribute-paying or imperial social formation (as in the Ottoman millet system), and assimilation. Other options are territorial segregation, population transfer, and genocide.

Assimilation has been a major strategy to control difference, for instance, the compulsory conversion of Jews and Moors after the Reconquest of the Iberian Peninsula and the Inquisition. A familiar version of assimilation is the American melting pot. In nineteenth-century Latin America *mestizaje* served as a hegemonic ideology of "whitening" and "Europeanization." These are forms of monoculturalism, or nationalism framed by a cultural hegemony and center of gravity, which in the U.S. for a long time used to be WASP hegemony. Group boundaries are taken to be fluid *except* those of the dominant group; all groups are expected to gradually melt and converge on the center, the cultural identity of Americanism, which itself was not supposed to change. A précis of classic responses to cultural difference is in Table 5.1.

An early perspective on the coexistence of cultural groups is *plural society*, a notion coined by J. S. Furnivall to describe the situation in the Dutch East Indies and colonial Burma. In the Dutch East Indies different populations (Javanese and other island peoples, Chinese, Dutch, and a scattering of Arabs) allegedly coexisted without mingling; they interacted only in the

Table 5.1.   **Responses to group differences**

Responses	Key words	Examples
Status differences	Ascribed status	Caste, helots, slavery, estates, colonial color bar, Apartheid
Relative autonomy	Local peoples can follow their religion and culture	Dhimma, Ottoman millet system, tributary systems, indirect rule
Segregation	Territorial confinement (and different legal status)	Ghettos, reservations, Jim Crow laws, Bantustans
Assimilation	Convergence on a given center	Conversion, melting pot, nineteenth-century mestizaje
Migration	Population transfer (forced or voluntary)	Pogroms, ethnic cleansing, Indian Removal, expulsions from Turkey
Genocide		Armenians, Shoah

marketplace and thus made up a plural economy.[29] The idea of plural society has also been applied to other social formations such as the Caribbean, the southern United States, and the Philippines, and criticized in the process.[30]

Plural society fails to capture many nuances. Thus many Chinese in Java and elsewhere in Southeast Asia became integrated over time and intermarried with the indigenous population, giving rise to mestizo groups. In the Malay world they were called "peranakan Chinese," in contrast to Chinese newcomers. The Dutch included newcomers from the Netherlands, and the Indo-Dutch, who had been living in the East for generations, intermarried with locals and developed a mixed colonial culture (known as "tempo doeloe"). Indos, the offspring of relations between locals and the Dutch, who assimilated within the native population, were an in-between group of lower status. The local population in turn consisted of many different groups and strata. In England, too, multiculturalism and the way in which cultural difference is recognized were originally patterned on the colonial experience.[31] The limitations of plural society are relevant to the further discussion.

- It treats group differences as permanent;
- It ignores intermarriage and mingling across groups;
- It ignores varieties within groups;
- It ignores or downplays status differences between groups in the colonial power hierarchy; and
- It echoes late colonial fictions on the separation between population groups (which developed in the mid-nineteenth century in reaction to ideas of "race" imported from Europe) and gives a view "from above" rather than accurately describing actual intergroup relations.

Another approach to the coexistence of different cultural groups is *pillar-ization*, which derives from the settlement achieved in the wake of the *Kul-turkampf* in the Netherlands. Pillarization was the Dutch mode of cultural pluralism from the 1910s to the 1970s. Pillarization refers to the history of religious differences within the nation, between Catholics, Protestants, and the non–church affiliated. Equal rights in terms of state support for education was granted to Catholics only by 1917. Government funding of schools founded by religious organizations established the system of pillarization, also known as the "silver strings" between the state and Christian denominations. Over time it gave rise to different trade unions, universities, newspapers, and broadcasting for Protestants, Catholics, socialists, and liberals.[32] At a later stage this served as a template for multiculturalism:

> In the 1980s there was talk of the return of pillarization with a view to immi-grants. Pillarization seemed a logical mode in which to incorporate the new-comers. Thus Christian Democrats spoke of "emancipation within one's own circle," just as sixty years earlier this applied to Catholics and Protestants, who each received state subsidies for their schools and denominational insti-tutions. There are, however, differences between denominational and multi-cultural pillarization. The religious pillars communicated among one another at the top, together their elites constituted a roof over the pillarized society. But the mini-pillars of the newcomers with their low socioeconomic status do not reach that high. This truncated mini-pillarization did involve subsidies for immigrant institutions. The second difference was the timing: multicul-tural pillarization set in when religious pillarization was past, in an urban-ized and secularized society in which denominational differences were becoming a background rumour. . . . In the course of the 1980s the pillariza-tion model gave way to greater emphasis on integration, advocated by social democrats and liberals. In the 1990s this takes the form of emphasis on learn-ing the language, courses in "citizenship skills," and plans for immigrant employment schemes with a reporting system for companies.[33]

The Dutch political scientist Arend Lijphart was inspired by Furnivall's work on plural society and the policy of pillarization, which he combined in the influential model of *consociationalism*.[34] In ethnic conflict regulation consociationalism or power sharing is still the leading prescriptive model.[35] The main objections to consociationalism are fairly familiar:

- It reworks the plural society and pillarization models.
- It does not sufficiently problematize "ethnicity" or group boundaries.
- It promotes patronage and clientelist politics.
- It produces static multiculturalism as a mosaic of ghettos and static communities.

- New mini-pillars do not reach to the roof. Under classic pillarization the elites of the different groups fraternized at the roof, but the new multicultural pillars don't reach the upper echelons of society.
- It overlooks the hybrids, the in-betweens.

In this context, the proposal for accommodating ethnicity in African politics mentioned earlier does not really go beyond consociationalism. It represents an advance on conventional approaches to democracy in Africa that leave cultural difference out of the equation and incorporates alternative development perspectives. The multilevel distribution of authority as in Ethiopian ethnic federalism (state autonomy at federal levels and ethnic organization at local and regional levels) matches the pillarization and consociationalism approaches. There are no safeguards in this approach against patronage politics or against ethnic rivalry spilling over political watersheds and contaminating or taking over higher levels of governance, resulting in ethnic polarization and ethnocracy. If local and regional power bases become ethnic vote banks, state autonomy is at risk. If this approach goes together with participatory democracy and therefore decentralization, it would clash with the strict separation between levels of authority required by pillarization. Accordingly the emancipation model of ethnicity *tout court* leads to recycling patronage politics, a classic predicament in African politics.

Experiences in the North with immigration and minorities dominate the discussion of multiculturalism, whereas experiences in the South are discussed under headings such as ethnic segmentation or communalism. Since what is at stake in multiculturalism is political rights, normative political theory is the leading discourse on multiculturalism. Political theory speaks to policy, whereas sociology and cultural studies tend to play interpretative and critical roles. Combining ethnicities and multiculturalisms serves to combine experiences and perspectives North and South and place discussions of multiculturalism on a wider canvas.

The historical lineages of perspectives on multiculturalism include nineteenth-century "race science," Victorian anthropology, and social Darwinism, but the main sources of conceptions of multiculturalism are the following:

- Old local arrangements of regional and cultural differences and minorities;
- Colonial societies (such as plural society);
- Settlements of the *Kulturkampf* in European countries (such as the emancipation of minorities and pillarization);
- Combinations of the latter two (consociationalism);

- Adaptations to changing demography and hegemony in colonial settler societies, notably in the U.S. and Canada; and
- Corporate marketing strategies (such as ethnomarketing).

The various notions of multiculturalism reflect these lineages. Multiculturalism on the model of pillarization is a static, conservative archipelago
of cultural groups or communities, a mosaic of ghettos. Peter McLaren
distinguishes conservative, liberal, left-liberal, and critical or resistance
multiculturalism. Hollinger contrasts pluralist multiculturalism, in which
groups are permanent, enduring and the subject of group rights, and cosmopolitan multiculturalism, which involves shifting group boundaries,
multiple affiliations, and hybrid identities and is based on individual
rights.[36] If cultures are viewed as porous and interpenetrating, rather than
as billiard balls, *interculturalism* might be a better term.[37]

A familiar line of criticism dismisses multiculturalism as the cultural
wallpaper of late capitalism, as the "bourgeois eclecticism" of corporate or
consumerist multiculturalism à la Benetton.[38] These forms of "managed
multiculturalism" come in corporate and administrative varieties and
reflect a "standard pluralism that not only leaves groups constituted as
givens but entrenches the boundaries fixing group demarcations as unal-
terable."[39] The problem, however, is not that these forms of multiculturalism are managed (political rights imply a relationship to the state and thus
some form of institutional "management"); the problem is the terms on
which they are managed. The view that multiculturalism equals late capitalism overlooks that multiethnicity matters also prior to capitalism, recognizes but one variety of multiculturalism and one variety of capitalism,
"late capitalism," and by implying that "identity can wait" reproduces
class reductionism.[40]

Forms of "multiculturalism from above" do not address power relations and if we accept that multiculturalism is about political rights and
power relations in postcolonial settings, managerial multiculturalisms
miss the point. Alternative options are critical, transformative, or revolutionary multiculturalism.[41] These views have been criticized for being
"culturalist" and requiring stronger political economy,[42] which is valid,
although it echoes points made in critical multiculturalism itself; the work
of critique is never finished. Critical multiculturalism does not treat
cultural differences as givens but problematizes them as differences-in-
relation, and by incorporating class analysis, power relations and political
rights, it brings politics back into the babble of diversity.

Table 5.2 presents a schema of different multiculturalisms. The axes on
which they are constructed are perspectives on difference, the nature of
group boundaries and notions of rights. The boxes are not mutually exclusive. What underlie these varieties of multiculturalism are assumptions

Table 5.2.   **Multiculturalisms**

Multiculturalism	*Key words*	*Related notions*
Conservative	Groups and differences are enduring; group rights	Plural society, pillarization, consociationalism; pluralist multiculturalism
Liberal	A natural equality underlies differences; inequality indicates lack of opportunity	Diversity; corporate, boutique, ludic, consumerist multiculturalism
Left-liberal	Differences are viewed as "essence"	Identity politics, standpoint theory, "strategic essentialism," "Show one's identity papers before dialogue can begin" (McLaren)
Critical	Differences in relation (McLaren)	Resistance, transformative multiculturalism
Fluid	Shifting group boundaries, multiple	Cosmopolitan multiculturalism, interculturalism or hybrid identities, individual rights (Kymlicka)

concerning identity, group boundaries and the nature of the state. A general backdrop to understandings of multiculturalism is the liberal state (chapter 4). All multiculturalisms in this table, except the plural society model, assume common citizenship and thus a commitment to individual rights while ignoring noncitizens.

The question is how individual rights and collective rights interrelate. In North America a classic friction runs between the politics of recognition and redistribution. In an exchange with Iris Young, Nancy Fraser argues that these are not reducible to one another and that the cultural left and the ideological left are divided.[43] Young argues for a coalition politics that bridges these differences and Fraser responds that in reality such differences are being reproduced within these politics.

Canadian multiculturalism is more fluid than U.S. multiculturalism. This debate calls to mind William Julius Wilson's plea to shift from race to class and economic criteria of entitlement. Another way of phrasing this is that what is at issue is the need to strengthen the welfare state. In Europe the friction between recognition and redistribution is tempered by the welfare state. In most European Union countries the recognition of collective rights based on cultural difference assumes fixed group boundaries, but since citizenship provides more basic entitlements than the residual American welfare state (or workfare state), the pressure for group affiliation and identification is reduced.

This is where notions of identity come in and where the varieties of multiculturalism meet with the varieties of ethnicity, as twin sets of assumptions concerning identity and group boundaries. Consider, for instance, Will Kymlicka's views in relation to "American multiculturalism":

> the appropriate form of multiculturalism must be fluid in conception of groups and group boundaries (new groups may emerge, older groups may coalesce or disappear); voluntary in its conception of group affiliation (individuals should be free to decide whether and how to affiliate with their community of descent); and nonexclusive in its conception of group identity (being a member of one group does not preclude identification with another, or with the larger American nation).[44]

This adds up to the following conditions for intergroup relations: fluid group boundaries, voluntary group affiliation, and multiple identities. These ideas would go a long way in addressing the question of domination-within-domination, but they raise several problems. In essence, this treats ethnicity as if it is optional, while the realities it refers to are probably conditions of competition ethnicity. If the stipulated conditions would indeed exist there would be no need for ethnic competition. The emphasis on individual choice in Kymlicka's view may be specific to North American conditions. This begs the question. If individual choice indeed exists as a viable option, what is the problem? In addition, if cultural identity is understood as a matter of individual agency it clashes with the allocation of group rights, which assumes ascribed status. In addition, the perspective is from the outside, from the viewpoint of the state and multiculturalism, not from the viewpoint of the groups. The problem is, how is this to be institutionalized? Collective rights may be granted to right past discrimination and disadvantage, but once granted they rigidify group boundaries—how else to know who are entitled? So the side effect of some remedies is that they sustain or aggravate the problem of difference. There is a clash between collective rights and fluid group boundaries: collective rights turn group membership into an ascribed status, not a voluntary choice. Collective rights foster ethnic organization and hence patronage. To the extent that this approach is relevant to multiethnicity it does not settle the question of multinational societies and indigenous peoples, such as Native Americans. Here, if collective rights are granted (such as tax exemption, welfare benefits and free crossborder traffic) group membership is an ascribed status, not a voluntary choice.

A related problem is the question of hybrids and in-betweens. Nationalism (dominant culture, ethnocracy) and ethnic mobilization have both been highly visible and the field is usually seen as the friction between these two. But what about the in-betweens who are "neither and both," who belong in neither camp or in both? For instance, in the United States, demographers speak of a silent explosion in the number of mixed-race people. Between 1960 and 1990, the number of interracial married couples went from 150,000 to more than 1.1 million, and the number of interracial children leaped accordingly: "Since 1970, the number of mixed-race children in the United States has quadrupled. And there are six times as many intermarriages today as there were in 1960." Thus, in addition to the choice of sixteen racial categories the U.S. Census Bureau offers Americans, some propose a new "multiracial" category. This infuriated those African American leaders who regard it as undermining black solidarity: "African-American leaders also object to a multiracial category because race data are used to enforce civil rights legislation in employment, voting rights, housing and mortgage lending, health care services and educational opportunities."[45] Proponents argue that this category—and a "category of 'multiethnic' origin, which most Americans might wish to check"—would help soften the racial and ethnic divisions that now run through American society. Amid ample controversy, the 2000 U.S. Census for the first time offered Americans the option of multiple identification. This is one example of the clash between the allocation of collective rights and the idea of multiple identity and fluid group boundaries.

If we juxtapose the varieties of ethnicity and multiculturalism the problems become apparent. Domination ethnicity (monocultural nationalism) suppresses differences through assimilation policies. Enclosure ethnicity suppresses differences through territorial segregation, often accompanied by ascribing a different legal status to different groups. Liberal citizenship forecloses both these options. Here the real problem zone is competition ethnicity. Liberal multiculturalism sidesteps the question of competition by viewing inequality as lack of opportunity, thereby denying the problem of difference itself: a cultural division of labor that privileges some groups. Left-liberal multiculturalism recognizes this problem but in the process reifies and essentializes identities, so that what is a solution in one sphere (recognizing difference) becomes a problem in another (reifying difference). Fluid and cosmopolitan multiculturalism sidestep the problem of competition by treating ethnic identity as if it is optional already. Thus they mix up what might be the likely outcome over time (ethnic identity as choice) with the ongoing process (competition on the basis of identities). Table 5.3 gives an overview combining ethnicities and multiculturalisms.

We can leave assimilation and hegemony out of the equation since they are essentially variations on monoculturalism. Multiculturalism concerns the redefinition of political rights in societies in which the composition of the population and the political balance of power have been changing. North America and Europe dominate in the discussion on multiculturalism, but changing demographics and shifting cultural hegemony pertain throughout the world.

Table 5.3. Ethnicities and multiculturalisms

Ethnicities	Intergroup relations	Multiculturalisms
Domination	Assimilation	No (monoculturalism)
Enclosure	Segregation	No (Apartheid)
Competition	Bicultural rivalries	Liberal, left-liberal, critical
Optional	Hybridity, post-ethnicity	Fluid, cosmopolitan

In these situations what matters is neither pure and uncontested hierarchy nor enclosure (with reified or fixed cultural boundaries) nor optional identities (shopping for identity, ethnic chic, ethnicity lite, confetti culture), but the in-between zone of differences in relation, the zone where groups are sufficiently similar to compete for the same resources while falling short of convergence upon sameness of identity or degree of mobility. It follows that in the realities of culturally inscribed inequality of the multiculturalisms discussed above only critical multiculturalism is a pertinent option. As a critical perspective it poses more questions than it answers, but the questions are pertinent. Collective learning as a contextual process involves the awareness that each settlement is provisional, contextual. A settlement must have in-built provisos that avoid closure and make it open to amendment. Standard pluralism shuffles stereotypes, whereas fluid or cosmopolitan pluralism overlooks stereotypes, assumes liquidity of identity, and thus serves as a cure for which there is no ailment.

Notes

1. Cf. Nederveen Pieterse 2002.
2. Lake 1995, 3; emphasis added.
3. Examples are Moynihan 1992 and Kaplan 2000.
4. Salih 1999, 3; emphasis added.
5. For instance, the historian Ernest Wamba-dia-Wamba, who long argued against the "imperial state" in Africa as a colonial imposition (1991), later became a spokesperson of the rebels in eastern Congo.
6. According to Algis Prazauskas, "In the modern world, ethnic nationalism looks larger than life mainly because it has received wide coverage in the mass media and the lion's share of ethno-political research deals with secessionist movements and regions of ethnic strife rather than with progress of national integration in much larger areas" (1998, 2).
7. A discussion of these views in the context of humanitarian action and intervention is Nederveen Pieterse 1998.
8. Cf. Rupesinghe and Tishkov 1996; Wimmer et al. 2004.
9. Bayart, Ellis, and Hibou 1999; Chabal and Daloz 1999.

10. Mkandawire 2002, 184, 186, 190–91.

11. Social learning is a salient theme in fields such as organization theory, social movements, industrial districts, development studies, and research methodology, discussed in Nederveen Pieterse 2001.

12. See, for example, Jenkins 1999; Bulmer and Solomos 1999; and chapter 2, this volume.

13. Taylor 1999, 121.

14. "Most rural Africa is still largely divided into ethnic territories homelands or enclaves inhabited by one or more dominant ethnic group. . . . Ethnic or primary affiliations still provide the basis on which individuals and groups gain access to land" (Salih 1999, 8).

15. The distinction between "culture" and "cultures" is discussed in the conclusion to this volume.

16. An example is Lake 1995; a discussion is Nederveen Pieterse 1998b.

17. Uvin 1999.

18. Dorronsoro 2004.

19. Richards 1996.

20. This is a growing awareness in Sri Lanka; for example, Nithiyanandam 2000; Uyangoda 2005.

21. Ramet 1996, 76, 72, 75.

22. Denitch 1994; Humphrey 1997.

23. Dwyer 1996, 4.

24. For example, on the Nation of Islam, see Marable 1998.

25. Huntington 2004a, 2004b.

26. Waters 1996, 238.

27. Waters 1996, 23–24.

28. We could argue that ethnicity implies ethnicities and therefore multiculturalism for the coexistence of ethnicities always involves a normative component and collective representations and ideologies of differences-in-relation. But this would stretch "multiculturalism" beyond its usual meaning of positive recognition of cultural diversity to *any* valuation of cultural difference, that is, anti-Semitism, Jim Crow, and Apartheid would then be forms of multiculturalism too. But multiculturalism is not merely a demographic condition.

29. Furnivall 1939, 1956. Furnivall's original 1939 term "plural economy" was later stretched to plural society.

30. Hollander et al. 1966.

31. Ali 1992, 104.

32. Goudsblom 1967; Knippenberg and de Pater 1988.

33. Nederveen Pieterse 1997, 192–93.

34. Lijphart 1975, 1977.

35. Taylor 1999.

36. McLaren 1995, 120–32; Hollinger 1995. Cf. Turner's "difference multiculturalism" (1994).

37. Bernasconi 1998.

38. Jameson 1991; Zizek 1997. A related notion is "hegemonic multiculturalism" (Matustík 1998).

39. Goldberg 1994, 7.

40. As a rejoinder, McLaren proposes a materialist multiculturalism (2001, 416–17).

41. Chicago Cultural Studies Group 1994; McLaren 1997; Martin 1998; May 1999.

42. McLennan 2001.

43. Fraser 1998; Young 1998.

44. Kymlicka 1998, 73.

45. A. Etzioni, "'Other' Americans help break down racial barriers," *International Herald Tribune*, May 10, 1997.

6

❖

Multiculturalism and museums

Representing others in the age of globalization

If it is true that knowledge is power and that, therefore, as Umberto Eco argued, the library is the central institution of western culture, this also applies to the museum, for the museum is the library on display, turned inside out. The key to the museum is "its role in making visible the foundational and originary narrative structures of western knowledge about the nature of the world."[1] "We think of museums as places of objects. In fact, they are places of ideas."[2]

Exhibitions are "privileged arenas for presenting images of self and 'other,'"[3] and ethnological museums, in particular, provide narratives about "others." That may be why ethnographic museums have never been in the limelight of prestige. Prestige went to national history museums and art galleries and then to the modern art museum as the central sites of the museums' "rituals of citizenship."[4] Ethnographic museums were never museums of influence, models to other museums. Often they have been scenes of neglect and underfunded institutions, standing in relation to other museums like the Third World to the First.[5] Occupying a derivative status as a political, moral, and scientific annex of the majority museums, excluded from the leading museums' rituals of citizenship, ethnological museums serve as a counterpoint to them, politically marginal while symbolically central.

In the words of American president William McKinley, "Exhibitions are the timekeepers of progress." The colonial exhibitions of the late nineteenth century, which were the origins of many ethnographic museums, offered panoramas of power in which imperial hierarchies were on display. As the public storehouse of the legacy of empire, the ethnological museum is, as Julie Marcus observes, a monument of imperial tropes: the acquisition of objects (trophies of empire, taken by armies, as if decapitating the natives by taking their sacred objects), the collector as hero (salvaging the object from the decay of oriental meltdown), the charisma of the object (and the claim to "undisputed origin" as the mark of authenticity), the intersection of taxonomy and chronology (situating the object while structuring the institutional world of museums).[6]

In recent times the entire field has radically changed for all museums. In the era of accelerated globalization, national museums are losing their function and becoming shrines of nostalgia.[7] Citizenship is in the process of becoming global, civilizational, regional, and local. Thus the German Historical Museum founded in 1987 in Berlin adopted a "postnationalist" view of German history as part of European history, also to sidestep the vexed question of "one nation, two states."[8] Earlier the modern art museum initiated the principle of the transnational aesthetic. Postmodernism further undermines conventional exhibiting strategies.[9]

Ethnographic museums are deeply affected by these wider trends, to the point that they now seem quaint. They "exhibit ideas about the 'other' in the earlier, cruder forms left over from the time in which the ideas came into being, and not in the glossier disguised forms into which they have developed and in which they are found in many art and history museums."[10] They are directly affected by two epochal shifts, decolonization and multiculturalism. The function of offering vivid evidence of the West's triumphal stride has shrunk since decolonization. Ethnographic museums can no longer afford to be shrines of colonialism, display windows of empire, or indirect testimonies of national grandeur, though some museums quietly linger on in this mode, probably as much on the grounds of inertia as on principle. The Museum for Central Africa in Tervuren, Belgium, is notorious in museum land as King Leopold's empire display and for its pristine prewar aura: "In none of the museum's twenty large exhibition galleries is there the slightest hint that millions of Congolese met unnatural deaths."[11]

Postcolonialism unsettles ethnographic museums as it does ethnography and anthropology. The time of ethnographic museums may be past altogether: "The collections and displays are overwhelmingly of the shield, spear, boomerang, and war-canoe type"; they emphasize "traditional culture" and thus "encourage a patronizing and escapist attitude toward the people involved."[12]

Multiculturalism has brought the natives home in the post-imperial countries and occasions the need to redefine citizenship. Multiculturalism unhinges the citizenship rituals of the national museums and museums of modernism. It opens up a new field of cultural flux—of "insurgence of subjugated knowledges," of nomadic knowledge and crosscultural translation. Museums and other media are in the forefront of this arena. Multicul-turalism, as discussed earlier, is about sharing access to public resources and the public sphere, so media and museums as institutions of public rep-resentation are strategic venues for multicultural engagement. Several ethnographic museums have been reinstituted as *world museums*, essen-tially dedicated to multiculturalism and migration—as in Rotterdam, Gothenburg, Chicago, and Copenhagen—or have adopted radically differ-ent exhibition formats. In the 1990s the National Museum for Ethnography in Stockholm adopted an exhibition approach under the heading "The knowledge-creating human."[13] In this time of transition several exhibiting strategies have come into prominence in a curious mélange of newness and nostalgia.

In the first part of this chapter I discuss the thesis that representations of others are either exoticizing (emphasizing difference) or assimilating (emphasizing similarities). Thus, displaying ethnographic objects as art follows an assimilative approach, whereas in situ exhibitions (reconstruct-ing habitats) tend to be exoticizing, and encyclopedic exhibitions follow mixed strategies. In the second part I consider the perspectives on culture that inform display strategies. Cultural relativism and evolutionism in anthropology reproduce different gazes of the Enlightenment: modernist, displaying roadmaps to modernity, or Romantic and differentialist. The actual politics of representation are further affected by the *rapport de forces* in different settings, such as light or strong multiculturalism, cultures with a stable center or canon, and those that are in flux. In the third section of this chapter I address changing notions of self and others. The dichotomy of self and other is destabilized by accelerated globalization. The conven-tional Enlightenment subjectivities (national, imperial, modern) are thus refracted in multiple identities (local, regional, transnational, global, sex-ual, urban, and so forth), and "the other" becomes "others" (differentiated by "race," class, gender, national origin, lifestyle, and so forth). The idea that representations of others must either be exoticizing or assimilating ignores other options—such as recognizing difference without exoticism, viewing others as counterparts in dialogue, and viewing oneself as an other. Section four concerns the alternative display agendas that reflect and produce these changes, each of which poses different questions. Plu-ralism—but is there still a center? Dialogue—but who sets the stage and who is in control? Self-representation—but who speaks for indigenous and other communities? Hybridity—but what are the terms of mixture? And finally, reflexive representation—zeroing in on and thematizing the dilemmas of representation itself.

In the closing section I address the core dilemma of exhibiting power. Representation tends to keep the power of representation out of view. Thus colonialism frames ethnographic exhibitions but is rarely addressed by it. Exhibitions fetishize (or sometimes neutralize) rather than examine the charisma of power. This follows from exhibiting as a gesture of power and museums as sites of power. Reflexive representation can transform exhibitions into laboratories of collective learning. From sites of power, links in the chain reproduction of desire, museums can become laboratories of social reflexivity and transformation.

Exhibiting strategies

> The Museum of the Indian in Manaus, the capital of the state of Amazonas, is run by the Silesian Mission. Upon entering the museum, one sees a Neanderthal-looking figure made out of some sort of plastic depicting a "Typical Amazonian Indian" fishing in a pond made of broken pieces of tile set in concrete. The caption reads, "Typical Uaupés River Landscape."
>
> —Jimmy Durham and M. T. Alves (1993)

In the volume *Exhibiting Cultures*, Ivan Karp observes, "Discourse about the 'other' requires similarity as well as difference" and "exhibiting strategies in which differences predominate I call *exoticizing*, and one that highlights similarities I call *assimilating*."[14]

The most prominent contemporary exhibiting strategy is to display ethnographic objects as art. "Treatment of artifacts as fine art is currently one of the most effective ways to communicate cross-culturally a sense of quality, meaning, and importance," notes anthropologist James Clifford.[15] The art-culture approach tends to follow an assimilationist strategy, seeking to emphasize similarities between the aesthetic of the viewers and of the makers of the objects. This is generally done on the basis of purely formal criteria and structural considerations—not to mention the commodification of ethnographic objects. The stage was set by the Museum of Modern Art exhibition "Primitivism in 20th-Century Art." "I want to understand the Primitive sculptures," wrote William Rubin in the exhibition catalogue, "in terms of the western context in which modern artists 'discovered' them."[16] Rubin wanted to retrace the steps that Picasso, Braque, and other artists made through the ethnological museum on their way to the studio. This attempts to reproduce an experience that was decontextualized in the first place. In a classic instance of an assimilationist approach, Rubin desired to "place 'primitive' aesthetics on a par with modernist aesthetics. In the end, however, he only assimilates the aesthetics of other cultural traditions to a particular moment within his own tradition. . . . He ends up constructing cultural 'others' whose beliefs, values, institutions, and histories are significant only as a resource used in the making of modern art."[17]

The art-culture system prevails wherever ethnographic objects are set apart in glass cases under boutique lighting. The "Magiciens de la terre" exhibition in Paris 1989 was another step from the ethnographic to the modern art museum, this time avoiding the category art for the category magic, which recalls the witchcraft routine, an old cliché of ethnography: the other as magical mystery other. The curatorial preference for self-taught artists or "people who have no training"[18] is emancipatory, though it may also reinvent exoticism.

The Musée du Quay Branly, which opened in Paris in 2006 and is dedicated to the art of indigenous peoples, rehouses many objects from the ethnological Musée de l'Homme and thus institutionalizes the reclassification of objects from ethnology to art. The museum's architecture set in a jungle garden suggests nature, rather than history, as the setting. The display is apolitical too in that it doesn't refer to France's colonial past when the objects were obtained.

The quasi-jungle setting of this museum suggests an in situ approach, which is another prominent exhibiting strategy. Barbara Kirshenblatt-Gimblett distinguishes between *in situ* and *in context* strategies. In situ exhibits practice the art of mimesis, re-creating native habitats and reenacting rituals. Such environmental and re-creative displays may include live persons, preferably representatives of the cultures on display. The hyper-realism of in situ exhibits highlights difference and tends to be exoticizing. It builds on the tradition of colonial exhibitions with native villages rebuilt on the fair grounds along with live specimens of natives doing what natives do, under the ethnographic gaze. There are several problems with this approach. "'Wholes' are not given but constituted" and often hotly contested. There is a further question of "social pornography"—as in slumming and tourism in general. In the process a "neighborhood, village or region becomes . . . a living museum in situ."[19] This can lead to the conversion of living spaces into "historical" sites and museums, as in the following newspaper announcement:

> UNESCO is about to launch next year an international appeal for the restoration of the old imperial city of Fès, in Morocco. A blueprint, elaborated by international experts . . . provides that the historic buildings should be restored and their inhabitants rehoused elsewhere, in order to create centres dedicated to Islamic arts and thought.[20]

In this case an elite "view of how Islam is to be practiced, studied, taught, and authorized" prevails. In other situations the dilemma is "Import the tourist? Or export the village and festival?"[21] In situ exhibits are substitute tourism, feeding the hunger for difference, re-creating the travel experience at a remove. Visitors can imagine themselves in a street in Cairo, Yemen, Mexico, or India. A related exhibition formula is the *festival* (Festival of India, etc.). This is hegemony in action, treating "the life world of others as our playground."[22] In the 1980s in Australia grandiose schemes for life-sized Aboriginal villages re-created on museum grounds were quite popular. Ethnic theme parks are in vogue in China and Japan.[23] On the large grounds of the Yunnan Nationalities Villages in Kunming representatives of ethnic groups display their culture in characteristic costumes, buildings, and temples with food and other folk customs. A tourist guide book notes that in Yunnan "there live people of 26 diligent and brave ethnic groups." They range from Dai and Tibetans to Wa. The well-maintained grounds and pavilions demonstrate not only theme park multiculturalism as a global display style but also the decorative, cheerful facade of state-controlled ethnicity.[24]

In context strategies pose different problems, in particular, the problem of the interpretive frame of reference. In context approaches "exert strong cognitive control over the objects, asserting the power of classification and arrangement to order large numbers of artifacts." "Viewers need principles for looking" but of course "There are as many strategies for an object as there interpretive strategies."[25] The frame of western ethnography, the gaze of modernity, is now itself under scrutiny and is no longer an unproblematic guide.

A different strategy is encyclopedic exhibitions such as "Japan und Europa, 1543–1929" (Berlin, 1993), "The Turks: A Journey of a Thousand Years, 600–1600" (London), "Europa und die Orient" (Berlin), and "Al-Andalus: The Art of Islamic Spain," "The Art of Pre-Columbian America," and "Art of the Aztecs" (all New York). In one sense these are harbingers of global consciousness, milestones on the grand trunk road of globalization. In displaying civilizational aesthetics and trajectories they evoke cross-civilizational sensibilities. As their titles indicate these exhibitions display what Clifford calls "the sweep, the nonoppositional completeness characteristic of majority History."[26] They seek to be authoritative, encompassing, definitive. They nourish the panoramic urge of the panoptic gaze. Through blockbuster exhibitions "museums confront and resolve the lost unities (and certainties) of modernism, by offering an expanded consuming public the opportunity to experience the awe generated by the control of time, space and object which is inherent within them."[27]

Allowing for occasional oppositional views is part of their nonoppositional, pluralist, encyclopedic intent. They take us past ethnographic curiosity into the state of awe for Great Civilizations; they follow the tracks of, in Redfield's terms, great traditions rather than little traditions. They tend to be reverential, showing shrines and relics of humanity's great forward march. The global consciousness articulated in these exhibitions is partial, confined to Great Civilizations, typically situated in the past and viewed from the center of power. The imperial era was obsessed with great civilizations—Rome, Greece, Egypt, China, India, Persia—and there was no contradiction between this awe and Victorian evolutionism. Eurocentrism and racism pursue and display the same hierarchical view of civilization.

Multiculturalisms

> We are now in a period of looking at our history from the standpoint of all of our citizens, not just from the perspective of a single group or even the majority. We are also coming to understand that no group is monolithic in its view point.
>
> —Willard L. Boyd, president emeritus of the Field Museum, 1999

We can distinguish between static and closed and fluid and open views of culture and these yield contrasting perspectives on multiculturalism. Static perspectives on culture follow territorial and essentialist understandings, view cultures as pieces in a mosaic (fixed and discrete) rather than as flows and treat the coexistence of cultures as a set of cohabiting ghettos, in fact, a form of neo-apartheid (discussed in chapters 4 and 5).

Different perspectives on multiculturalism parallel leading perspectives in anthropology. William Roseberry points to three episodes in the development of American anthropology: the period when *cultural relativism* dominated from the 1890s to 1940, when the United States faced a great influx of new immigrants and many anthropologists themselves were immigrants, often Jewish, such as Franz Boas; 1940 to 1980, when *systems-anthropology* predominated, concerned with large-scale evolutionary dynamics and structures of global inequality, which coincided with the American rise to globalism when the overriding problematic was that of public power; and the period from the 1980s to the present, marked by the crisis of categories and assumptions, a time when multiculturalism again ranks high on the agenda, resembling the pluralism of the early twentieth century.

Cultural relativism in anthropology took shape at a time when nation, race, Volk and *Gemeinschaft* were near synonyms. Herder's romantic view of nation/language/culture informed cultural relativism and produced a similar outlook of "national character" and cultural determinism. Culture, reified and homogenized, is manipulated in the same way as "history." Roseberry refers to cultural relativism's "image of neatly bounded, discrete cultures with clearly defined traditions, imparting a singular set of values" and observes, "On its own, the assumption of cultural boundedness and essentialism may seem harmless enough, but it also serves as an ingredient to a dangerous variety of claims to cultural authenticity and the uniqueness of particular cultural visions. . . . The distance between academic claims of epistemological privilege along racial, cultural, or gendered lines and ideologies of 'ethnic cleansing' is not that great."[28]

Disseminated through the media, static notions of culture may function as an acceptable form of intellectual racism and thus serve as a legitimation of the racism of the street and skinheads. Fluid views of culture and identity treat culture as a construction that is perennially in motion and under construction. The epistemology is constructivist: Cultural identities are not given but contingent and produced. Multiculturalism is not the cohabitation of neatly bounded cultural communities but a field of crossover, recombination, and the formation of new, mixed identities. Culture is not simply "cultures" but also civilization and, at a deeper level, human software and ongoing, open-ended learning.

Evolutionism, another stream in anthropology, alongside diffusionism and functionalism, also put its mark on ethnological exhibiting strategies. The strongest example of the evolutionist-inspired display is the Pitt-Rivers Museum in Oxford, where items are arranged not by origin but primarily according to levels of skill (e.g., from basic to refined arrowheads).

A different distinction runs between strong or deep multiculturalism as in the United States and the light multiculturalism of societies that have recently become immigrant countries (as in most of Europe) or where nationalities other than the dominant majority are relatively few in number (as in Canada outside Québec). The difference lies in the general rapport de forces. Strong multiculturalism sets the stage for developed power struggles in the arena of cultural politics. "The struggle is not only over what is to be represented, but over who will control the means of representing."[29] Emerging social forces recode and dethrone the canon and the old elite may lose its clout (though not its marbles). These distinctions are all relative. The civil rights movement made great strides, yet in the wake of civil rights legislation, southern Democrats switched sides and contributed to the Republican majority that brought Reagan and the Bush administrations to power. Winning battles is not the same as winning wars. The global recession of 1974 produced another major turning point.[30]

A further distinction runs between societies with a stable cultural center and those that are in flux. In the former, multiculturalism refers to majority-minority relations or peripheral differences arranged around a stable hegemony, whereas the latter has been termed "polycentric multiculturalism"[31] or, alternatively, interculturalism.

Marked shifts in the balance of forces between groups—such as decolonization, the shift from dictatorship to democracy, the transition in Eastern Europe—make for realignments in cultural politics. One of the issues this raises in postcolonial societies is that of renaming—towns, universities, streets, and squares, though there are still many Victoria streets and Albert streets.[32] Or relocating the government center, as in Sri Lanka.[33] Post-apartheid in South Africa sparked a national symbols debate on what to do with the monuments of white supremacy and apartheid—museums of white settler history, monuments commemorating colonial wars such as the Voortrekkers Monument, or claims to cultural hegemony such as the Taal Monument. Should they be taken down or kept as "histories of record"? Generally the latter option is being followed but they have been resignified, often with local community participation.[34]

Upon closer consideration the two exhibiting strategies outlined by Ivan Karp, the assimilating and exoticizing strategies, are both hegemonic, both defined from the viewpoint of the center, both instances of "discourse about the other." The exoticizing strategy insists on difference, whereas the assimilating strategy eliminates difference or reworks it in a wider modernizing perspective. The exoticizing approach essentializes difference and parallels cultural relativism and static notions of multiculturalism-as-mosaic with their insistence on the purity and boundedness of cultural "wholes." The assimilating strategy subsumes difference and reinscribes it as a subtext of modernity.

These discourses about others, then, represent twin faces of the Enlightenment: the romantic gaze and the modern gaze. The romantic gaze highlights the diversity of cultures and infuses it with meaning—as in reverence for the *bon sauvage*, the noble savage, authenticity and "roots." The modernist gaze views different cultures as so many paths leading towards the citadel of modernity. These twin gazes produce the familiar tension between *Lebenswelt* and system, *Gemeinschaft* and *Gesellschaft*, thematized in phenomenology (Brentano, Husserl, Heidegger, Merleau-Ponty, Schutz) and poststructuralism. Their relationship produces the dialectics of Enlightenment addressed in critical theory.

Ethnological museums have been strongly influenced by the perception of cultures as distinct configurations that could be represented through "typical" specimens. Cultural relativism and the notion of cultures as separate wholes revive in the age of multiculturalism. Thus a conference of European ethnological museums called for European solidarity in pushing back xenophobia and "conserving the cultural identity of minorities." In a report on the conference, the president of the International Committee of Museums of Ethnography noted, "The cultural wealth of the peoples of the world must be conserved, to avoid a worldwide standardization."[35] This is a familiar refrain in critiques of globalization. Is there no middle way then between cultural apartheid and global homogenization?

Selves and others

Fundamental to the question of representation is the relationship between self and other. This underlies both exoticizing and assimilating strategies. The dichotomy of self and other parallels and overlaps with the worn-out dichotomies of colonizer-colonized, center-periphery, Occident-Orient, North-South. The dichotomy of self-other has been enshrined in structuralist anthropology, mined in hermeneutics, problematized in poststructuralism, and unpacked in deconstruction as one more binarism. In conversation with Michel Foucault, Gilles Deleuze remarks, "You were the first to teach us something absolutely fundamental: the indignity of speaking for others." Deleuze concludes by appreciating the "fact that only those directly concerned can speak in a practical way on their own behalf."[36] Maurice Berger observes that "every representation—every painting, photograph, film, video or advertisement—is a function of 'someone's investment in sending a message.'"[37]

This awareness matches several trends in anthropology: the crisis of ethnographic representation[38] and experimentation with new methods of representation. Anthropology in the postcolonial era shares affinities with postmodernism and the techniques of collage, montage, and dialogue. Self-representation—such as ethnic community museums, the Pokot in west Kenya running their own museum, and Yanomamo filming themselves—is part of the reorientation away from the *National Geographic* tradition.

The relationship between self and others that went into the foundations of museum display has been undergoing profound changes. The identities that framed the age of the museum, from about 1840 to 1930, were national, imperial, and modern.[39] National identity was constructed in history museums and national art galleries (and military and war museums); imperial identities were produced in colonial and ethnographic museums and displays; and modern identities have been staged in world exhibitions[40] and science and modern art museums. These Enlightenment subjectivities were in turn articulated and framed by race, class, and gender.

Accelerated globalization gradually opened up these identity frames. Major phases of accelerated globalization were the turn of the century new imperialism (along with new technologies, transport revolution, industrial war, and international treaties) and postwar American hegemony (in tandem with the Bretton Woods system, the communications revolution and informatization). The high modern or postmodern turn decentered the universal Enlightenment subject and introduced the multiplicity of identities. In widening the range of organizational frameworks, accelerated globalization widens the range of identity repertoires: "Multiple identities and the decentering of the social subject are grounded in the ability of individuals to avail themselves of several organizational options at the same time. Thus globalization is the framework for the amplification and diversification of 'sources of the self.'"[41]

Gradually different identities come to the foreground. Community identities are constructed in local community museums. Migration histories are presented in displays of diaspora journeys. Intercultural art exhibits produce multicultural identities. Transnational identities are articulated in "festivals" and encyclopedic civilization displays. Exhibits such as "Africa: The Art of a Continent," staged in London; "Africa in the Field Museum in Chicago"; or "Asian Modernism" in Tokyo produce macro-regional, continental identities.[42] Beyond the old town museums, urban identities are reconstructed in displays of urban space and architecture. Gender awareness yields different inflections, also in modern art, as in Manhattan's Guerrilla Girls' "Conscience of the Art World": "Do women have to be naked to get into the Metropolitan Museum?" Sexual preferences inform exhibits devoted to gay history. Age awareness is a factor in displays geared to children (play and touch exhibits, theme parks). These identities don't replace the old ones but coexist and interact with them in novel combinations.

Just as the self is not what it used to be, "the other" is no longer a stable or even meaningful category. The time of structuralist pontificating on "the question of the Other"[43] is past. "The other" is now a hopelessly static notion.[44] The current terminology is "others" because, of course, there are many different kinds of others. "Others," plural, because of the big three—race, class, gender—and in view of national origin, religion, lifestyle, sexual preference, and age. That self and others necessarily stand to one another in a polarized relationship is in question. Martin Buber in *I and Thou* and Emmanuel Levinas viewed alterity as a relational concept and a framework for dialogue. Freud spoke of the unconscious as the ego's other. According to Foucault, "modern thought is advancing to that region where man's Other must become the Same as himself."[45] In feminism and poststructuralism otherness makes place for difference, a subtler notion in which alterity combines with philosophical queries into what constitutes identity, where notions of otherness originated in the first place.[46] Cultural differences are but one dimension in the spectrum of differences (ontological, metaphysical, and transcendental, as noted in chapter 4).

Table 6.1 gives a simplified schema of how various ideas of self and others correspond with exhibitions and types of museums. The point is that

Table 6.1.   Identities and exhibitions before/after accelerated globalization

Selves	Exhibitions, museums
National	History, art
Imperial, colonial	Ethnography
Modern, transnational	Modern art, science, technology
Local, regional	Community, folklore, folk
Macro-regional, continental	Civilizational
Transnational, hybrid	Diaspora, crosscultural
Global	Globo-art, planetary common concerns (ecology, water, etc.)

in relation to contemporary hybrid and global identities there are no more
"others."

Museums are institutions of modernity. Their concern with conservation reflects the modern esprit of control and appropriation through classification and taxonomy and as such museum displays are the triumphal
processions of modernity. The history of museums parallels the career of
modernity, which also means that museums take part in reflexive modernity and thus become sites of reflexivity, both in terms of modernity's evolution (new modernity, postmodernism) and in multicultural takes on
modernity (or modernities).

Alternative agendas

> Put simply, does the growing popularity of collaborative exhibits signal
> a new era of social agency for museums, or does it make the museum a
> space where symbolic restitution is made for the injustices of the colo-
> nial era in lieu of more concrete forms of social, economic and political
> redress?
>
> —Ruth Phillips, quoted in Clifford (2003)

If there is a general principle for exhibiting strategies in the age of accelerated globalization it is abandoning discourse about the other. First, the
very dichotomy of self/other is being surpassed in the process of globalization which involves the osmosis of cultures worldwide, the merging of
histories over time, and the growing awareness of this happening, and
second, because of the epistemological and political arrogance of representing others.

The division of labor among history, art, and ethnography museums
reflects a waning nineteenth-century order. Ethnographic objects are now
also on display in art museums and colonialism can also be addressed in
history museums. In global history the separation between "their" history
and "our" history is abandoned, so whether there are grounds for a separate agenda for ethnographic museums is increasingly doubtful. It might be
argued that because of their institutional history ethnographic museums
have a special responsibility in addressing the so-called North-South gap.
The notion of Third World is no longer adequate because of growing differentiation in the global South and territorializing poverty is no longer tenable since rich-poor divides crosscut geographies (the North is in the South
and the South is in the North), yet about three billion people live on less
than two dollars a day. Displays inspired by solidarity, however, are
double-edged. They construct a moral high ground and, while showing it is
"them" not "us" who suffer, the viewing gaze remains outside the frame.[47]

How then can a reorientation be implemented? The general reorientation of cohabitation in globalization can be summed up, in Clifford's phrase, as a shift from a colonial to a cooperative museology.[48]

An obvious question is, "How can museums make space for the voices of indigenous experts, members of communities represented in exhibitions, and artists?" The postmodern answer is to "turn the conflict of interpretations into an exhibition tool."[49] Thus the imperial voice, the voice of classic ethnography, is contrasted to the indigenous voice of agency and recuperation. The question is on what terms these voices are combined.

Pluralism as a political and aesthetic strategy for incorporating alternative representations is contested: "Pluralism as an ideology makes a peripheral place for new possibilities without allowing them to challenge the central idioms of 'Euro-centered art.'"[50] "Other" cultural and aesthetic expressions in the West have often been categorized as "ethnic art."[51] Pluralism as such doesn't address the underlying question of cultural center and periphery.

A *dialogical* approach can take the form of joint exhibitions organized by museums North and South or mainstream and periphery institutions. A transnational cooperative museology can address matters of global common concern such as human ancestry and ecological changes. Joint exhibitions are increasingly common, though the format is usually decided by sponsors, foundations or museums in Europe, North America, or Japan.

It may be argued that the guiding principle should be *self-representation*, that is, representations produced, staged, and developed by "others" in question. An example is "Picturing Us: African-American identity in photography."[52] Under conditions of repression and danger, self-representation may be the only option. John Berger introduces a collection of drawings by Palestinian children in the Occupied Territories thus: "Where the TV cameras were banned and journalists forbidden, schoolchildren painted for the world in watercolors."[53]

Tribal and African American museums in North America display community perspectives and local, alternative history, rather than majority history, as in the Schomburg Center in Harlem, New York. The past president of a major museum in Chicago notes, "It is standard Field Museum practice to include as active participants on the exhibit planning team representatives of cultures that are the focus of the exhibit."[54] This option is open to multicultural societies with substantive minorities with local historical memory of sufficient depth. At some point, however, the logic of self-representation wears thin. For if there is no other, who is self? The twin terms of the dichotomy are interdependent and if one goes so does the other. There is a comparable dilemma in the indigenization of knowledge—the repudiation of Eurocentric knowledge and the affirmation of indigenous knowledge. What is indigenous and who decides? What are its boundaries, its circumference? Who belongs and who doesn't? What is essential and what is not? Who speaks for "others"? Once we repudiate the representation of others across cultural boundaries, it naturally leads to questioning them across boundaries of gender, class, age, status, region, and language within cultures and groups. The question of representation extends infinitesimally: in the process of representation as a manifestation of power, *all* others represented are "others."

Museums that exhibit community histories—such as histories of immigrant groups in the U.S. or Britain—are not beyond contestation. Though they may reflect community values better than an outsider view, no community is homogeneous. Different generation cohorts, for instance, hold different perspectives. Self-representations staged by museums in postcolonial countries, by Arab Cultural Centers in Manhattan or London or the Institut du Monde Arabe in Paris may be constrained by elite constructions of Arab culture. Cultural self-representation as a principle does not settle the question of representation and power, but shifts it from the intercultural to the intracultural sphere. Cultural insiders contest the ways in which culture is constructed and represented. Self-representation requires resources that may be available to postcolonial societies or in conditions of strong multiculturalism. "Museums have far more relevance to the powerful—those capable of housing art and artifacts—than they do to the disempowered," note Jonaitis and Inglis. "Moreover, there is no such entity as the Native voice, one that speaks with authority for the entire community. There exist many voices, some of which speak for upholders of cultural traditions, others that address band and tribal politics, and still others that concern themselves with social issues."[55]

African American critic Greg Tate criticizes an exhibition on "Black Art, Ancestral Legacy" (Dallas Museum of Art, 1991) for its cultural nationalism and ghettoization of black art, "as if Western art history never happened," collapsing "all Black art into an ethnically pure African reclamation project."[56] To avoid ghettoization and modes of self-representation that freeze identities rather than open up to identities in the making, *hybridity* is a radically different approach. This means breaking with inward-looking cultural nationalism and opening the windows. Hybridity is the pivot where analysis and positioning in the anti-colonial and national liberation mode end and positioning in the postcolonial and post-imperial mode begins. Hybridity foregrounds the openness and fluidity of identities, the cut 'n' mix zone of selves and others, as in Stuart Hall's "new ethnicity" (rather than freezing existing ethnic identities). In British arts it inspired the "long march from 'Ethnic Arts' to 'New Internationalism.'"[57]

Crosscultural mixing is not just a subject matter of exhibitions but also an exhibiting strategy. As a strategy, instead of highlighting the separateness of cultures, it shows the mélange of cultures over time and the emergence of crossover cultural forms. A point of reference is UNESCO's Silk Routes project.[58] Numerous terrains of cultural mixing, past and present, come to mind: technology, knowledge, language, medicines, migration, trade, foods, arts and crafts, consumption, music, and fashion.[59] It undermines the romantic view by pointing to differences within and unsettles the modernist thesis by relativizing the rupture of modernity. Yet hybridity should not be allowed to become a new mask: "Deterritorialisation, hybridisation and multiculturality should not turn into new totalisations hiding new structures of power."[60] Hybridity compels us to examine the terms under which mixing occurs in the process of recoding power relations.[61]

A further option is what we might term, in analogy with reflexive anthropology and reflexive sociology, *reflexive representation*. Reflexive in the sense of self-questioning and problematizing the politics of representation. In exhibiting strategies this refers to exhibits not about others but about the relationship between selves and others, about the process and the logics of othering. In an ethnological context it involves self-examination of the ethnographic gaze, questioning the colonial matrix of anthropology and the relationship between ethnography and "national history." In white settler colonies such as Australia and South Africa ethnography was traditionally subsumed under natural history and native peoples were displayed in natural history museums, whereas "white" ("our") history was displayed in art and history museums.[62] Until recently the National Museum in Cape Town displayed dioramas with life-sized models of San in situ next to dinosaur skeleton models.

Presently, if this is an age of ethnicity, the distinction between nation and ethnicity, between *éthnos* and *ethnikós*, is being unsettled (chapters 1 and 2). From a generalized "ethnic" viewpoint national history is a monocultural project, national museums are ceremonial sites of ethnocratic citizenship, and oppositional exhibiting strategies are forms of ethno-criticism, exercises in the decolonization of imagination. One option for reflexive representation is anthropology in reverse: looking at the West or at the majority with the same gaze and cognitive tools that have been directed at others. Since the late eighteenth century the ethnographic gaze fashioned overseas has influenced the perception of rural and folk cultures in Europe: "From the study of manners and customs in Tahiti or among the Iroquois it was only a step for French intellectuals to look at their own peasants, scarcely less distant from them (they thought) in beliefs and style of life."[63] Ethnography and urban anthropology practiced in the West have long been influenced by anthropology "outre mer." The next step is looking at the West through the eyes of others, turning the tables, of which there are ample examples.[64] This involves scrutinizing the power of the ethnographic gaze and the creation and classification of ethnographic objects, engaging the history of colonialism and the culture of empire of which ethnography is a part.

An example of a reflexive exhibition is "Race and Representation" (Hunter College Art Gallery, New York, 1987). The "White on Black" exhibition (Tropen Museum, Amsterdam, 1990) is another. Based on a large collection of representations of Africa and blacks in western popular culture over two hundred years, it was a self-reflection exercise that aimed to decondition viewers' stereotypes.[65]

Several exhibitions have dealt with the "gaze of others" directed at Europeans. "Colon" (Munich, 1983) exhibited African images of Europeans.[66] "Exotic Europeans" (London, 1991) featured Nigerian, Japanese, Chinese, Indian, and Native American images of Europeans. Black analyses of the "white eye" and critiques of white stereotyping of blacks are amply represented in literature, but not as well in exhibitions. Several that have been organized—such as "Ethnic Notions" (Berkeley Art Center, 1982) and "Distorted Images" in a Brooklyn community museum (1984)—typically took place in African American community settings. The setting is significant in view of the importance of exhibits as occasions of public presencing. These exhibits did not take place in museums. There remain definite boundaries to collective remembering and reflexivity and limits to what can be shared, whether it can be shared and where it can be shared. "Minorities never get to represent more than their marginality," according to the Latino curator Chon Noriega.[67] An exhibit that did gain access to museum grounds was "The Black Image in American Art"—note the framing title—in the Corcoran Gallery of Art.[68]

Juxtaposing contrasting exhibiting strategies is another mode of reflexive representation. Fred Wilson, an African American artist, created an installation in which discarded slave shackles were displayed next to a silver tea set, and handcrafted armchairs side by side with a handmade whipping post (Contemporary Museum, Baltimore).[69] This used museum resources as tools to reflect on the role of museums and exhibiting strategies.

Clifford notes "how differences in power and perspective radically affect exhibiting voices": "even museums with opposed cultural policies can be united in the style of their discourse, universalizing in the case of majority museums and oppositional in the case of alternative kinds of museums."[70] This may be why some exhibitions, based on interesting ideas, have been inconsistent in conceptualization and implementation. The "Exotische Welten/Europäische Phantasien" exhibit (Stuttgart, 1987) was premised on the idea that exotic worlds are European fantasies, but the exhibit and the extensive catalogues were uneven and displayed many items in conventional terms, as "treasures of the Orient."

A cooperative museology must address the repatriation of trophies of colonialism—sacred objects of indigenous peoples, antiquities and art works taken without proper authorization—and acknowledge that accountability is no longer national but global. At times conservation interests may clash with indigenous interests and the construction of both positions may be problematic. In fact, what is at issue are wider questions of indigenous intellectual property rights and traditional resource rights.[71]

The alternative agendas discussed so far—pluralist, dialogical, hybrid, reflexive—refer primarily to western, metropolitan countries. In many postcolonial countries, nation building is ongoing, national identity is privileged, and the marginalization of women, minorities, tribals, ethnic groups out of favor is often a harsh reality. Public culture is defined narrowly, often in statist terms. The National Museum in Colombo, Sri Lanka, is not a good venue to learn about Tamil history or culture. In Latin America national identities are more secure and the desire to make up for international marginality by means of internal colonialism is less. A major concern in Brazil is democratization of access to museums. In Buenos Aires, the Naval Mechanics School, the main torture center during the dictatorship, is being turned into a Museum of Memory.[72] Everywhere, exhibits and museums are situated in landscapes of power whose parameters are as wide as the public culture allows.

Exhibiting power

Following turn of the century European aesthetic trends—Orientalism and Japonisme—Australian artists and institutions embraced *Asia* as style: homogeneous, traditional and static, exotic and serene. On the one hand, the people were viewed with derision, on the other, the culture was framed in desire.

—Donna McAlear (1994)

Brian Wallis recounts how cultural festivals staged in the United States devoted to "Turkey: The Continuing Magnificence" (1987–88), "Indonesia" (1990–92) and "Mexico: Splendor of Thirty Centuries" (1990) have been "intricate, multilayered engines of global diplomacy" that "function as huge public relations gambits, designed to 'sell' the nation's image in the United States." Aimed at the American public, these "festivals mark a specific moment in the realignment of international political and economic power relations." "All of the countries that have had festivals in the United States have shared an economic profile. They all have huge international debts (mainly to the United States); cheap, docile labor markets (attractive to U.S. businesses); and valuable exports managed by U.S. multinational corporations (principally oil). All of them have recently privatized state industries (with encouragement from the United States and the International Monetary Fund)."[73] They involve the governments hiring major American public relations firms and the sponsorship of multinational corporations, and they are "symptomatic of the trend toward using the aura of culture to attract capital." Yet "national cultural festivals mask the contemporary situations in the countries, especially the factionalism, by papering it over with catchphrases like the Indonesian national motto, Unity in Diversity."[74]

The role of art and culture in international relations and diplomacy is familiar. Thus the CIA promoted abstract expressionism as a counter to Soviet realism during the cold war.[75] Australia, seeking to improve its relations with dynamic Asia, has been sponsoring artists and cultural events in Asian countries to change its image away from koalas, kangaroos, and the white Australia policy.[76] This is the tip of the iceberg of wider, more or less subtle correlations of aesthetics and power.[77]

Indeed, with a slight shift of angle, power itself appears as a charm operation, a theatrical performance in the manufacture and stage management of charisma. Museums are regarded as educators of the gaze, reformatories of manners,[78] but when it comes to power, museums and exhibitions prefer to reproduce the charms of power. "Treasures of," "Gold of," "Splendor of" exhibits invite the public to luxuriate in the aura of power, moonstruck by the accumulated glitter of palaces and temples turned inside out. Under the heading of education museums provide gratification.[79]

"In some dim but important way we expect museums to be decorous rather than challenging"[80] and that is an understatement. With the backing of the "institutional power of speech . . . the exhibit takes on the quality of an oracle."[81] Pierre Bourdieu focused on schools and media but museums too are links in the chain of social reproduction.[82] Museums are power places, "ceremonial monuments." Tucked amid national monuments, statues of statesmen, mausoleums of nation builders, triumphal arches, and obelisks commemorating national achievements, museums are part of the landscape of power, dedicated to documenting the giant steps taken by the nation's history. "Museums do not simply resemble temples architecturally; they *work* like temples, shrines, and other such monuments." They induce a "willingness to shift into a state of receptivity."[83] In short, they exemplify and contribute to the hypnotism of power. Multicultural representation is one angle on revisioning museums and democracy is another.

The point of reflexive representation is to zero in on representation as power. Yet representations tend to keep the power of representation out of view. Power itself is rarely the object of display. It frames the context of display rather than being addressed by it. Power is more often fetishized in exhibitions than interrogated by it. The fetishism of power involves the culture of empire as a culture of power. As Roseberry notes, although power and colonialism are often referred to in poststructuralist anthropology, "One is often struck, however, by how little the authors actually have to *say* about colonialism and the state."[84] It is certainly insufficiently addressed in ethnographic museums. Matching the museum culture of conventionality and telling "culturally authoritative" stories,[85] the decorous, edifying side of empire is on display, rather than its bloodstained record. Indeed colonialism as a subject is excluded from ethnological museums: it frames the ethnological museum but is not addressed by it. In cultural festival type exhibits, the postcolonial state is diplomatically kept out of view, is the sponsor and beneficiary of the exhibit, "self-orientalizing" the entire nation for the sake of tourism glamour.

An obstacle that runs deeper still is the sentimentality about empire and the discreet affection for colonialism because, though this is an unfashionable sentiment in the postcolonial age, it is viewed as part of modernization led from the West. Besides, it is a matter of national pride. Why in Belgium has there not been a major exhibit devoted to King Leopold II's colonialism and the "Congo atrocities" beyond the national rhetoric of civilizing mercy? Statues in Brussels' Jubilee Park still celebrate Belgium's colonial magnanimity, much like the grateful natives that surround Prince Albert in his Memorial Monument in London's Kensington Gardens. The same applies to France, the Netherlands, Portugal, Spain, and Germany and their colonial past. In the Netherlands an exhibit could focus on the colonization of the East Indies—not on Indonesia's cultural treasures, not on Javanese gamelan and Balinese dancing, not on the exotic cultures of the island peoples, not on *tempo doeloe,* but on the plantation system, the frontier society of Deli in Sumatra, colonial divide and rule, the conquests of Bali and Lombok, the Aceh wars and the military efforts to forestall Indonesian independence.[86]

Colonialism is past, but repressed rather than assimilated. The critical assimilation of empire has not taken place in museums nor, by and large, in film or theater. To some extent it has taken place in literature and scholarship. In the public sphere and popular culture, up to the present, a docile view of colonialism prevails, particularly of one's own nation's colonialism, essentially because the general power structure that sponsored colonialism is still in place. The empire nostalgia industry is an annex of the heritage industry and thrives on a saccharine view of empire in productions such as the British TV series *Jewel in the Crown.* In the U.S. the exhibit "The West as America" (National Museum of American Art) challenged the decorous clichés of "how the West was won," unpacked the ideological messages and techniques in the cherished art depicting the frontier, and reaped a storm of protest from the media to Congress.[87] A populist tradition of aversion to big government, multiculturalism strong in numbers and deep in time, an immigrant society with an open imaginary, and yet every step must be fought for.

"From Totem to Lifestyle" (Amsterdam, 1987) was an exhibit based on the provocative idea of juxtaposing the "totems" of non-western cultures to totems of the West. The former were represented by sacred objects and the latter by consumer lifestyle segments used in marketing.[88] But the actual totems of the West—the church, the pope, the state, the nation, the monarchy, science, technology, media—remained completely outside the picture. This produced a glaring asymmetry in which sacred objects of non-western cultures were placed side by side with icons of western consumerism. A steep asymmetry in time (traditional/modern) and in the status of symbols was intrinsic to the exhibition concept, making the trite point that "our" worship is the market.

The main obstacle in getting a focus on power is people's desire to be hypnotized by power. While contesting its gestures, public media reproduce the cult of leadership and indulge the obsession with the official realm of politics, even if it is no longer the center of actual political decision making. As Derrida observes, to renounce is also to invoke. The standardized aesthetics of power and methodologies of the manufacture of charisma have become part of the cultural landscape. "Fascism is theater," according to Jean Genet. Why hasn't there been a major exhibit devoted to the Nazi era—not to *Entartete Kunst* (degenerate art) and music (both have been the theme of exhibits in Germany) but to *Entartete Politik?* To avoid erecting shrines to Nazism, what exhibits have been organized have produced "feminized," domesticated renderings of the Nazi era, so viewers identify with the victims of Nazi politics.[89] Significant exhibits have been devoted to totalitarian art and architecture (such as "Art and Power: Europe under the Dictators, 1930–45"),[90] but there is no general format or forum and no exhibition strategy for probing and deconstructing power. The spell of power reproduces power.

Meanwhile, these are boom times for museums. In the U.S. "more people go to museums than to sports events."[91] In Japan some fifteen hundred new museums were opened between the 1970s and 2000. At the same time museums have become more dependent on earned income: "Rather than edifying, the museum increasingly plays to the masses in competition with tourist sites, amusement parks, cultural centers, bookstores, and shopping malls. As such the museum exhibition has become much more event-oriented—in roughly the same way as motion pictures during this period—while the museum now offers a wide range of revenue-generating services and activities beyond that of the exhibition proper."[92]

The mural movement, happenings and the performance art of the 1960s were forms of public art in which artists communicate directly with communities and public spaces, streets and sidewalks become venues for political dialogue.[93] Willard Boyd, past president of the Field Museum in Chicago, notes, "Controversy is now a way of life for museums. . . . Exhibits should be designed to permit the expression of dissent" and "Museums need to be open and consultative in collecting and exhibiting."[94] The "active, transactional museum" engages the public: "We should now aim for interpretation to be a transaction between the public and the curator, a shared task."[95] In the Ethnography Gallery of Birmingham Museum, "one section of the gallery displays objects from Papua New Guinea, which the visitor can then find out about through using an interactive video program. In this, the objects are interpreted in four different ways, by a nineteenth-century collector, by a Christian missionary, by a museum curator, and by a present-day New Guinean."[96] Public participation and interactive, experiential strategies—talk backs, public seminars, sorting archaeological finds, examining reserve collections, involving communities in the production of their own past—have become common to address the fluidity of interpretation.

In the end, discourse about others is a function of uneven development. The power of representation is anchored in discourses and taxonomies that correlate with forms of hard power, economic and political. Political power because influence counts and institutions are path dependent, and economic power because representation is for sale. Discourse about others is old fashioned but will remain with us as long as there is unequal development. A growing reflexivity about this condition has been gained in the shift from colonial to postcolonial times, and produced a shift from discourse about others to discourse about othering, but this doesn't necessarily change the power relations themselves. Museums face "the demand that there should be parity of representation for all groups and cultures within the collecting, exhibition and conservation activities of the museums, and the demand that the members of all social groups should have equal practical as well as theoretical rights of access to museums."[97] Yet "the museum itself increasingly operates within a political and corporate environment seemingly removed from such concerns."[98] Curator Chon Noriega makes a sobering point about alternative display agendas in the U.S. that has wider relevance:

> a market-based approach to social issues emerged in the late 1970s and has been official state policy since the 1980s. Ironically, while government support decreased, its significance increased, serving as the staging ground for ideological conflicts over the public sphere. Racial and sexual minorities received the lion's share of the attention in the press and public debate, but the real change had less to do with minorities per se than with the role of the federal government in securing public institutions to serve a diverse nation. To be blunt, inclusion required either more space to accommodate the new groups knocking at the door or that whites accept the possibility that the public sphere that they once claimed as their own might no longer be their exclusive domain. The former proved economically unsustainable in a Cold War economy and what is now a global economy; the latter proved politically untenable for a still largely white electorate.[99]

Thus the politics of representation faces similar constraints as that of redistribution. At a time when multiculturalism requires a more capacious and responsive welfare state, the welfare state is cut back; at a time when multicultural representation seeks more responsive museums, museums are more dependent on corporate funders that look to museums as profit centers or sources of prestige.

Notes

1. Marcus 1991, 11.
2. Boyd 1999, 185.
3. Karp 1991a, 15.
4. Duncan 1991.
5. Hudson 1991; Karp 1991a.
6. Marcus 1991.
7. Prösler 1996.
8. Stölzl 1988; cf. Craig 1991.
9. Negrin notes that "postmodernist art practice is even more dependent on the museum than was modernism. For postmodernism, even more so than modernism, is an art about art" (1993, 123).
10. Karp 1991b, 379.
11. Adam Hochschild, quoted in Boyd 1999, 195.
12. Hudson 1991, 460, 464.
13. "Den Kunskapande Människan," Wagner 1997.
14. Karp 1991b, 375.
15. Clifford 1991, 225.
16. Rubin 1984, 1, 1; Nicodemus 1993.
17. Karp 1991b, 377.
18. Picton 1993.
19. Kirshenblatt-Gimblett 1991, 389, 413.
20. *Le Monde*, quoted in Gilsenan 1982, 211.
21. Kirshenblatt-Gimblett 1991, 419.
22. Kirshenblatt-Gimblett 1991, 419.
23. The documentary *Global Villages: The Globalization of Ethnic Display* (Tamar Gordon, 2004) is devoted to ethnic theme parks in China (the Splendid China Miniature Scenic Spot near Shenzhen Special Economic Zone, and the Yunnan Nationalities Villages in Kunming) and Japan (Huis Ten Bosch in Nagasaki and Parque España in western Japan).
24. Yunnan Nationalities Villages n.d.; Can 2004.
25. Kirshenblatt-Gimblett 1991, 390.
26. Clifford 1991, 240.
27. Marcus 1991, 12.
28. Roseberry 1992, 849.
29. Karp 1991a, 15.
30. Notes Noriega: "Wholesale changes took place in that one year: rights-based movements were supplanted by cultural nationalism and identity-based

politics; and diverse public-affairs programming on network television ended, replaced over time by corporate-funded and -produced finance programs and conservative talk shows on public television. . . . This abrupt change brought an end to the media reform movement, while it required that minority civil rights and community-based organizations turn to the private sector—the very arena that they had been created to challenge. Given this context in the arts, 1974 serves as perhaps the best (and most materially consequential) year with which to mark the shift from the modernist avant-garde to postmodernism" (1999, 62).

31. Shohat and Stam 1994.

32. In a dispute in South Africa about whether to change the names of towns such as East London and Grahamstown, the *Cape Argus* editorial page contrasts two views: "Changing place names does not bridge divides, it only deepens them" and "Names have meaning and must reflect social realities" (August 4, 2006, 15).

33. Perera 2005 and, more widely, Geisler 2005.

34. This was a theme of research at University of KwaZulu Natal. Tomaselli and Mpofu 1997; Shepperson 1996. On the shift from Rhodesia to Zimbabwe, see Munjeri 1991.

35. *European Conference of Ethnological and Social History Museums: museums and societies in a Europe of different cultures*, Paris 1993. The statement cited first is from the opening speech by the French president; the second is by the president of the International Committee of Museums of Ethnography in a conference report in Stein 1993.

36. In Sheridan 1980, 114.

37. Berger 1987, 10.

38. Clifford and Marcus 1986; Marcus and Fischer 1986; Sangren 1988.

39. Phillips 1995.

40. Rydell 1993.

41. Nederveen Pieterse 2003, 68.

42. Furuchi and Nakamoto 1995.

43. For example, Todorov 1988.

44. As part of a postconventional approach to otherness, Sue Golding 1997 discusses such forms of otherness as nomadism, contamination, cruelty, and noise; cf. Spivak 1993.

45. Quoted in Sheridan 1980, 80.

46. Gatsché 1994.

47. Edwards 1991; Back and Quaade 1993.

48. Clifford 1991, 224.

49. Lavine 1991b, 151, 155.

50. Ybarro-Frausto, quoted in Lavine 1991a, 83.

51. Araeen 1989.

52. Willis-Braithwaite 1993.

53. Quoted in Boullata 1990, 10.

54. Boyd 1999, 210.

55. Aldona Jonaitis and Richard Inglis, quoted in Clifford 2003, 17. Clifford's treatment of indigenes in Alaska offers a sensitive discussion of problems of self-representation.

56. Tate 1992, 245, 251.

57. Papastergiadis 1994, 42. Cf. Gupta 1993; Bhabha 1994; Nederveen Pieterse 2003.

58. See *Significance of the silk roads* 1992.

59. Nederveen Pieterse 1994b, 2003.

60. Mosquera 1993, 91.

61. Nederveen Pieterse 2003 discusses hybridity and power.

62. Marcus 1991, 15.

63. Burke 1978, 14.

64. For example, Fohrbeck und Wiesand 1983; Theye 1985.

65. Nederveen Pieterse 1992b.

66. Jahn 1983.

67. Noriega 1999, 59.

68. McElroy 1990.

69. Wilson 1993.

70. In Lavine 1991b, 157.

71. See Posey 1994 on intellectual and cultural property rights and traditional resource rights.

72. Rother, "Debate rises in Argentina on Museum of Abuses," *New York Times*, April 19, 2004, A13.

73. Wallis 1994, 267, 266, 277.

74. Wallis 1994, 277, 274. International exhibits increasingly travel intercontinentally—now also to China and Africa—and can serve as a conduit of intercultural communication. P. Aspden, "The museum as global mediator," *Financial Times*, March 28, 2006, 14.

75. Saunders 1998.

76. McAlear 1994, 5.

77. Duncan 1993; Zolberg 1995; Nederveen Pieterse 1993.

78. Katz 1991; Bennett 1995; Kaplan 1994; Macdonald and Fyfe 1996; Prior 2002.

79. In Disney World "the fantasies of the powerless are magically projected onto landscape developed by the powerful" (Sharon Zukin 1991, 218). This also applies to "Splendor of" and festival exhibits that cater to middle-class fantasies by staging fairytales of cultural utopias.

80. Fulford 1991, 28.

81. Boyd 1999, 200.

82. Bourdieu and Passeron 1990.

83. Duncan 1991, 90, 91.

84. Roseberry 1992, 850.

85. Macdonald 1998, 19. "Museums . . . are institutions in which the forces of historical inertia (or 'cultural lag') are profoundly, perhaps inescapably implicated" (George Stocking, quoted in Boyd 1999, 210).

86. In the exhibit "Counter Images of Tempo Doeloe" (Ethnological Museum, Leiden, 1993), the style of display made the counter images peripheral to the standard decorous nostalgia images of Tempo Doeloe that occupied center stage. See Vanvugt 1993.

87. Truettner 1991.

88. Fohrbeck and Kuijpers 1987.

89. Rogoff 1994.

90. Britt 1995. Cf. Hudson 1994; Groys 1992.

91. Pitman 1999, 12.

92. Noriega 1999, 64.
93. Noriega 1999, 74.
94. Boyd 1999, 217, 211, 224.
95. Merriman 1992, 138.
96. Merriman 1992, 138.
97. Bennett 1995, 9, quoted in Noriega 1999, 63.
98. Noriega 1999, 63.
99. Noriega 1999, 62.

7

❖

Islam and cosmopolitanism

The effort to "understand Islam," to locate it, describe it, and reduce it to intelligible summary, is caught up in the excitements of the present moment. It is a thing of responses and reactions—of warnings, reassurances, advices, attacks.

—Clifford Geertz (2003)

One association that cosmopolitanism brings to mind is its western legacy, but what about non-western cosmopolitanisms? We can view cosmopolitanism, broadly, as perspectives and sensibilities that stress human bonds and interconnectedness across cultural and political boundaries. These can be found also in Buddhism, Hinduism, Confucianism, and so forth.[1] This discussion focuses on Islamic cosmopolitanism and the historical role and self-perception of the Islamic world as a "middle nation," a bridging civilization. A further question is whether and how this applies to contemporary radical political Islam, which is often viewed as an anti-modern and anti-western bunker mentality.

It was not so long ago that political Islam was acknowledged, though not necessarily welcomed, as a major alternative to western modernity. Khomeini's revolution in Iran, Hezbollah, Islamic Jihad, and a host of Islamist movements were part of this momentum. But after the end of the Cold War and once the Afghan freedom fighters became the Taliban and the mujahideen turned into "Arab Afghans" who challenged governments in Algeria and Egypt, political Islam slipped off the map of emancipatory struggle. Still, many of today's conflicts concern the Middle East, Palestine, Iraq, Afghanistan, and the sprawling war on terrorism. It is as if

155

there are parallel universes, one in which "global civil society" such as the World Social Forum takes on the Washington consensus and an entirely different one in which militant Islam confronts American hegemony. The two universes of global civil society and "Muslim defiance" don't seem to intersect. Militant Islam seems to be a rare instance in which hegemonic policy, mainstream views, and majority progressive views converge.

Cosmopolitanism is a theme with a considerable lineage and resonance. Unlike globalization, it carries a normative charge and cultural and intellectual depth. Cosmopolitanism used to come with elite and urban overtones, but in recent times it has been revisited in wider contexts, in discussions of modernity, international relations, migration and multiculturalism. Ulrich Beck advocates "methodological cosmopolitanism."[2] We may choose to bracket cosmopolitanism, we may prefer global solidarity or resignify cosmopolitanism as globalization in the affirmative. Whatever our views on cosmopolitanism, it enables us to discuss globalization in a normative way and with some historical perspective.

Cosmopolitanism is at a dramatic cusp. Technological developments enable unprecedented worldwide interconnections across all dimensions of social life. But complex high-density interdependence also brings major conflagrations, a configuration that James Rosenau refers to as "fragmegration" (fragmentation-and-integration).[3] As the capability for transnational rapport is growing, also at an institutional level, as in the International Criminal Court and the Kyoto Protocol, so are conflicts and claims for global justice.

How should cosmopolitanism be rethought in twenty-first-century conditions of crisis-prone neoliberalism and belligerent American hegemony? Are the typical legacies of cosmopolitanism and internationalism such as European humanism and labor internationalism still adequate or too Eurocentric? What is the contribution of cosmopolitanism in view of notions such as Huntington's clash of civilizations and "the age of Muslim wars"?[4] Should we view political Islam as part of contemporary cosmopolitanism or place political Islam and Islamism beyond the pale of modernity and globalization? Cosmopolitan horizons of global solidarity are sidelined by grim narratives of global divide such as the clash of civilizations and assessments of global threats.

"Islamo-fascism" has become a new ideological target. Slavoj Zizek counsels that we shouldn't distinguish between Islamic fundamentalism and Islam. "Instead," he argues, "one should gather the courage to recognize the obvious fact that there is a deep strain of violence and intolerance in Islam—that, to put it bluntly, something in Islam resists the liberal-capitalist world order." After dismissing Muslim civilization, he wonders whether Islamic resentment could perhaps be redirected toward socialism.[5] American neoconservatives and their counterparts in Europe, such as Bernard-Henri Lévi and Oriana Fallaci, offer similar views.[6] Etzioni uses a term from pathology in speaking of "virulent Islam."[7] Conservatives and liberals alike urge strong American intervention in the Middle East because radical Islam presents a threat to the West.

Real as the risks of transnational terrorism and crime may be, threat inflation may become a habitus and since threat inflation produces force inflation, the remedy may be worse than the disease. Neoliberal policies wreak economic havoc on many societies. The war on terrorism is destabilizing and produces a dangerous world too. What perspectives point beyond planetary perplexity? There is no cosmopolitanism without access to collective history and collective memory as the threshold to a collective future. A cosmopolitanism that is informed from one part of the world only, that monopolizes the world by a single language and a single cultural style, such as liberal pluralism, is not cosmopolitanism but hegemony and a "standardization of dissent" of the kind that Ashis Nandy cautioned against.[8]

The first section in this treatment discusses the cosmopolitan scope of Islamic culture. How does this fare when the Islamic world loses its intercontinental middleman position during the era of European dominance? This is taken up in the second section. The third section focuses on contemporary political Islam and its relationship to American hegemony and the closing section reflects on how clichés of "Islamic fundamentalism" translate into American national security perspectives on the Islamic world.

Recentering Islam

In social science the relationship between theory and history is often uneven, and so it is in Islamic studies. Theoretical work in the tradition of anti-foundationalism[9] offers important critiques of essentialist treatments of Islamàla "fundamentalism," but sometimes sophisticated theory is premised on conventional history. Al-Azmeh repeatedly refers to universalism as a western legacy and thus shortchanges the Islamic contributions to universalism.[10] Many authors note how globalization enables Islamism,[11] but few recognize how Islam enables globalization. It is important to step back and combine what Abdel Malek calls the depth of the historical field with the breadth of the historical field. Part of this record is well known, but for a complete picture it is worth recontextualizing recent historical assessments of Islam alongside recent historical perspectives on Asia and then revisiting theory.

In discussing Islamic cosmopolitanism I propose a triple movement of recentering, decentering, and again recentering the Islamic world—in a broad geopolitical, geo-economic, and cultural sense. In each round Islam makes different contributions to cosmopolitanism:

- Recentering the Islamic world by acknowledging the central place of the Orient and Islam in early globalization and early modernity. During this phase the Islamic world makes foundational contributions to cosmopolitanism.
- Decentering Islam in view of its loss of status during the centuries of European dominance. During this period Islam spreads widely beyond the Arab world and reform movements reshape Islam, so the Muslim world becomes more cosmopolitan and Muslim cosmopolitanism becomes more diverse and less Arab-centric.
- Recentering the Islamic world from the twentieth century onward because of the strategic significance of fossil fuels and the Middle East. This involves accounting for the codependence of American hegemony and the rise of Islamism. In this phase the Muslim diaspora spreads to the West and Islam takes the form of an alternative and rival globalization project.

Recentering Islam involves a twofold logic, historical and theoretical. Historically it means viewing the Middle East and Asia as an early modernity in terms of trade, merchant capital, productivity, population densities, and urbanization. Janet Abu-Lughod pushes the time line of early capitalism back to the thirteenth century, locates it in the Middle East, and notes that "the fall of the East precedes the rise of the West."[12] Andre Gunder Frank views the early world economy as centered not in northern Europe, but in East and South Asia as part of an Afro-Eurasian world economy.[13] Recent global history studies go further back in time. John Hobson dates the central role of the Middle East in the emerging world economy from about 500 CE, lasting till about 1000 CE when China and India play a propelling role in the world economy.[14] A strong version of this view is the thesis of *oriental globalization* that overturns Eurocentrism and views the Middle East and Asia as the first globalizing forces.[15] The economic dynamism centered in the Middle East and then in China and India, traveling via Silk Routes by land and sea via Hormuz and the Persian Gulf to Mesopotamia and the Mediterranean, is then the infrastructure of early globalization. The Middle Eastern and Asian bazaars are the world's oldest.

According to Sheldon Pollock, the Latin cosmopolis and the Sanskrit cosmopolis coincided in time, the former initially clustered around the Roman Empire and the latter existing as a civilizational framework. Both went into decline around the same time and gave way to the increasing use of vernacular languages.[16] The Muslim cosmopolis—in part centered on Arabic but extending far beyond the Arab world—was the major successor to these cosmopolitan worlds, arose geographically and culturally in between them, touched many more cultures, and lasted far longer and into the present.

Marshall Hodgson's *Venture of Islam* took Islamic history beyond its conventional focus on the Middle East to cover the entire region from Morocco to China and could thus appreciate Islam's global expanse. Richard Eaton, following Hodgson and William McNeill, treats Islamic history as global history and the Islamic world as "history's first truly global civilization":

> For the Arab conquests inaugurated a thousand-year era, lasting from the seventh till the seventeenth century, when all the major civilizations of the Old World—Greco-Roman, Irano-Semitic, Sanskritic, Malay-Javanese, and Chinese—were for the first time brought into contact with one another by and within a single overarching civilization. What is more, Muslims synthesized elements from those other civilizations—especially the Greek, Persian, and Indian—with those of their Arab heritage to evolve a distinctive civilization that proved one of the most vital and durable the world has ever seen.[17]

Eaton compares the travels of Marco Polo, who was a stranger everywhere he went, with those of his near-contemporary Ibn Battuta, who traveled much farther, from Andalusia to China: "In contrast, Ibn Battuta, in his intercontinental wanderings, moved through a single cultural universe in which he was utterly at home. Most of his travels took place in what Muslims have always called *Dâr al-Islâm*, the 'abode of Islam.' . . . If Ibn Battuta intuitively understood that the Muslim world of his day constituted a truly global civilization . . . it has taken Western historians some considerable time to understand it as such."[18]

By comparison, the lineages of European cosmopolitanism—such as the transnational networks of nobles and clergy during the middle ages and of humanists and Nietzsche's *freie Denker*—appear provincial, for they are largely confined to the European peninsula and Christendom. How, for instance, to accommodate information such as the following in a Eurocentric framework? "Around 900 C.E. ibn Khordâdbeh, postmaster of the Arab province of al-Jibâl in Persia, compiled his eight-volume *Book of the Roads and Countries* as a guide for the postal system. He described roads and sea routes as far as Korea, giving detailed directions, distances, weather conditions, and road security." This is echoed in Korean records of Arab traders in the ninth century.[19]

Islam may be the most cosmopolitan of the world religions, if only for geographical reasons: no other major religion has been geographically adjacent to so many different continents and cultures and mingled with them over so long a time. Historical considerations are that Islam emerged when Mecca and Baghdad were major long-distance trade hubs, peaked during the high tide of Asian economic dynamism and as a "middle civilization" relayed Asian dynamism to the Mediterranean world and Europe. The world of Islam is crisscrossed by long-distance trade networks and diasporas, caravan trails, and Silk Routes and dotted by caravanserais, trading ports, and emporia. It encompasses many languages and cultures such as Persian, Turkic, and Uyghurs in Central Asia. The presence of Muslim traders also influenced China. "Beginning in the 10th century," according to Ramesh, "Muslim traders played a significant role in globalising China's economy. They filled the gap caused by the demise of Indian Buddhism and promoted Sino-Indian trade."[20]

Islam's role as "middle civilization" is a major part of Islamic self-awareness. Osman Bakar notes, "The idea of Islam as the *middle nation* is not an after-thought or a later invention made after it had established itself as an empire, a world religion and world civilisation." The idea is to be found in the Koran where the new faith and its followers are described as *"ummatan wasatan,* meaning the middle nation": "Thus have we made you a middle nation that you might be witnesses over the whole human family or the world community (2:143)."[21] As a religion and a culture, Islam is and seeks to be "a bridge between East and West": "In Islam, civilisation-consciousness is deeply rooted in such Quranic ideas as common human ancestry, common humanity, universal goodness of the human being, universality of divine favours to the human race, the wisdom of ethnic and cultural pluralism. . . . Islam is very much interested in the idea of a *universal civilisation."*[22] This is one of the reasons why Huntington's thesis of a clash of civilizations is so fundamentally misplaced, as well as alien to Muslim thinkers.[23]

The deep tradition of tolerance in Islam is scripted in the Koran.[24] Emerging *after* Judaism and Christianity as the other Abrahamic religions, Islam acknowledges their legacies, a gesture that has not generally been reciprocated. This is not merely an abstract or theological point. In the system of *dhimmis* or protected peoples the rights of adherents of other religions were recognized under Muslim law and payment of a poll tax entitled non-Muslims to the protection of the Muslim state.[25] The Muslim record of centuries of peaceful coexistence of peoples of the book contrasts with the European pogroms of Jews and Crusades against Muslims. There is no record of genocide, pogroms, or Inquisition in Islamic culture or under Islamic rule.[26] The fluorescence of al Andalus hinged on the creative cohabitation of Muslims, Jews and Christians and inspired Europe's Renaissance. The Ottoman millet system is an early instance of what we now call multiculturalism. Europe, ensconced in a more bigoted culture, lagged behind: "In the Turko-Arab-Islamic World, the Ottoman state codified coexistence at a time when the Latin Church exorcised peaceful ethnoreligious relations from its realm."[27] Centuries of Muslim rule from Andalusia to the Mughal Empire extended this cosmopolitan history and gave depth to Islamic jurisprudence. Law was "the master science of the Islamic world." The Sri Lankan Supreme Court judge and scholar Weeramantry's study of Islamic jurisprudence provides a painstaking account of

Islamic legal schools, legal ideas and perspectives on tolerance, human rights and international law.[28]

These cosmopolitan episodes enabled and shaped European modernity, which would be unthinkable without it. Acknowledging the scope of Islam, then, means provincializing and decentering Europe and its precedence as the pioneer and exemplar of modernity and capitalism. European modernity is layered and includes, as Edward Tiryakian argues, strata of chthonic Greek legacies and Gnostic Christianity.[29] Islamic legacies are among these strands. The steps in this line of thinking are to some extent familiar and can be briefly reiterated.

Hellenism in the Mediterranean world was a mélange culture of oriental and occidental elements.[30] To the more advanced civilizations, Europe until 1100 appeared backward: "Muslim Iberia was an 'urban' society in 1000 C.E. compared not only to Christian Iberia, with the single city of León, but also to the rest of Europe."[31] In the middle ages the Mediterranean was a "Muslim lake" and the Renaissance, especially the twelfth-century Renaissance, built on the efflorescence in the Muslim world. Many features that are held to be characteristic of European civilization are of external origin: "The central element of the Gothic style, the pointed arch, was Arabic in origin and was probably introduced by men returning from crusades."[32] The medieval European division of the world into three parts according to the three sons of Noah derives from medieval Arab-Islamic culture.[33] Influences from the Orient shaped European technology, philosophy and aesthetics, as in the application of geometry in architecture and the design of gardens, in notions of luxury and sensuousness, the tradition of the troubadours and understandings of love.[34]

European capitalism was propelled by the Levant trade. Oriental influence also indirectly concerns another cornerstone of modernity, the modern state system established in the 1648 Treaty of Münster (discussed in chapter 1). The victory of the Protestant powers over the Catholic-Habsburg axis was enabled by the political and military cooperation between the Ottomans and the Protestant powers united against their common enemy, the Catholics.[35] This influence extends to international law. For Victoria in Spain and Grotius in the United Provinces, Muslim international law was the only sophisticated literature that was available to build on and was far ahead in the treatment of prisoners of war and civilians, the right to asylum and safe conduct, and the prohibition of killing noncombatants.

The first encyclopedia was published in Basra in 980 CE in fifty-two volumes, brought to Spain before 1066 and translated in English by Abelard of Bath, Europe's first Arabist.[36] The model of Islamic institutions of learning inspired the formation of European universities,[37] and Islamic scholarship influenced the *philosophes* and their *Encyclopédie*. Rousseau held Muslim

Table 7.1.   Early globalization and Islam

Regional dynamics	Islamic world	Islamic cosmopolitanism
Middle East: center of first globalization, 500–1000 CE	Central to world economy, conquests	A bridging civilization passing on legacies of Egypt, Mesopotamia, and Hellenism
East to South Asia: early globalization, 1000–1850	Middleman and go-between 1000–1850	Middling between Asia, Africa, Europe
Africa: gold trade; later slave trade	Andalusia, Maghreb	Enabling European reconnaissance (navigation); Islamic jurisprudence
Rise of Europe	Ottoman Empire	Links with Jews and Protestants, support for Reformation; Islam spreads to Africa and Asia; Islamic reform movements

thinking in high regard (unlike Voltaire), and some argue that his theory of general will may have been influenced by the Islamic notion of *Ijma* or consensus. Montesquieu referred, in passing, to the Koran, biographies of Mohammed, and reports by travelers in Muslim lands (in the *Lettres Persanes* and *De l'Esprit des lois*). His observations on the relationship between climate and culture echo those of Ibn Khaldun centuries earlier. Ibn Khaldun's comparative historical method has been seminal in sociology.[38]

This reorientation of history suggests that we must decenter Eurocentric social theory and instead develop a historicist theory of modernities. As the emphasis shifts to examining how Asia and the Islamic world shape and inform European development and modernity, Eurocentric perspectives on modernity increasingly come across as ethnocentric. Marx's Asian mode of production is a myth, Weber's view of Islam is biased and the Protestant ethic is *not* a general requirement of modernity.[39] In this light, European cosmopolitanism emerges as a late, derivative, and reluctant cosmopolitanism. Table 7.1 gives a simplified, incomplete sketch of Islamic contributions to cosmopolitanism during early phases of globalization.

Decentering Islam

The Islamic world was shaken by the attack of the Mongols that destroyed the Abbasid caliphate of Baghdad in 1258. From the sixteenth century onward it gradually lost its position as intercontinental go-between to the Portuguese, the Dutch, and other European entrants in the Indian Ocean and Asian and African trade. During the Crusades the European objective was to break through the Muslim encirclement and establish direct links with the fabled world of the Orient and the Spice Islands. What the Crusades did not accomplish, Vasco da Gama and other voyagers did. European infiltration into the Arab trading networks in Asia and Africa gradually undermined the middleman role of the Middle East. Precious metals from the Americas gave Europeans an edge that outflanked Muslim traders.

For the Arab world, geopolitical trauma due to the rise of the Mongols in the East and geo-economic trauma due to the expansion of the Europeans merged in a growing marginalization. Nevertheless, this period also saw the rise and expansion of the Ottoman Empire. Marshall Hodgson doesn't treat the history of Islam after 1258 as one of protracted decline but recognizes "the coincidence of and relationship between political fragmentation and cultural fluorescence in Islamic history. . . . It was only in the centuries after 1258 that the Islamic religion, as a belief system *and* as a world civilization, grew among the peoples of Asia and Africa."[40] Studies of Islamization have come to view it not as a process of expansion or imposition but rather in terms of assimilation,[41] or what we would now call hybridization. Besides, these were times of active reform. As Mortimer notes, "Alterations in patterns of trade helped to disrupt Muslim and partly Muslim societies, and this may in turn account for the rapid spread of the reform movements."[42]

A related question is how Islamic is Islam? This question is as appropriate in relation to the Islamic world as it is in relation to Europe.[43] Islam is not merely a religion but a civilization with a legacy of pre-Islamic cultural resources from Mesopotamia, Egypt, Persia, Greece, and so forth. William McNeill described the expansion of the charioteers and the early Middle Eastern empires under the heading "Cosmopolitanism in the Middle East 1700–500 BC," which illustrates that cross-civilizational linkages had a vast scope already early on.[44]

Sufism in particular serves as a link to older civilizational strata,[45] a sensibility that has found wide resonance in Rumi's poetry. Local pre-Islamic cultures and non-Islamic contributions such as Hellenism and Persian and Turkic culture shaped the Arab world.[46] These lineages inform the layered texture and sprawling diversity of Islamic culture and generate many Islams. "Like other religions, Islam is not a generic essence, but a nominal entity that conjoins, by means of a name, a variety of societies, cultures, histories and polities."[47] Islam is multitextured and includes folk Islam, urban and clerical Islam, Sunni and Shia Islam, and Sufism.[48]

Nineteenth-century modernization in the Islamic world took multiple forms, such as the Tanzimat reforms in the Ottoman Empire and efforts at industrialization in Egypt and Persia. The latter were sabotaged by the British for the same reason as the Indian manufacturing sector was sabotaged.[49] The Nahda in the Arab world ushered in nationalism and Pan movements such as Pan-Islam, Pan-Arabism, and Pan-Turkism. Reform movements of Young Turks and Young Persians led to secular parties and modernizing regimes such as that of Mustafa Kemal Ataturk and new combinations of Islam and nationalism (as in al Afghani), Marxism (as in Ali Shariati and Sukarno), and philosophy (as in Muhammad Iqbal).

Recentering Islam: McJihad

In the course of the twentieth century the Middle East returned to the center of geopolitics through its petroleum resources. This situation peaked in 1973 with the OPEC oil boycott. At the same time the region incurred what economists refer to as the resource curse: rent seeking, oligarchies, and unbalanced development. This pattern of uneven and dependent development produced a social condition that has been characterized as neo-patriarchy. Its lasting imprint is documented in the Arab Human Development Reports.[50] The growing role played by militant political Islam is part of this equation.

Whereas Benjamin Barber contrasts *Jihad vs. McWorld*, Timothy Mitchell offers a radically different view under the heading "McJihad":

> If conservative religious reform movements such as the *muwahhidan* in Saudi Arabia or the Muslim Brotherhood in Egypt have been essential to maintaining the power and authority of these states and if, as we are often told, the stability of the governments of Egypt and Saudi Arabia, perhaps more than that of any other governments in the global South, are vital to the protection of U.S. strategic and economic interests, in particular the control of oil, it would seem to follow that political Islam plays an unacknowledged role in the making of global capitalism.[51]

The warlord Ibn Saud came to power in what later became Saudi Arabia with the help of British oil companies and military forces and the Ikhwan, a local conservative Islamic movement. In 1930 he defeated the Ikhwan, switched from British to American protection, and developed a new compromise in which the religious establishment tolerated the role of the foreign oil company and in return received funding for their program of converting Arabia to puritanical Islam from the proceeds from oil. Several forces came together in this ensemble: the Arabian American Oil Company (Aramco) provided funds and technical and material assistance; the U.S. government provided security support and training through its military base in Dhahran, established in 1945; and the religious establishment created the moral and legal order of the state and suppressed political dissent. In the late 1950s, in response to denunciations of corruption and misuse of "Arab oil" from nationalist governments in Egypt and Iraq, "the government of Saudi Arabia used oil money to enable the religious establishment to promote its program of moral authority and social conservatism abroad."[52] They funded the revival of an Islamic political movement in Egypt, Pakistan, and beyond and supported a U.S. military coup in Iraq that brought the Ba'ath, the party of Saddam Hussein, to power in 1963. Mitchell concludes,

> Given the features of the political economy of oil—the enormous rents available, the difficulty in securing these rents due to the overabundance of supply, the pivotal role of Saudi Arabia in maintaining scarcity, and the collapse of older colonial methods of imposing antimarket corporate control of the Saudi oil fields—oil profits depended on working with those forces that could guarantee the political control of Arabia, the House of Saud in alliance with the *muwahiddun*. . . . "Jihad" was not simply a local force antithetical to the development of "McWorld." McWorld, it turns out, was really McJihad, a necessary combination of a variety of social logics and forces.[53]

Fatema Mernissi refers to this constellation as "palace fundamentalism."[54] Over time this dynamic unfolded to affect developments in Iran, Afghanistan, Sudan, and Somalia, and other elements came into play: the role of Israel, international banks recycling petrodollars (which later precipitate the debt crisis in the global South), arms exporters, and the IMF and structural adjustment. According to Mitchell, "We live in an age of 'McJihad' . . . an age in which the mechanisms of capitalism appear to operate, in certain critical instances, only by adopting the social force and moral authority of Islamic conservative movements. . . . It follows that such religious movements have played a small but pivotal part in the global political economy."[55] McJihad exemplifies the deficiency of capitalism: "Seen as a process of McJihad, capitalism no longer appears self-sufficient. Its success depends on other forces, which are both essential to the process we call capitalist development and disjunctive with it."[56]

The Cold War is a specific episode within this process. The Cold War "green belt" strategy sponsored Muslim allies as counterweights against left-wing forces and local popular dissent, thus nourishing Islamism. To outflank left-wing forces, western and pro-western governments forged alliances with conservative religious movements such as Moral Rearmament, evangelical Christians, and various Islamic movements.[57] Gandhi and Gramsci, as contemporaries, were aware of the importance of popular religion.[58] Teaming up with popular religion has been a strategy of insurgency and counterinsurgency all along, notably in the decolonization struggles. In Egypt president Sadat legalized the Muslim Brotherhood; Moroccan and Algerian governments leaned over to the mosques; Israel sponsored Hamas as a counterpoint to Fatah and the PLO; and the U.S., together with Pakistan, Saudi Arabia, and Israel, funded, supplied, and trained the mujahideen in the Afghan war. The Soviets were aligned with the northerners in Afghanistan while the U.S. supported the mujahideen in the South, who were mostly Pashtuns. The ensuing "Talibanization" is a variant of McJihad.[59] The CIA term is "blowback": blowback from the Afghan war and "Arab Afghans" returning to Egypt, Algeria, and later Bosnia with new military skills further nourished Islamic radicalism.[60]

Mahmood Mamdani views this episode as part of the wider American effort to enlist proxy forces against communism and militant nationalist regimes, such as Unita in Angola, Renamo in Mozambique, the Contras in Nicaragua, right-wing paramilitaries in Colombia, and the Afghan mujahideen.[61] Toward the end of the Cold War the Reagan administration relied on low-intensity conflict and in the process created a privatized and ideologically stateless resistance force and transnational cadres of uprooted individuals across the Middle East. State terrorism has a long lineage, but this period is significant in the evolution of political terrorism also because it coincides with lethal arms becoming cheaper and more widely available. The green belt of the Cold War era has returned as the contemporary "arc of extremism."

This is not to suggest a reductionist interpretation. Conservative trends in Islam are several and have diverse sources. They have been nourished by Wahhabism and its puritanical influence and by madrassas in Muslim countries and the Muslim diaspora. State Islam (such as Al-Azhar in Egypt and Dyanet in Turkey) plays a conservative role of a different hue.[62] The early Muslim labor migration to Europe often consisted of immigrants of rural background led by imams with little education. Information technology enables the spread of alternatives from the Zapatistas to the World Social Forum and Islamism. Trendy Muslim Web sites in the West, for all their techno savvy, often disseminate orthodox Islam because of their disconnection from the dynamics of Islamic renewal.[63]

Several of these trends are codependent with western developments, typically clustered around fossil fuels, geopolitics, and the Cold War. As the Cold War came to a close, western attitudes toward Islam changed. Liberal democracy seemed to be the sole victor; proxy forces had to be brought back under control, and yesterday's freedom fighters became the new enemy. In this U-turn, Huntington's 1993 article on the clash of civilizations was a signal moment. According to Huntington, "Islam has bloody borders."[64]

Globalization involves projects on the part of many diverse actors (corporations, feminists, human rights campaigners, etc.). The umma is one among several globalizations, and contemporary Islam is both codependent with western modernity and deeply wired to the career of global capitalism and neoliberalism *and* an alternative cosmopolitanism that is interspersed with many cultures. In Bryan Turner's words, "Islam is now able to self-thematize Islamic religion as a self-reflective global system of

Table 7.2. Contemporary globalization and Islamism

Dimensions	Episodes	Outcomes
Fossil fuels	U.S.-Saudi-Wahhabi complex, palace fundamentalism	McJihad, petrodollars
Coercive modernization	Kemalism, Nasser, Iran (Shah), Ba'ath parties, Tunisia	Backlash: Muslim Brotherhood, Iranian revolution, Alevis
Cold War anti-communism	Support Islam against the left: Egypt, Morocco, Algeria, Israel, U.S.	Blowback: Cold War dialectics
Low-intensity conflict	U.S. recruiting proxies (Mujahideen)	Blowback: transnational resistance
Neoliberalism	Infitah in Egypt, Turkey, Lebanon, Jordan	Rise of Islamist social services
Postmodernism	Muslim diaspora	Decentering of the West, multiculturalism
Information technology	Virtual umma Virtual caliphate	Virtual Mecca, Web sites Al Qaeda

cultural identity over and against the diversity and pluralism involved in the new consumer culture."[65] In Turkey this involves an Islamic consumerism and entrepreneurialism that, though it has a history of its own, assimilates a neoliberal ethos.[66]

The umma suggests greater unity than exists and is fragmented along many lines. In this setting Islamism of various kinds has become not merely an alternative globalization[67] but a rival project. Al Qaeda and 9/11 are part of this equation. Al Qaeda's sources go back to the Saudi connection, Wahhabism, the Egyptian Ikhwan, the Afghan war and the Arab Afghans, and the United States is involved in each of these junctures. Table 7.2 gives a simplified overview of ways in which contemporary globalization and Islamism are interrelated.[68]

In this light let's revisit the usual accounts of "Islamic fundamentalism." Islamism is interpreted as a reaction or backlash against modernity, a bastion outside the modern and a backwater of globalization, as argued by Bernard Lewis, Fouad Ajami, Daniel Pipes, Samuel Huntington, Martin Kramer, Bassam Tibi, Thomas Meyer, and others. This view is shared by Enlightenment rationalists, western feminists, terrorism experts, and others who find a foe in Islamic fundamentalism. This outlook generally shares the following features:

- It focuses on ideas, values and politics that are divorced from political economy.

- These ideas are seen as arising from internal conditions that are divorced from the role of external forces (oil companies, western powers, arms exporters, etc.).
- Western modernity is viewed in its postcard image divorced from its dark side (such as colonialism and racism) and dialectics.

This representation glosses over the interrelations between modernity and Islam past and present. Although the alleged foe of modernity is "fundamentalism," in the United States, conservative Christianity is a major electoral base of the Republican Party.[69] In this outlook Muslim societies are deemed less capable of development and democracy. According to Etzioni, "It is an elementary fact that Islamic cultures are less amenable to fast-paced development than East Asian societies,"[70] which apparently overlooks Malaysia, Turkey, and the United Arab Emirates.

This discussion yields fundamentally different claims. The Islamic world has been a hub and driving force of early globalization and has made fundamental contributions to cosmopolitanism. Transnational networks such as *hawal* banking build on old infrastructures of Muslim globalization. When the Islamic world lost its intercontinental middling position, Islam spread beyond the Middle East and mixed with cultures in Asia, Africa, and, eventually, the Americas, giving Islamic cosmopolitanism a more diverse profile. This is what Malcolm X encountered on his hajj in Mecca. Contemporary radical Islamism is, as many have argued, a political rather than a religious phenomenon. Radical Islam, in contrast to the cliché view of fundamentalism, is an essentially modern Islamic Jacobinism.[71] The traditionalist account of fundamentalism ignores the ongoing reforms and internal modernization within Islamism such as the "new Islamism" and the "renewal of renewal" in Egypt.[72] Militant Islam is codependent with global capitalism and American hegemony, a relationship that may be summed up as McJihad. Part of this is blowback of the Cold War, including the role of American proxies. Networks such as Al Qaeda build on these far-flung links. Militant Islamic movements primarily concern struggles within Muslim countries. The turn against the United States, which culminated in the attacks of September 11, 2001, has come since the American U-turn after the end of the Cold War. The U.S. abandoned its former allies (as in Afghanistan) and in the next round declared them the new enemy.

The polemical account of "Islamic fundamentalism" for general consumption is at odds with American national security accounts of Islamic threats. The former presents Islamism as an irrelevant anti-modernity, whereas the latter treats it as a major threat and views Bin Laden as the CEO of Al Qaeda, a modern transnational enterprise.[73]

Assimilating the new enemy with the old under the heading of totalitarianism has been a long-term concern of Bernard Lewis, who argues that "Oriental despotism" predisposed Muslim societies to communist totalitarianism.[74] "Islamic fascism," a theme that emerged in 2006 and in the U.S. elections, makes a similar case. The aim is to equate the war against "Islamo-fascism" with the wars against Hitler, fascism, and Leninism, as a war for civilization, and as "the ideological war of the twenty-first century."

Islam and U.S. national security

The point of departure of a brief study of the Rand Corporation is that "the outside world should try to encourage a moderate, democratic interpretation and representation of Islam," and this has "gained great urgency after September 11, 2001."[75] The exercise carries some weight because Rand is a research subcontractor of the CIA and the Pentagon and because it generally matches the Washington approach in the "war for civilization."[76] The author is the wife of Zamil Khalilzad, the former U.S. ambassador to Afghanistan and Iraq, and from 2007 to the United Nations. Let's examine this approach as a summing up of emerging core tenets of American national security policy vis-à-vis Islam. Cheryl Benard distinguishes four essential positions in Islam as overlapping segments on a continuum:

- *Fundamentalists*, who put forth an aggressive, expansionist version of Islam. This includes scriptural fundamentalists (Iranian Shia and Sunni Wahhabis) and radical fundamentalists (such as Al Qaeda and the Taliban).
- *Traditionalists*, including conservative (resisting change) and reformist varieties (cautious adaptation to change).
- *Modernists*, who believe in the historicity of Islam and seek far-reaching changes in orthodoxy.
- *Secularists*, who believe in the separation of state and religion.[77]

In addition, Benard mentions that Sufism "represents an open, intellectual interpretation of Islam." Of the modernists, she says, "The modernist vision matches our own. Of all the groups, this one is most congenial to the values and the spirit of modern democratic society."[78] The modernists, however, face two handicaps: financial (fundamentalists receive far more funding) and political. After setting forth the positions of these groups on a wide range of issues, Benard proposes a strategy along the following lines:

- Support the modernists first, enhancing their vision of Islam over that of the traditionalists by providing them with a broad platform to articulate and disseminate their views.
- Back the traditionalists enough to keep them viable against the fundamentalists . . . and to prevent a closer alliance between these two groups. Encourage disagreements between traditionalists and fundamentalists. Encourage the popularity and acceptance of Sufism.
- Confront and oppose the fundamentalists. Encourage divisions among fundamentalists.
- Selectively support secularists.[79]

Let's unpack this approach. First, it is a variation on the New Policy Agenda that USAID and OECD agencies adopted in the nineties throughout the developing world: "building democracy by fostering civil society."[80] This report echoes this premise in practically identical wording: "This approach seeks to strengthen and foster the development of civil, democratic Islam and of modernization and development."[81] In a speech to the Heritage Foundation in 2002, then–secretary of state Colin Powell announced a new "U.S.–Middle East Partnership Initiative" that would "provide American support and $29 million of initial funding for a variety of programmes to promote civil society, political participation and democracy in the Arab world."[82] This Rand study is a policy study of how best to allocate such funds.

The report is ahistorical—understandable in a brief study, yet even so, historical memory is strikingly absent. Erasing history comes with the modernizing, engineering approach to Islamic societies in which history doesn't count or counts only as obstacle—replicating the modernization approach in development, which is long bankrupt.[83]

The unproblematic perspective on modernity reveals a deeper binary structure. The fundamental matrix of American perspectives on Islam is a binary view in which the West is modern and democratic, and Islam, especially militant political Islam, is pre-modern or anti-modern. A differentiated view that allows for nuances and subdivisions within the Islamic world doesn't belie this matrix, as this passage suggests: "The modernist vision matches our own. Of all the groups, this one is most congenial to the values and the spirit of modern democratic society." The implication is that *we* are modern and *they* are not (but some of them are like us). The casual binarism in American perceptions also comes across in views on occupied Iraq, as in this headline: "Iraq navigates between Islam and democracy."[84] This approach echoes an American attitude to development: the search for their mirror image, the middle class, and the entrepreneur as culture hero, another trend that goes back to early postwar development policy.

The weaknesses of the modernists, according to Benard, are financial and political. Absent in this account is class analysis and political economy. Modernists are viewed as key allies, but there is no analysis of the political economy of modernism and no recognition of the way in which policies such as structural adjustment (in the Middle East known as *infitah*, or "opening") and OECD trade barriers *impede* the development of a middle class in Muslim societies.[85] National security perspectives and political economy don't interact; the paradigms don't meet. The institutional foundation of policy incoherence is the compartmentalization of knowledge.

Strengthening the modernists is taken as a matter of outside ideological intervention, and the imagined American capability for intervening in the Islamic world and engineering ideological change is large and taken to great lengths. "Publish and distribute their works at subsidized cost," Benard suggests, for example. "Encourage them to write for mass audiences and for youth. Introduce their views into the curriculum of Islamic education" and so on. This approach does not reflect on the political and ethical implications of this kind of engineering and the blowback it may produce, such as growing domestic suspicions of modernist positions. The time frame is immediate, now, so there is no developmental perspective to this strategy. A remarkable passage in her study notes, "While U.S. officialdom appears to be seeking *a symbolic rapprochement* with Islam on the level of outward lifestyle issues, European leaders seem more inclined to try for *a rapprochement on political issues* they believe to be important to Muslims. The split between the United States and Europe over Iraq is in part attributable to this difference" (emphasis added).[86] This reveals the true-blue American approach; it is essentially a matter of ideological repackaging. There is not a single mention of the obvious, commonsense way to strengthen moderates in Muslim societies: simply by adopting more evenhanded policies in the Middle East.

Viewed in this light, this edifice of modernists and traditionalists, moderates and hardliners, is contrived and circumvents the real issue: the United States wants the Middle East to change on its terms and doesn't want to change itself. Hence there is no real dialogue. There cannot be because the U.S. does not even contemplate changing its policies on Israel or its alliance with Saudi Arabia and other regimes, according to the Friendly Tyrant principle. However, ideological engineering and propaganda will have no effect as long as the real issues—Israel, Palestine, and American hegemony itself—are no-go zones of U.S. policy. This is another policy study that is studiously devoid of self-reflection or reflection on American policies and doesn't acknowledge blowback. The attitudes of Muslim fundamentalists and traditionalists are described but not explained; they are presented as ideological dispositions (read: Muslim rage) rather than as reactions to policies, including American policies. Instead, the emphasis is on ideas (democracy, civil society, modernity), which are taken in the abstract and decontextualized from Middle East realities.

"Islam's current crisis," according to Benard, "has two main components: a failure to thrive and a loss of connection to the global mainstream."[87] Richard Falk refers to the geopolitics of exclusion.[88] But exclusion is not entirely accurate. The instances of exclusion that Falk mentions—double standards, a discriminatory nonproliferation regime for nuclear weapons, policies in the world economy, responses to terrorist incidents, the stigmatization of "rogue states"—are rather instances of asymmetric inclusion or *integration* in a world order on unequal terms. Indeed, exclusion does not sync with decades of global economic integration via the oil industry and political integration under the tutelage of American hegemony.

The Rand approach is not entirely without self-criticism; it criticizes the "official Muslim Life in America Web site" of the U.S. State Department for being "exclusively dedicated to traditionalist content." And it cautions, "Accommodating traditionalists to an excessive degree can weaken our credibility and moral persuasiveness. An uncritical alliance with traditionalists can be misunderstood as appeasement and fear."[89] In other words, it counsels against "going soft." This intervention is a one-dimensional approach of Americanizing the Middle East, ideological, Machiavellian, and unreflexive.

Awareness of Islam's long cosmopolitan lineage should inspire a sense of historical modesty. For over a millennium the Muslim world has mixed and mingled with many cultures from Africa to Asia and Europe. This gives it a unique depth, sprawl, and resilience. Awareness of this background should lead to a dialogue with the worlds of Islam and Islamism. This dialogue should be civilizational, political, and reflexive. It should be civilizational in recognizing Islamic cosmopolitanism past and present; political in taking seriously the concrete grievances of Muslims, in particular, the question of Palestine; and reflexive in considering one's own role in the process and in recognizing global dynamics.

This should also include reflexivity and willingness to come to terms with the past in the Muslim world. Nostalgia for the caliphate and for past Muslim cultural splendor and accomplishment is no substitute for coming to terms with the geopolitical, geo-economic, and geocultural trauma that the Muslim world suffered by losing its intercontinental middleman role. The second trauma that afflicted the Muslim world is the resource curse of fossil fuels and its conservative ramifications, including McJihad. The third trauma that afflicts Islam is that since the end of the Cold War targeting Islam and "fundamentalism" has become an ideological and cultural successor to attacking communism. I discuss some of these attacks in the next chapter. They have a polarizing effect within Islam, strengthen hardliners, and crowd out precisely the humanistic and cosmopolitan strains of Islam.[90] It requires profound sophistication on the part of Muslims to address these three traumas, but it is the only way to recover Islamic cosmopolitanism.

Notes

1. Cf. Camilleri and Muzaffar 1998.
2. Beck 2006.
3. Rosenau 1990.
4. Huntington 2003.
5. Zizek 2004, 3.
6. Fallaci 2002.
7. Etzioni 2002.
8. Nandy 1989.
9. Such as Al-Azmeh 1993; Sayyid 2003.
10. Al-Azmeh makes the ethnocentric claim that "the very notion that there could be a 'universal civilization' is a Western idea" (1993, 41).
11. Baker 1999; Lubeck 1999; Sayyid 2003.
12. Abu-Lughod 1989. Gunn's *First Globalization* (2003) draws attention to the role of Southeast Asia but echoes the western preoccupation with the sixteenth century that prevails from Marx to Wallerstein.
13. Frank 1998.
14. Hobson 2004.
15. This literature is too large to reference here; note Subrahmanyam 1997, 1998; Pomeranz 2000; Hobson 2004; and references in Nederveen Pieterse 2006.
16. Pollock 2000.
17. Eaton 1993, 12; cf. McNeill 1979; Burke 1979.
18. Eaton 1993, 32.
19. Hoerder 2002, 31. On the Korean side, see Cohen 2000.
20. Ramesh 2005, 26.
21. Bakar 1996, 1.
22. Bakar 1996, 2.
23. For example, Rashid 1997.
24. "Let there be no compulsion in religion" (Koran 2:256), quoted in Weeramantry 1988, 85.
25. Weeramantry 1988, 90.
26. According to Mazrui, this reflects the "relatively nonracial nature" of Islam. He also notes, "While Islam may generate more political violence than Western culture, Western culture generates more street violence than Islam" (1997, 129, 130).
27. Hoerder 2002, 109.
28. Weeramantry 1988.

29. Tiryakian 1996.
30. Bernal 1987.
31. Hoerder 2002, 51.
32. Hoerder 2002, 85.
33. Al-Azmeh 2003, 15.
34. Boase 1977, 1978; Nederveen Pieterse 1989, 1994b.
35. Atasoy 1999.
36. Weeramantry 1988, 98.
37. Alatas 2006b; Makdisi 1981.
38. Alatas 2006a.
39. Turner 1992.
40. Eaton 1993, 24.
41. Levtzion 1979.
42. Mortimer 1982, 71.
43. Elsewhere I ask, "How European is Europe?" (Nederveen Pieterse 1994b).
44. McNeill 1979, ch. 3; cf. Veenhof 1997.
45. Ernst 1992.
46. Amin 1978.
47. Al-Azmeh 1993, 60.
48. Geertz 1968.
49. Stavrianos 1981.
50. Sharabi 1988 and UNDP 2003, 2004.
51. Mitchell 2002, 3.
52. Mitchell 2002, 11.
53. Mitchell 2002, 11.
54. Mernissi 2003.
55. Mitchell 2002, 3.
56. Mitchell 2002, 12.
57. Nederveen Pieterse 1992a.
58. Pantham 1995.
59. Rashid 2001; Ahmed 2003.
60. Johnson 2000; Rashid 2002; Cooley 1999.
61. Mamdani 2004.
62. Barraclough 1998.
63. Khatib 2006.
64. Huntington 1996. An early treatment is Said 1981; recent discussions are Qureshi and Sells 2003.
65. Turner 1994, 90.
66. Göle 2000; Adas 2003.
67. Beeley 1992.
68. Besides those mentioned in previous notes, sources include Sayeed 1997; Johnson 2000; Abdo 2000; Ahmed 1992; Lubeck 1999; Simons 2003; Noor 2000.
69. On Christianity and capitalism, see Frank 2000.
70. Etzioni 2002, 34.
71. Esposito 1992; Ray 1993; Nederveen Pieterse 1994a; Achcar 2003; Simons 2003.
72. Baker 2004; Hamzawy 2004.

73. Nederveen Pieterse 2004, 48.

74. Sabra 2003. "Oriental despotism" is Karl Wittfogel's old and disqualified thesis.

75. Benard 2003, 1.

76. For example, Satloff 2004.

77. Benard 2003, 8f.

78. Benard 2003, 36, 37.

79. Benard 2003, 47, xi–xii.

80. Bernard et al. 1998.

81. Benard 2003, 47.

82. Gordon 2003, 161.

83. Nederveen Pieterse 2001.

84. Susan Sachs, "Iraq navigates between Islam and democracy," *New York Times*, March 7, 2004, WK 3.

85. Cf. Kuran 2002.

86. Benard 2003, 35.

87. Benard 2003, ix.

88. Falk 1996.

89. Benard 2003, 36.

90. A point made by E. Qureshi, "The Islam the riots drowned out," *New York Times*, February 12, 2006, WK 15. Cf. Qureshi and Sells 2003.

8

❖

Global multiculture, flexible acculturation

Multiculture, said critics, is only different wallpaper and a wider choice in restaurants. But the Danish cartoon episode, the murder of Theo van Gogh in Amsterdam, the July 7, 2005, bombings in London, and the 2005 car burnings in the French banlieues show that more is at stake. Multiculturalism is a global arena. Yet most treatments still conceive of multiculturalism as a national arena. Muslim women's headscarves from Istanbul and Cairo to Tehran and Lyon display a wide register of meanings but in the French national assembly have been signified in just one. Multiculturalism means global engagement. To engage with the world is to engage with its conflicts. Multiculturalism is not no-man's-land. Multiculturalism is not consensus. There is no consensus in Britain about the war in Iraq, and there isn't among immigrants either. The "securitization" of cultural difference confirms the interplay between international and multicultural frictions. Multiculturalism is one of the faces of globalization; and globalization, at its Sunday best, is human history conscious of itself, which by the way isn't always nice.

Multiculturalism in contemporary accelerated globalization is profoundly different from the past. In the past migrants chose between two environments that were often radically different; now communication and travel back and forth are relatively ordinary. In the past migrants often chose between two overall monocultural settings; now they navigate between two or more multicultural environments. Indians resident in the U.S. can tune in to Indian TV news, alternate with an American show, and tune back to Indian satellite programs, and in India foreign broadcasts are more widely available. Immigrant neighborhoods in Germany, the Netherlands, and Sweden are fields of satellite dishes. Many Turks abroad lead multicultural lives, tuned to Turkish, German, and other European broadcasts. They follow Turkish news, music, and shows and choose between Hollywood, Bollywood, or Cairo films. Jet travel has made vacations in the home country easier for migrant workers and their families. Retiring and buying a home in the country of origin is now more frequent. Migrant remittances are major revenue flows for the Philippines, Mexico, Pakistan, India, and so on. Irish and Scottish politicians canvas expatriates overseas, and Mexican politicians campaign among Mexicans living in the U.S. Transnational relations are no longer simply two-way between country of origin and migration but across diasporic settlements in multiple continents. Gujaratis are continually in touch with family members in the UK, U.S., Canada, and Australia and compare notes about where it is best and most advantageous to study, start a business, find a companion, or enjoy a vacation. Diasporas are linked transnationally and intercontinentally like pearls on a string. Meanwhile, in the throes of neoliberal globalization, global inequality is increasing and multiculturalism carries a heavier burden.

Multiculturalism has gone global over time and in rapid pace particularly since information and communication technology (ICT) and cheaper air travel in the 1990s. Just as ICT revolutionized production (flexible accumulation, offshoring, outsourcing), finance (24/7 global reach), and firms (decentralization), it revolutionizes migration and multiculturalism. Migrants can now work in one space and culturally inhabit another. A consequence is that, as Michael Storper notes, in contemporary globalization the differences *between* localities have lessened and the variety *within* localities has increased.[1]

The nation state is no longer the "container" of multiculturalism. Yet the multiculturalism literature remains overwhelmingly focused on the relationship between migrants and the destination country and national policy options. This is unrealistic. It overlooks that for migrants and their offspring the conversation with the host nation is one among several, a conversation in which participation is optional and partial. The cultural ambience of the host nation is no longer encompassing; e-media tune to many worlds. Second, it underplays the dynamics of the host country—assimilation into what? The Netherlands, Germany, and the UK require integration courses for immigrants. But integration policies overlook that the "nation" is a series of vortices of change—local, regional, national, macro-regional, and transnational. Asians in the UK function locally in their workplaces, neighborhoods, and cities, regionally, in Yorkshire, and so on, nationally, in the context of British policies and culture, move in the European Union with British passports, and relate to country of origin culture and transnational Islam or Hinduism. Third, this overlooks the role of rainbow conversations and economies across cultures—such as Cape

Town Malays studying Islam in Karachi or Turks selling Belgian carpets to Moroccans in the Netherlands (as discussed in chapter 3). Fourth, it ignores the emergence of intermediary formations such as "Euro-Islam" ("a hybrid that attempts to reconcile the principles laid out in the Koran with life in a secular, democratic Europe"),[2] which is neither national nor belongs to another civilization.

Multiculture is global too because several diasporas outnumber the nations. The seventy-three million people of Irish descent worldwide dwarf the four million living in the Irish Republic; out of almost fifteen million Jewish people worldwide, about five million live in Israel; and similar equations apply to Greeks, Lebanese, and Armenians. Multiethnicity exists worldwide, and multiculturalism discourse and policy is spreading widely.

Postnationalism may be exaggerated shorthand, but surely the national center and space hold much less than they did in the past. Multiculturalism debates suffer from methodological and policy nationalism. Most discussions of multiculturalism are too preoccupied with questions of national policy to cope with multiculturalism issues that spill over boundaries. The July 7 bombings in London and the threats of August 2006 created a culture shock (the attackers were born in Britain and grew up as British lads) that multiculturalism debate has not been able to address adequately. It doesn't work to revisit the customary policy choice of integration or assimilation.[3] Global multiculture is a complex field that includes engagement with global conflict. Nations and cultures are no longer 360-degree environments. Danish cartoons are seen in Islamabad and Cairo, Illinois and Sarajevo. A joke made by a German commentator is heard in Istanbul. A speech by George W. Bush to veterans in Cincinnati plays the following day in Baghdad and on Al Manar TV.

Discussions of globalization and culture are dominated by shorthand such as McDonaldization and the clash of civilizations, which are ideological shortcuts rather than analytics. And the approach in terms of general norms—freedom of speech, democracy, human rights—without contextual fine print risks becoming part of institutionalized hypocrisy.

Multiculturalism conflicts

Some cases may illustrate contemporary dynamics—the Danish cartoons mocking Islam and the murder of Theo van Gogh in the Netherlands. I give brief outlines because the cases have been widely covered in international media and detailed information is readily available.

The Danish cartoons originated in a contest for cartoons mocking Islam issued by one of the country's leading morning newspapers, *Jyllands-Posten*.

Twelve cartoons were published on September 30, 2005, alongside this editorial note:

> The modern, secular society is rejected by some Muslims. They demand a special position, insisting on special consideration of their own religious feelings. It is incompatible with contemporary democracy and freedom of speech, where you must be ready to put up with insults, mockery and ridicule. It is certainly not always attractive and nice to look at, and it does not mean that religious feelings should be made fun of at any price, but that is of minor importance in the present context. . . . We are on our way to a slippery slope where no-one can tell how the self-censorship will end. That is why Morgenavisen Jyllands-Posten has invited members of the Danish editorial cartoonists union to draw Muhammad as they see him.[4]

The idea of a cartoon competition came from the newspaper's cultural editor, Flemming Rose, a Ukrainian Jew with ties to Israel and the Likud party.[5] A year earlier he traveled to Philadelphia to interview Daniel Pipes and wrote an admiring article about him.[6] Daniel Pipes, a fervent neoconservative Zionist who equates militant Islam with fascism (the familiar "Islamic fascism" idea) and sees total Israeli military victory as the only path to Middle East peace,[7] had been involved in the Danish multiculturalism debate since 2002, when he launched a virulent attack on Muslim immigrants in a newspaper article coauthored with a right-wing Danish journalist and historian.[8] The article sparked a debate on multiculturalism with Danish parliamentarians. By interviewing Pipes in 2004, Flemming Rose revived an attack on Muslims in Denmark that had been in motion for years. This suggests that from their conception the inflammatory cartoons were part of a transnational arena and reflect an elective affinity with American neoconservative agendas. The way they are framed, using free speech as an intercultural wedge issue, suggests that this is not a happy time to be Muslim in Denmark. The idea of sparking tensions with the Islamic world is not far from the surface.

In October Islamic ambassadors sought a meeting with the Danish prime minister, which he declined. In November and December imams from Denmark took the cartoons to meetings with Muslim leaders in the Middle East and the Islamic Organization Conference. Meanwhile, the cartoons were being reprinted in fifty countries. What ensued was an orchestrated response of anti-Danish demonstrations and boycotts virtually across the Islamic world in early 2006. Thus, a multicultural tussle sparked an almost worldwide conflagration. The fine print, however, indicates that from the outset it was designed to provoke Muslims, to manufacture a "clash of civilizations" around an artificial arena: free speech versus Muslim rage. "The exercise was no more benign than commissioning caricatures of African-Americans would have been during the

1960's civil rights struggle," one commentator noted.[9] A deliberate provocation met with an organized response. This is multiculturalism as a transnational arena. Discussing this under the heading of the do's and don'ts, pros and cons of free speech is beside the point, or, rather, frames the issue in the way the provocation sought to achieve. No one now claims that painting Swastikas and anti-Semitic slogans is a matter of free speech. They are hate speech and gestures of ethnic cleansing. The cartoons reflect a similar outlook. Notes Simon Jenkins, "Speech is free only on a mountain top; all else is editing."[10]

Until recently Denmark was an exemplary progressive and strongly pro-welfare Nordic country. In the 1990s an anti-tax party had not succeeded in winning votes. An alternative is to keep the social contract but to limit entry by appealing to what Habermas calls the "chauvinism of prosperity." Using this ladder right-wing parties have climbed to power by mobilizing anti-immigrant sentiment. Similar frictions run through many European countries—slow growth and welfare states under pressure from neoliberal constituencies who frame globalization in terms of competition. Right-wing parties have used anti-immigrant sentiment in Austria, Belgium, France, the Netherlands, and Italy, usually to limited or temporary effect. With the passing of communism, Europe's right-wing parties also face an enemy deficit. This entails various strands of political chauvinism—to advance party interests (Haider's FPÖ in Austria, the National Front in France, Vlaams Belang in Flanders, Fortuyn's Leefbaar Nederland), to advance regional interests (Lega Nord in Italy) or to bring a rightwing coalition to power and move economic agendas to the right (Berlusconi's coalition in Italy, the DLP and Japanese nationalism).

In November 2004 the Dutch filmmaker Theo van Gogh was murdered in Amsterdam while riding his bike to work in the morning. In August his latest film, *Submission Part I*, was shown on national television. This eleven-minute work featured seminaked young women with Arabic Koran texts written on their bare bodies, seen through transparent veils, tokens of their submission to Islam. A play on words because "Islam" means submission. On his talk show on Amsterdam TV, van Gogh referred to Muslims as "goat fuckers." Van Gogh was stabbed to death by a twenty-six-year-old Dutch Muslim of Moroccan immigrant descent, Mohammed Bouyeri, who left a five-page letter on van Gogh's body threatening Ayaan Hirsi Ali and was arrested within hours.

A Somali-born woman, Ayaan Hirsi Ali conceived and co-wrote the film. As a Labor Party policy adviser, she described herself as a "lapsed Muslim" and declared Islam a "backward religion" and Mohammed "a pervert and tyrant." She advised the party policy unit to close all forty-one Islamic schools, put a brake on immigration, and change Article 23 in the Dutch constitution, which establishes the rights for setting up separate schools and institutions—a central pillar of the Dutch system and a foundation of multicultural orthodoxy since the 1960s. The party rejected these extreme recommendations. In the wake of September 11, she published articles arguing that Islam is not capable of integrating into Dutch society. In 2002 she stood as a member of parliament for the free market Liberal Party (VVD) and was elected.

Émigrés who act as cultural mediators are often granted a privileged status of authenticity: "the native informant knows best." Tariq Ali once contrasted V. S. Naipaul's journey ("Naipaul came from Trinidad, a tiny colony, to the center of empire, and became an empire loyalist") with that of Juan Goytisolo (the Spanish writer who seeks to "recover the vanished glory of Andalusia which was destroyed by Catholicism").[11] As a character in the multiculturalism psychodrama, Hirsi Ali plays the part of the immigrant who is more western than westerners. Some Muslims in the Netherlands accuse her of "pandering to the Dutch," and some people tire of her hijacking emancipation agendas for populist polarizing.

The political setting is welfare cuts, health-care privatization, "pension tension," state crackdowns on illegal immigrants and immigrant youth delinquency, restrictive drugs policies, and a difficult discussion on multiculturalism that argues that it has failed, largely because of the immigrants' failure to integrate. Pim Fortuyn used anti-immigrant, anti-Muslim sentiment to garner votes, stating, "There is a tension between the values of modern society and the principles of Islam" and "As far as I'm concerned, no Muslim will ever come in."[12] He also took position against Turkey becoming a member of the EU. These figures—Fortuyn ("the right to freely talk crap"), van Gogh ("the Jerry Springer of Dutch social-political discourse"), Hirsi Ali ("no ruckus, no debate")—were (are), in popular parlance, "attention getters," loud, in your face.[13] Fortuyn, at a time when his political numbers were rapidly rising, was assassinated by a young animal rights activist; van Gogh was killed by a Muslim of Moroccan descent; Hirsi Ali continued as MP under police protection and left the Netherlands in 2006 to join the neoconservative American Enterprise Institute in Washington, D.C. Wilders, a right-wing MP and would-be successor to Fortuyn, also known for his anti-Muslim pronouncements, is also under police protection. Ideological murders and MPs under police protection are unprecedented in the Netherlands. In 2006 Hirsi Ali's denaturalization (she lost her passport and resigned as MP) and then renaturalization led to the fall of the Dutch government and early elections. Through this episode her influence was reassessed in the media.[14] Her book *Caged Virgin* was reviewed as "sloppy and factually inaccurate."[15]

There are further twists to the situation. For years van Gogh's killer had been an exemplar of integration in Dutch society: employed in a neighborhood youth center, active in local Amsterdam politics, but then had a falling out with his employers, became alienated, and joined Muslim militants. A television documentary gave (unconfirmed) indications that he had been a Dutch intelligence service (AIVD) plant in militant Muslim youth circles but the service lost control of him.[16] In the municipal elections of March 2006 the government coalition parties and the Fortuyn-type parties suffered a massive defeat in a landslide swing toward left-wing parties, in large measure due to immigrants voting en masse against the anti-immigrant bias of the governing coalition. This is a different kind of multiculturalism backlash.[17] The immigrant vote is counting more also in the U.S., Canada, and the UK.

In both episodes in Denmark and the Netherlands, conflict was sparked by willed provocations: symbolic violence begat violence. Transnational affinities played a key part in both episodes. In both episodes the conflicts were about the character of the public sphere, a central arena of multiculturalism. In both cases appeals were made on behalf of "western values" (free speech, modernity) and involved a politics of tension targeting Islam or Islamism, and in effect marginal immigrants. It seems inappropriate to discuss this in normative terms of free speech or blasphemy; it should be addressed first in political terms: cui bono, who benefits from fomenting strife between Muslims and Denmark or Europe? In both cases the target is Islam and the backdrop to these multiculturalism skirmishes is heightened tension in relation to the Middle East. Recent literature in European countries examines these skirmishes and typically does so in terms of the "limits of tolerance." The gist is that it's appropriate that multicultural societies are tolerant; however, extending this to militant Islam means tolerating intolerance.[18] Missing in this kind of approach is recognition that the arena is not merely that of particular European countries and of the failure to accept limits in western policies in the Middle East. It is appropriate to consider the link between Islam and global multiculture.

The Middle East has long been an arena of geopolitical conflict (chapter 7). What Samuel Huntington calls a clash of civilizations is no clash of civilizations at all but the political ramifications of interventions in the Middle East that go back for over half a century. McJihad and "palace fundamentalism" includes many actors (oil companies, the U.S. government, arms sales, the Saudi royal family, wahhabite clergy, and transnational networks of conservative Islam). The conservative Islamic network is codependent with modern capitalism, a holdover of anti-communism and now a source of blowback.

American policies in the Middle East alienate many in the region. Since political avenues other than Islam are generally closed off, radical Islam is a major avenue of political expression. The U.S. declares that it seeks accommodation in the region through cooperation with moderate governments and moderate Islam through public diplomacy, promoting democracy and civil society; its policies, however, are not moderate and alienate the very moderates it claims it wants to cultivate. Since Middle East policies are not under discussion in the United States the situation is addressed through ideological repackaging and public diplomacy.[19] This targets Islamism as part of a discourse that places Islam on the outskirts of modernity—along the lines of Bernard Lewis, Fouad Ajami, Daniel Pipes, Thomas Friedman, and Bassam Tibi, usually in binarisms (tradition-modernity, conservative-progressive, pro- and anti-western, etc.). As mentioned before, it is difficult to synch this diagnosis with the region's decades of global economic integration via the oil industry and political integration under American tutelage.

How does this affect global multiculture? Recent escalations reverberate in every circuit. The ongoing stalemate and frustrations felt in the region and the expanding confrontations with the Islamic world have wide ripple effects. Consider a news item such as this: "The Bush administration . . . proposed Wednesday to spend $85 million to promote political change inside Iran by subsidizing dissident groups, unions, student fellowships and television and radio broadcasts."[20] According to secretary of state Rice, "We will use this money to develop support networks for Iranian reformers, political dissidents and human rights activists." The policy will probably make progressive ideas in Iran suspect and bolster hardliners, as have past policies such as declaring Iran part of an axis of evil. If hegemonic power acts across borders and pursues regime change from within as policy, why then should migrants be required to integrate in national society rather than integrating, likewise, along crossborder lines?

Multicircuit identification

Cultural difference as a marker, frontier, vocabulary, vortex, and arena of conflict is as old as the hills. Multiculturalism as a manifestation of contemporary globalization is a sequel to multiethnicity, which is as old as the stone age, when hunter-gatherers, cultivators, and pastoralists cohabited and mingled (see chapter 1). What is now different by degree is that not just local, domestic differences matter, but conflicts that originate elsewhere also are fought out in the arenas of multiculturalism. Different by degree; in the religious wars of sixteenth and seventeenth century Europe translocal differences counted locally, too. Contemporary times have been characterized, from a European viewpoint, as neo-medieval in that they show a similar overlap of jurisdictions and loyalties as in the middle ages.[21] In hindsight the nation state era with its exclusive sovereignty might well appear as an anomalous historical interlude. The idea of nations as insular containers—with a national economy, national market, national firms, national bourgeoisie, national character, national culture, national politics—may seem an interval in a much longer and now resumed experience of crossborder flows that occupy center stage. Historically the translation of crossborder conflicts into local disputes is quite ordinary. In this sense contemporary global multiculture is historically normal, more normal than the inward-looking nation state epoch.

Multicircuit acculturation is as old as the phenomenon of subcultures that offer variable acculturation, as old as the situation imagined in the song "By the Rivers of Babylon." What is new is the scope and degree of multicircuit identification. During the Nazi era in the 1930s some emigrated from Germany and others opted for "inner migration," taking their thoughts and hopes to imaginary realms.[22] In the U.S. many blacks live on the other side of the tracks in poor housing and receive substandard education and services but participate in alternative circuits—churches, music circuits of blues and hip hop, the sports world in which their stars shine, the Black Entertainment channel, circuits of drugs and crime. These circuits offer belonging, recognition, and a sense of feeling at home. Flexible acculturation is an exercise of agency by picking and choosing, mixing and matching cultural affiliation in multicircuit settings.

Asian Muslims in northern English cities, North African *beurs* in French banlieues, and many other migrants and their offspring share experiences of social exclusion and are increasingly ghettoized: "Asian communities living in several UK cities face social isolation as severe as that experienced in the black ghettoes of divided American cities like Chicago and Miami." UK cities are rising in the world rankings of segregation. "The idea was that people would assimilate. The danger is that the assimilation process is so slow that for many it is just not possible."[23]

Exclusion in many instances is not occasional but institutionalized. In France *le crise des banlieues* is grounded in urban planning policies that privileged modern high rises à la Le Corbusier, like the high rises on the south side of Chicago and the Bijlmer in Amsterdam Southeast, which combined gigantism and uniformity. Amsterdam and Rotterdam have razed these housing complexes.[24] According to a different view, the issue is not the architecture or the housing, but the location, far from employment.[25]

It is not occasional also because multiculturalism often combines with institutionalized amnesia and the refusal to view the country's colonial past in other than a benevolent light. This is a factor notably in France, Belgium, Japan, and, to a lesser extent, the UK. According to Article 4 of a law passed on February 23, 2005, it is now "compulsory in France to emphasise the positive dimension of the French colonial era in high school history courses and textbooks. When the Socialist party tried to overturn this controversial law recently, it was defeated in the National Assembly by a conservative majority that may have moved further to the right as a result of the recent violence."[26]

Dominique Moisi comments, "By imposing political correctness on the teaching of the past, the National Assembly has committed more than a crime. It has made a crucial error. If one of the big challenges confronting France in the global age is that of integrating its minorities, then the imposition of a unilateral reading of history on all French people whatever their origins is not only anachronistic but offensive." The law has been declared unconstitutional by the Constitutional Court and is inoperative, but it indicates the refusal to come to terms with the French imperial past and the Algerian war, which combines with reluctance to view Algerian immigrants as permanent residents and citizens. The French law banning overt religious signs in schools, directed at the wearing of the hijab, fits the same pattern of integration of minorities on terms set by the French elite, in other words, monocultural multiculturalism.[27] As Wallerstein observes, "France is a multicultural society par excellence still living the Jacobin dream of uniformity."[28]

Exclusion is not occasional also because multiculturalism is under multiple pressures: entrepreneurial globalization translates into pressure on welfare states and in view of the securitization of migration (discussed below) immigrants face increasing demands to conform and decreasing resources and incentives to integrate. The welfare state is shrinking precisely when demand for welfare services is expanding. Right-wing forces focus on migrants as a soft target and in several countries the political center has moved to the right on multiculturalism. Multiculturalism in Europe has been polarized almost from the outset, but the "soft" period of multiculturalism—when a slogan displayed in Berlin read "Liebe Ausländer, lasst uns nicht mit diesen Deutschen allein" (Dear foreigners, don't leave us alone with these Germans) and when cultural differences seemed all that mattered—is no more. Immigrants too adjust to multiculturalism in myriad different ways, many by ignoring it altogether except for its basic provisions.

Global multiculture provides multiple circuits of identification and integration that can make up for social exclusion at least symbolically. Alternative circuits are appealing when mainstream circuits are alienating; in social psychology this two-way flow is termed interactive acculturation.[29] It takes two to tango. The wider the gap between multiculturalism rhetoric and actual socioeconomic integration, the greater the appeal of alternative and symbolic spaces of identification; simple, but that seems to be the basic geometry of flexible acculturation. In France, "the immigrant origin populations turn to Islam, not only out of fidelity to the values and religion of their parents but also because it gives meaning to an existence in a society which tends to despise them, to discredit them or to exclude them. . . . Here religion is part of an endeavour to participate in modernity rather than to exclude oneself from it."[30] This may refer to an alternative modernity. Multicircuit multiculturalism includes tea houses, cyberspace, mosques, malls, and "Muslim by day, disco at night."[31] *Beur* youths synchronized their riot actions across Paris quartiers and other cities via Web sites and mobile phones. The easy media terminology—"riots"—underplays their degree of coordination and organization.

For many immigrants at the bottom rungs of society, multiculturalism is a bogus exercise, a regime of platitudes, a tedious "race relations industry" that mainly benefits a small elite. The reality of multiculturalism on the ground is often a furnace of discontent where grinding anger results in inner migration into imaginary worlds of cyberspace, subcultures of gangs and petty crime, or desire to strike back and affiliate with hostile forces. This is part of what looms behind the July 7, 2005, and August 2006 episodes in the UK: a backlash against bogus multiculturalism and alienation felt by Muslim youth in UK ghettoes and a response to the belligerent policies of the U.S. and UK in the Middle East, Palestine, and Iraq. The appeal of militant Islam is a matter of pull and push. It reflects the nature of conflict in the age of accelerated globalization—conflict is discursive, unfolds through representations, is channeled via media, is no longer spatially sequestered, moves with the speed of light, is subject to multiple interpretations, and evokes a wide variety of agency.

A standard response before and after the crisis and a response to the London bombings and the car burnings in France was to blame the victims of social exclusion for their lack of integration. Also in response to September 11, few bothered to mention the role of American policies in the Middle East. Collective self-reflection is in short supply, which indicates the degree to which hypocrisy and power-with-impunity have been institutionalized.

The structural features that underlie global multiculture and flexible acculturation match those that Robert Cooper, Prime Minister Tony Blair's foreign policy adviser, calls the "postmodern state," pertaining in the EU: a fuzzy boundary between domestic and foreign affairs, mutual interference in domestic affairs and mutual surveillance, and security based on interdependence and mutual vulnerability.[32] (In contrast, the U.S. state is characterized by "defensive modernism.")

The growing role of "intermestic" (international-domestic) affairs is a general trend. Global multiculture means engagement with conflicts worldwide. If societies are engaged globally it means that conflicts travel too. Conflicts cannot be contained locally. Multiculturalism and foreign policy are no longer separate domains. This has been part of global experience since the expulsion of the Jews from Spain and Portugal and part of recent experience for instance in the Kurdish presence in Germany and Sweden. Muslims are kept out of the Metropolitan Police elite VIP protection squad and Prime Minister Blair's security detail.[33] It is an unwritten rule in India's intelligence agencies and security apparatus that Sikhs and Muslims are not welcome.[34] Lines drawn in multiculturalism are often drawn globally, as in the French foulard affair: "The French debate has become 'global.' It has developed both locally and well beyond France, and has considerable diplomatic and geopolitical implications."[35] It reverberates from Turkey to North Africa. Conflicts in Somalia over the status of women are part of an animal husbanding society and a trading society on the coast, in the throes of change. Folk Islam mixed with patriarchy and neo-patriarchy is a party in this change. Dutch society with Somali immigrants also becomes a party in this change.

Multiple circuits of integration also mean multicircuit blowback. The Danish prime minister not meeting with Muslim ambassadors may score domestic points but loses points in umma politics. The Japanese prime minister's annual visits to the Yasukuni shrine score with Japanese nationalists but shrink Japan's standing in the region. George W. Bush's speeches assuring American audiences that Iraq is on the right track come across differently on Al Jazeera and in living rooms in Basra and Baghdad. The old compartmentalization of audiences and circuits is no more. Multicircuit multiculturalism is what Walter Anderson calls "communities in a world of open systems."[36]

Globalization amplifies the sources of the self and opens multiple organizational avenues, which is not particular to multiculturalism but a general trend. The Zapatistas mobilized in Chiapas and took their cause of democracy and dignity to the nation via savvy media skills and to the world via the internet and international *encuentros* against neoliberalism. Mobile phones played a key part in "people power" in the Philippines and Thailand, coordinating street action and bypassing mainstream media.

Migrant mobility and connectivity are variable and reflect class and migration history. The Indian diaspora is overall better educated and more prosperous and mobile than Pakistani and Bangladeshi migrants. Compared to Moroccans, Turks in Europe come from more urban backgrounds (many migrated to urban centers in Turkey before migrating abroad) and have more entrepreneurial experience, and the Turkish economy and diaspora provide greater economic depth.

The account of contemporary globalization as the "annihilation of distance" (the death of distance, end of geography, etc.) is shallow. What matters is social distance mediated by cultural affinity. So what is at issue is the arbitrage of distance; distance or exclusion in one circuit is compensated for by integration in another, though not in a linear fashion. Nor are the circuits comparable in the goods they provide. They refer to different sectors—economic, social, cultural, cyberspace, symbolic—and provide diverse benefits.

Flexible accumulation deploys flexible methods (production, product features, location, labor conditions) towards a single purpose (accumulation). *Flexible acculturation* deploys flexible methods (switching codes, mixing vocabularies and alternating circuits of affiliation) towards the general aim of belonging and being at home in the world. A parallel notion is Aihwa Ong's flexible citizenship: "I use the term *flexible citizenship* to refer especially to the strategies and effects of mobile managers, technocrats and professionals who seek to both circumvent *and* benefit from different nation-state regimes by selecting different sites for investments, work and family relocation. . . . They readily submit to the governmentality of capital, while plotting all the while to escape state discipline."[37]

This perspective differs from global multiculture in that the focus is on the Chinese diaspora, mainly on the Pacific Rim, and on elites (many are "well-heeled Hong Kongers") and their strategies of capitalist opportunism. Global multiculture includes elites but consists mostly of poor and less privileged migrants, it includes diasporas with long histories but also recent migration chains, and it includes economic opportunism but also a wider spectrum of interests. So although Ong's flexible citizenship also refers to diverse cultural politics, its ambit is narrower than flexible acculturation in global multiculture. Another instance of flexibility—spatial, economic, cultural, legal—is Xiangming Chen's work on de-bordering and re-bordering in East Asia's border regions and their "local cosmopolitanism."[38]

Flexible acculturation is multidirectional and exercised by migrants, authorities and other actors. Politicians and governments switch and alternate discourses and policies they apply to migrants and citizens of immigrant origin. Multiculturalism is one register; security and socioeconomics are others, including the political economy of the welfare state. As Ong notes, "Nation-states are reworking immigration law to attract capital-bearing subjects while limiting the entry of unskilled labor."[39] Canada, the U.S., the UK, and Australia adopt a "give us your best and your brightest" brain-drain policy that operates as a tax on poor nations or foreign aid in reverse.[40]

A major trend is to reframe migration in security terms. In Europe this goes back to "Fortress Europe" measures that differentiate between member state and third country nationals and seek to bring migration under control: the Schengen accord, the 1992 European Union Treaty, and the Treaty of Amsterdam, which brought immigration, asylum, and refugee matters under one heading.[41] By securitizing issues, political elites achieve that these issues "trump normal democratic processes of debate and negotiation" and trump justice "since national security takes precedence over justice, and since disloyal minorities have no legitimate claims anyway."[42]

The securitization of migration received a boost since September 11. The United States applied massive security measures, curtailing civil liberties, tightening visa requirements, eavesdropping, and carrying out renditions and detentions in Guantánamo and Bagram Airbase as part of the generalized preoccupation with terrorism. According to former national security adviser Richard Clarke, July 7 shows the United States the way: "The British experience this summer has lessons for us about finding terrorist sleeper cells." It involves "infiltrating undercover agents into the population from which sleepers are recruited" and seeking "the cooperation of the American Muslim community in identifying possible problem groups and individuals."[43] European governments participate in the surveillance and security discourse and practices. In Europe "minority nationalism only becomes securitized when it involves terrorism,"[44] but the definition of terrorism has widened.

Global multiculture exemplifies how technological and political changes affect the logics of globalization and conflict. Borders are not what they used to be, the state no longer holds the monopoly of means of violence, technological changes enable the "democratization" of lethal weapons (warlords, crime syndicates, gangs), and arenas cross territorial boundaries.[45] Gangs from East Los Angeles repatriate to El Salvador and move back again to operate in Louisiana.

Multiculturalism is inherently linked to inequality in the world, an articulation of global inequality. Most migration is labor migration. If it weren't for steep inequalities people wouldn't move as much. Secondly, the same trends that reinforce overall global inequality make conditions in many multicultural societies harder. For the world majority, neoliberal globalization creates a world that is harder to live in back home and in the metropolises. Welfare cutbacks make it harder to get by in multicultural societies, and scarce jobs, rising income inequality, reduced state spending, and privatization of utilities in low-income countries make it harder to get by there as well. Wal-Mart capitalism doesn't offer a benevolent script. This is the dark sea beneath migration and multiculturalism. Global multiculture enables migrants to compare notes on economic dynamics in motion. Global poverty is part of bogus multiculturalism backlash, but it is not appropriate to reduce the current tensions to economic deprivation. The imposition of reckless power politics astride the world unleashes pent-up tensions. A further element in the mix is the democratization of the means of violence.

There is now a strange disjuncture between general abstract principles and real-time applications. In March 2006 a group of writers issued a statement warning that Islamism is a form of totalitarianism which is now the world's main danger: "After having overcome fascism, Nazism, and Stalinism, the world now faces a new global threat: Islamism. . . . We, writers, journalists, intellectuals, call for resistance to religious totalitarianism and for the promotion of freedom, equal opportunity and secular values for all." The writers included Salman Rushdie, Christopher Hitchens, exiled Bangladeshi writer Taslima Nasreen, Ayaan Hirsi Ali, and Bernard-Henri Lévy. Ideas and ideologies have increasingly become a sphere of displaced politics (what politics doesn't want to solve, ideas and moral posturing should solve), so that in some real-time discursive regimes they seem to mean the opposite of what they represent.

An open letter to Prime Minister Blair sent by thirty-eight British Muslim organizations and most Muslim MPs after the airplane bomb threats of August 2006 accused the government of adopting policies that expose the nation to terrorist attack.[46] The general message is that multiculturalism and foreign policy cannot be treated separately. This is a keynote of global multiculture: National multiculturalism regards these domains as separate; global multiculture acknowledges that migrants are transnational agents who act in multiple domains.

A central struggle of multiculturalism concerns the public sphere, including access to public spaces, institutions, media, symbols, and curricula. The Danish cartoons and in a different way Hirsi Ali seek to marginalize Muslims in the public sphere. Contrast these accounts of European public spaces in 2006. London in August: "Terror arrests outside my park; multiethnic peace within."[47] And *Londonistan*, a book by a right-wing British columnist, the novel *Londonistani*, which in an unsentimental way gives a totally different account, and *Kasba Holland*, a scene of intercultural mixing according to upbeat Dutch writers.[48]

Over time, for structural demographic reasons, multicultural sharing of the public culture and institutions will arguably be a likely trend in the West and Japan.[49] The populations of Europe, Japan, and the U.S. are graying and cultural hegemony is not being reproduced demographically. In this sense multicultural Europe and the "Latinization" of America (12.5 percent of Americans are of Hispanic background) are a matter of time. In this light, the current skirmishes may be viewed as actions that seek to halt what is, for structural economic and demographic reasons, an unstoppable trend. But multiculturalism is part of a much wider configuration. The policy implications of this inquiry are, in outline, threefold. First, international migration should be addressed at multiple levels: local, national, regional, and global. Second, issues of migration and multiculturalism should be addressed also in terms of political economy, which includes recognizing the economic, social, and demographic contributions of migrants. As mentioned before, between 1990 and 2000, 89 percent of Europe's population growth was due to immigration. It includes assessing the international political economy in which migration is embedded with a view to its impact in developing countries. Combining migration and development—taken in the sense of global development as well—is one way of avoiding a western bunker mentality and remaining transfixed in the "chauvinism of prosperity." Thus an implication of global multiculture is to engage multiculture conflicts also at the source. In the concluding chapter I reflect on the wider meanings and ramifications of the global multiculture that is taking shape.

Notes

1. Storper 2001.

2. M. Simons, "Muslim women in Europe claim rights and keep faith: embracing Islam and independence," *New York Times*, December 29, 2005, 3; AlSayyad and Castells 2002.

3. Modood 2005.

4. The translation is from Wikipedia, under "Muhammad cartoons controversy," http://www.wikipedia.org/wiki/Muhammad_cartoons_controversy (January 24, 2007).

5. Petras 2006, 142.

6. Flemming Rose, "The threat of Islamism," *Jyllands-Posten*, October 29, 2004. Translated at the Bellaciao Web site, http://www.bellaciao.org/en/article .php3?id_article=10253 (February 6, 2006). Cf. Christopher Bollyn, "European media provoke Muslims to inflame Zionist 'clash of civilizations,'" *American Free Press*, February 3, 2006, http://www.rumormillnews.com/cgi-bin/forum.cgi ?read=84976 (February 3, 2006). Cf. Flemming Rose, "Why I published the cartoons," *Washington Post*, February 19, 2006, B01.

7. "The Palestinians are a miserable people . . . and they deserve to be." Daniel Pipes, *Washington Report on Middle East Affairs*, July 2001.

8. Daniel Pipes and Lars Hedegaard, "Something Rotten in Denmark?" *New York Post*, August 27, 2002 (and the *National Post*, in Danish). (Quote: "For years, Danes lauded multiculturalism and insisted they had no problem with the Muslim customs—until one day they found that they did. Some major issues: Living on the dole: Third-world immigrants—most of them Muslims—constitute 5 percent of the population but consume upwards of 40 percent of the welfare spending. Engaging in crime: Muslims are only 4 percent of Denmark's 5.4 million people but make up a majority of the country's convicted rapists. . . . Self-imposed isolation: Over time, as Muslim immigrants increase in numbers, they wish less to mix with the indigenous population. Importing unacceptable customs: Forced marriages . . . are one problem. Another is threats to kill Muslims who convert out of Islam. . . . Fomenting anti-Semitism: Muslim violence threatens Denmark's approximately 6,000 Jews, who increasingly depend on police protection. . . . Seeking Islamic law: Muslim leaders openly declare their goal of introducing Islamic law once Denmark's Muslim population grows large enough—a not-that-remote prospect. If present trends persist, one sociologist estimates, every third inhabitant of Denmark in 40 years will be Muslim.") The article sparked a debate with Danish parliamentarians.

9. Craig S. Smith, "Adding newsprint to the fire," *New York Times*, February 5, 2006, WK5.

10. "These cartoons don't defend free speech, they threaten it," *Sunday Times*, February 5, 2006.

11. Quoted in F. Eberstadt, "The anti-Orientalist," *New York Times Magazine*, April 16, 2006. Cf. Brennan 2006.

12. Kolbert 2002, 112, 108.

13. On Fortuyn, see Broertjes 2002. On van Gogh and Hirsi Ali, see Andrew Osborn, "Woman who defied Islam forced to flee" (*Guardian Weekly*, November 14–20, 2002, 3), Ayaan Hirsi Ali, "Ik bevraag de islam, een religie zonder zelfreflectie" (*De Volkskrant*, October 30, 2004, 6), Bruce Bawer, "Tolerant Dutch wrestle with tolerating intolerance" (*New York Times*, November 14, 2004, 3), Jon Henley, "I feel terribly guilty and very much afraid" (*Guardian Weekly*, November 17, 2004), Farida Majid, "How Van Gogh provoked Islamists" (*Daily Times*, December 1, 2004), Alan Riding, "Navigating expression and religious taboos" (*New York Times*, January 22, 2005, A25), Marie-Claire Cécilia, "Netherlands: the pillars are shaken" (*Le Monde diplomatique*, March 2005, 4–5), Marlise Simons, "2 Dutch deputies on the run, from Jihad death threats" (*New York Times*, March 4, 2005), "Living with Islam: the new Dutch model?" (*Economist*, April 2, 2005, 24–26), C. Caldwell, "Daughter of the Enlightenment" (*New York Times Magazine*, April 3, 2005, 26–31), and Alexander Linklater, "Danger woman" (*Guardian Weekly*, May 27–June 2, 2005, 17).

14. For example, R. Koopmans and R. Vliegenthart, "De schijn van heiligheid: onderzoek naar de politieke invloed van Ayaan Hirsi Ali," *NRC Handelsblad*, July 2–3, 2006, 35. S. Kuper, "Holland's crowded house," *Financial Times*, August 26–27, 2006, W21–22.

15. Hirsi Ali 2006, reviewed by Lalami 2006, 30.

16. Katja Schuurman, "Prettig weekend, ondanks alles," 2005. Fauwe and van Amerongen 2006 report on Bouyeri's family background.

17. After five years' residence immigrants have the right to vote and stand in municipal but not in national elections, so the leftward swing has been less marked in the 2006 parliamentary elections.

18. For example, Buruma 2006.

19. Steger 2005.

20. S. R. Weisman, "Rice is seeking millions to prod changes in Iran," *New York Times*, February 16, 2006, A1, A12.

21. For example, Kobrin 1998.

22. Another instance of flexible acculturation is the "fifth column" idea, which led to the internment of third country nationals with whom the nation is at war (such as the Japanese in the U.S. and Dutch nationals in the East Indies).

23. D. Adam, "UK Asians isolated in city enclaves," *Guardian*, September 1, 2005, 12; Ian Draper, "Britain: acceptance not integration," *Le Monde diplomatique*, March 2005, 5.

24. C. Caldwell, "Revolting high rises," *New York Times Magazine*, November 27, 2005, 28–30; cf. Hannerz 1992 on high rises and multiculturalism in Amsterdam.

25. "Their physical isolation sustains a sense of alienation, they become dormitory ghettos" (E. Heathcote, "How France's suburbs became dormitory ghettos," *Financial Times*, November 19–20, 2005).

26. Dominique Moisi, "France is haunted by an inability to confront its past," *Financial Times*, December 12, 2005, 15.

27. Dominique Vidal, "France: hate and the hijab," *Le Monde diplomatique*, February 2004, 4; Wieviorka 2004b.

28. Immanuel Wallerstein, "The inequalities that blazed in France will soon scorch the world," *Guardian*, December 3, 2005.

29. Bourhis et al. 1997.

30. Wieviorka 2004a, 284.

31. Nederveen Pieterse 1997.

32. Cooper 2000; Peters 2005, 110.

33. R. R. Lall, "Muslim policeman found too unsafe to guard Blair," *Times of India*, November 8, 2006: 23.

34. S. Datta and B. Vij-Aurora, "Muslims and Sikhs need not apply," *Outlook*, November 13, 2006: 36–42.

35. Wieviorka 2004b, 72.

36. Anderson 1999.

37. Ong 1998, 136, 156–57; Ong 1999.

38. Chen 2005, 40.

39. Ong 1998, 136.

40. Kapur and McHale 2005.

41. Waever 1996.

42. Kymlicka 2004, 157, following Waever 1995.

43. Richard A. Clarke, "Finding the sleeper cells: the London attackers can show us what to look for," *New York Times Magazine*, August 14, 2005, 16.

44. Kymlicka 2004, 159.

45. Cf. Nederveen Pieterse 2004, ch. 6 on technologies of work, war, and politics.

46. A. Cowell, "In open letter, British Muslims throw harsh criticism at Blair and his policies," *New York Times*, August 13, 2006, 4.

47. Michael Goldfarb, "This is London," *New York Times*, August 13, 2006, WK11.

48. Philips 2006; Malkani 2006; Fauwe and van Amerongen 2006.

49. Tiryakian 2003.

Conclusion
Global multiculture

In light of the arguments in this book, how do we understand and map contemporary cultural trends? And what does this suggest about the kind of world that is emerging? This closing reflection maps how culture plays out in relation to the changing careers of states and nations, and beyond. Let me start with an analytical note on culture and then turn to teasing out the meanings and implications of global multiculture.

My starting point is the distinction between *culture* and *cultures*; I have drawn this in previous work and only briefly sum it up here.[1] *Culture* in a general sense is human software and know-how, all that is learned in the process of being human. This learning is open-ended, never complete, always in flux, and not necessarily bound to a particular location. It is a medium of agency, creativity, and transformation. Then there is culture in the specific sense of "a culture" and *cultures*, or forms of emotional and cognitive learning that occur in social settings such as nations, ethnic groups, localities, and cities, which are usually embedded in civilizations and religions. *Cultures* interact, clash, or harmonize and are mediated through *culture*. It is a mistake to define culture as that which distinguishes people because culture is also what people share; this in fact sums up the two meanings of the word "culture." *Culture* is multilevel and includes commonalities and frictions between *culture* and *cultures*.

As I have noted before, most theories and perspectives consider ethnicity and multiculturalism in relation to the nation state. This is historically shallow because the nation state is a latecomer. And it is inadequate in contemporary times because it underestimates transnational relations. The failure to acknowledge or understand multiethnicity in the past hampers understanding multiethnicity in the present. Thus, bracketing the conventional nation state framework is a key concern. Essentially this concerns the political matrix of the past two hundred years. In international studies a major approach that questions the centrality of the nation state is neo-medievalism. In his 1977 book on the anarchical society, Hedley Bull defines neo-medievalism as a system of "overlapping authorities and crisscrossing loyalties."[2] This theme has been taken up in various approaches. Reflecting on information technology and cyberspace interactions that crosscut geographical boundaries and jurisdictions, Kobrin argues that the future is neo-medieval. The postmodern condition has also been understood as neo-medieval and postmodernism as a neo-baroque sensibility.[3]

A precedent often cited is the medieval city-state system in northern Italy. In urban studies neo-medievalism is a tool for understanding contemporary trends of gated communities and common interest developments (the "secession of the successful"), squatters and informal settlements ("quiet encroachment"), and camps, which along with various nodes of urban power have their precedents in medieval towns.[4] The medieval patterns of overlapping jurisdictions and crisscrossing loyalties are insightful for understanding global multiculture as well.

In the fourteenth century Ibn Khaldun noted the differences between nomadic and sedentary peoples, such as Berbers and Arabs in North Africa. The nomadism approach, taken up by Deleuze and Guattari and scholars of postmodernity, is another counterpoint to the view that assumes nation states as the point of departure and the implicit norm of social behavior. The starting point of global multiculture is that the balance between cultures (sedentary, stationary) and culture (not place bound), between sedentary (integration, assimilation, multiculturalism) and mobile trends (flexible acculturation, transnational culture), is changing toward greater influence of mobility.

Nations and states, the usual points of reference in this discussion, are themselves in flux. Many discussions implicitly overstate their role as frameworks and understate how the frameworks themselves are changing. During the heyday of nation state formation, broadly from 1840 to 1960, nations and states underwent many changes. Particularly since the mid-twentieth century, nation states have been accompanied, and in some respects gradually overtaken by, regional, transnational, and postnational trends. States will no doubt continue to be major strategic formations, but they are changing profoundly due to internationalization, the pooling of sovereignty, and regionalization. The internationalization of states refers to states' growing preoccupation with international regulations and agreements. When this is institutionalized in treaties, covenants, and supranational bodies, it represents a pooling of sovereignty. Regionalization, a growing trend since the mid-twentieth century, refers to regional cooperation from free trade agreements to the deep institutional cooperation of the European Union.

Nations are increasingly composite because of migration. That several diasporas outnumber the population in the nation of origin shows that these trends have been in motion for quite some time. Growing multiethnicity in the course of recent centuries produces a "declining congruence between the nation and the state."[5] In the past this congruence existed as an ideal—as in Herder's romantic identification of people and state—and not as a reality. Now, in view of growing crossborder flows, the reality is receding (rather than approaching), and the ideal is increasingly, though not entirely, passé. An accompanying trend is the "decreasing congruence between spatial location and social formation."[6]

Multiethnicity has been the infrastructure of global interconnectedness since time immemorial. Multiethnicity is perennial and predates and will outlive the nation state. Multiethnicity is regional well before it is national. Ethnicity is in the past and the future of nation states and in both spills over nation state boundaries. It has not merely been states that have been globalizing agents (though many accounts present it that way) but just as much groups and regions within nations and migrants straddling nations. The nation state is a provisional "container" of multiethnicity, strong while the center holds and loose at the seams when the center drifts or is decentered in regional formations or in the vortex of global change. This is a source of growing friction and inevitable conflict according to nineteenth-century notions of "hard sovereignty" and national identity, but sovereignty has been dynamic all along, and twenty-first-century trends are toward pooling of sovereignty and soft sovereignty in view of changing technologies, economies, culture, and polities. Identity is becoming more fluid and multicircuit. But this is not a straightforward process.

Not too long ago ethnic cleansing and forced population transfer were regarded as ordinary tools of statecraft and foreign policy. Examples are the expulsions of Greek Christians from Turkey and Muslims from Greece in the 1920s (regularized in the Lausanne Agreement of 1923),[7] of Palestinians during the creation of Israel, of ethnic Germans from Eastern Europe, and of South Asians from Uganda; the mass transfer that came with the partition of India and Pakistan; population transfers in Indonesia; and, in smaller numbers, the expulsion of Ghanaians from Nigeria.

A major trend is toward the blurring of international and domestic affairs, yet border controls harden in response to the pressures of global inequality and the securitization of migration. Globalization talk is schizophrenic; wide acclaim for the free movement of goods and capital goes together with restrictions on the movement of people and labor. Few economists are consistent and argue for the free movement of labor too.[8] There is a growing recognition that liberalizing migration has a much greater impact on reducing global inequality—particularly because of remittances—than liberalizing trade. However, although international migration ranks as a major problem and global inequality is the main cause behind international migration, liberalizing trade is a priority goal, and reducing global inequality is not.

Consider the structural trends. Global political economy promotes crossborder flows and fosters and requires global cultural literacy. Cyberspace is global, too. Social movements and NGOs straddle boundaries. The global anti-apartheid movement that emerged in the 1970s was one of the first planetary social movements.[9] Between 1970 and 2000 the number of international NGOs quintupled to twenty-five thousand, and between 1990 and 2000 their membership increased by 72 percent.[10] In these times of transnational corporations, world products, world marketing, global brands, planetary social and professional networks, intercontinental pen pals, mail-order brides, and astronaut families, the old accounts of a world neatly compartmentalized in civilizations, religions, nations, states, and their forms of allegiance and belonging no longer fit. We have long entered the post-cubist phase of identity. Global multiculture is an attempt to conceptualize this momentum.

The first, straightforward meaning of global multiculture is that multiculturalism discourse and policy is spreading globally under headings such as human rights and minority rights. Thus existing multiethnicity is increasingly recognized and regulated as "multiculturalism." In this sense some literature refers to global multiculturalism.[11] However, as a term, "global multiculturalism" has limited purchase because—besides general human rights standards—there are no multicultural policies or institutions at the global level.

According to the Swedish anthropologist Ulf Hannerz, there is now a *world culture*, which he gives a supple meaning: "There is now a world culture, but we had better make sure we understand what this means: not a replication of uniformity but an organization of diversity, an increasing interconnectedness of varied local cultures, as well as a development of cultures without a clear anchorage in any one territory. And to this interconnected diversity people can relate in different ways."[12] Interconnected diversity is perceptive, but I think the term "world culture" suggests too much a single cultural field which could be easily thought of as homogeneous. Transnational culture exists in global technology, industrial standards (ISO), world products, global brands, and forms of popular culture as a broad but thin slice of global multiculture. It is not as uniform as it may appear because global cultural signs are translated, domesticated, indigenized, and repackaged. Even science and laboratory practices are culturally diverse.

My interpretation of globalization is that it represents a historical trend for human social cooperation to widen and expand, made possible by growing human capabilities and technologies. However, this is not a linear process, a linear march toward a single destination. The process is uneven, irregular. New channels of communication and influence are taking shape. In 2006, for instance, many pubs in England follow soccer matches via Al Jazeera Sports Plus, with the volume down, because the subscription charges are much lower than the commercial British sports channels.[13] New codes and vocabularies come in vogue. English as a global lingua franca has given rise to "Globish," as a description of global English as a practice and as a movement under the heading "Don't speak English, parlez Globish."[14]

Second, social cooperation includes conflict. Contemporary asymmetric wars are transnational, conflicts and conflict networks straddle boundaries, from the Democratic Republic of Congo's coltan and casserite mines and niche war on the borders of Rwanda to the CIA's "extraordinary rendition" and Guantánamo prison as a transnational site. American security professionals speak of "netwar" and argue that to fight a network (such as Al Qaeda) it takes a network.[15] This cuts two ways. In response to the sprawling networks of the war on terror, surveillance systems and far-flung bases, other networks emerge. And so forth. As such episodes and sites suggest, global multiculture is an irregular, uneven ambience. To give a proper account would take a chaos theory of culture, with curves, fractals, and percolation networks, but for now geological metaphors of strata and marble may do.

The main strata of culture are transnational or global culture, followed by civilizations, religions, nations, ethnicities, subcultures, localities and cities, and the underlying layer of deep culture. In brief, I argue that the overall trend is toward more marble that cuts across strata and flows that permeate units.

The cultural stratum that is most widely shared is hidden beneath difference. Languages differ, but the capacity for language is universal. Grammars differ but are all premised on the possibility of grammar (as in Chomsky's thesis of a "universal grammar"). Nations differ, but they also differ in similar ways. Nation states all have national symbols, which are by definition different (flag, anthem, institutions). Ethnic groups may be similar in the way they articulate their differences, borrowing signs and motifs from the planetary database. In terms of deep culture, we're all in the same boat. Of course this goes much further than is generally acknowledged. Our awareness of human sameness beneath difference is gradually growing. It is growing because of our consciousness of the "blue sphere" as our rendezvous in the universe and because of common concerns such as ecological change and global turbulence.

The next cultural layer of widest generality is *transnational culture* or global culture. It is not always clear what to include in this. Water boils at 100 degrees Celsius the world over. But the metric system, though widely known, is not universally used. Certain developments in science, technology, medicine, product standards, and to some extent popular culture make up a planetary database. Gordon Matthews refers to the "global cultural supermarket."[16] Coca-Cola, McDonald's, Barbie, and Disney are proverbial but also meet growing resistance. Transnational culture largely consists of signs and conventions that are shared because of serendipity and convenience, rather than because of their intrinsic or metaphysical virtues. Time is experienced differently across cultures, but states have agreed on a Universal Standard Time (in 1884 Greenwich, England, was chosen as standard, and by 1929 all major countries had adopted time zones). Transport rules and codes—in airplanes, shipping, automobiles, and rail—are nearly universally shared. Electric appliances the world over have similar functions and, for some reason, different plugs. The use of icons in electronic appliances and computers facilitates communication across languages. The scale and content of transnational culture, by comparison to national culture, will expand as global problems and global problem solving grow. Both necessity and sensibility lead the way. Transnational aesthetics such as modern art and postmodern architecture spread as well.

The next strata that make up global multiculture—more or less in order of descending scale—are civilizations, religions, nations, ethnicities, localities, and cities. These templates of culture all involve a relationship to space. Religions vary in their relationship to place, which is very pronounced in the Abrahamic "religions of the book"; Confucianism, Daoism, and Hinduism are embedded in civilizations; indigenous religions are strongly place-based; whereas place is a distant background in Buddhism (though Buddhism too has its spatial referents, in particular, Sarnath, where Gautama Buddha achieved enlightenment).

The templates of culture are gradually reformatted in the course of use. The beddings remain, but as the water flows differently the contours change.

In the not-so-distant past, civilizations, nations, ethnicities, localities, and cities were the mainstays of culture. Through human history culture has mostly been the arena of *cultures* and their interactions and clashes. Nations profile their identity in contrast to other nations; civilizations demarcate themselves from other civilizations; religions position themselves in relation to other religions; empires contend with other empires and social formations; ethnicities rival other ethnicities or units; localities, cities, and subcultures cooperate and compete with other and wider units; and so forth. These goings-on have occupied most human energy. These interactions unfold both horizontally (nations vying with other nations, etc.) and vertically (such as nations positioning themselves vis-à-vis larger and smaller units, from religions or empires to regions or ethnic groups).

Glimpses of *culture* occasionally appear through the cracks of the interactions and clashes of cultures—culture in the sense of general human know-how and software and in the sense of *deep culture* or human sameness beneath difference. This awareness is often referred to as "transcendence" or rising above mundane differences in works of art, poetry or religious inspiration, or as an esoteric, deeper knowledge, the knowledge of mystery schools that teach that, ultimately, all religions are one and all human groups are similar in their differences. However, most of the time boundary policing takes the upper hand and turf interests, whether territorial or symbolic, prevail, so knowledge of deep culture remains at best dim background knowledge, remotely present but not functionally operative, just as knowing about relativity or quantum physics doesn't affect the Saturday car wash.

The novel factor X that has entered the fray during the past two hundred years, and rapidly so during contemporary accelerated globalization, is the rise of *transnational culture*. Transnational culture blurs the boundaries among units; the compartments separating them become increasingly porous because transnational culture borrows from them indiscriminately and produces novel and irregular combinations. High fashion borrows from ethnic motifs and creates a novel ethnic chic, and so on. Thus the compartments separating units and strata have become porous and transnational culture as a planetary database has grown in scope, is more widely accessible, and exercises its influence across all strata. Civilizations, nations, ethnicities, and localities increasingly involve local-global interplay. All strata of culture include references to and translations of planetary culture, usually in irregular and unpredictable patterns. In economics, politics, and social movements the local and the global are increasingly and intricately intertwined (the conventional term is "glocalization"), and so they are in culture as the conduit and software that enables all these interactions.

The keynotes of global multiculture are increasing glocalization and interplay across cultural strata. Interconnected diversity is one description; others are information and network society. Flows crosscutting levels and functional domains (such as engineering, architecture, transport, media, consumer electronics, finance, and governance) are increasing in frequency, volume, and density. The templates remain—civilizations, languages, religions, nations, subcultures, and ethnicities—but they are being radically transformed and cross-fertilized by influences that straddle boundaries. Eventually there is more marbling than there are strata, and more cross flow than distinct, separate units.

This is not another version of the story of Progress. It is not a straight-forward path to a global culture. Consider the perplexities. Why is it that the overall trend of globalization, or widening social cooperation, comes with—not uniformly so but in many instances—increasing or intensified nationalism, nativism, and ethnic and religious conflicts?

The countertrends are familiar. Thus macro-regionalism often means that micro-regions, released from the exclusive hold of the national center, become more active and reinvent their identity claims. In other words, the larger, expanding scale also activates smaller units. The reason why many smaller units don't nicely line up and merge into the larger framework is because of the legacy and ongoing process of uneven development, and the new emerging opportunity structure. Thus European unification is also a catalyst for a new "Europe of the regions" (northern Italy, Catalonia, Galicia, Brittany, Flanders, etc.). In general terms, smaller units seek to negotiate the terms of their association with larger and expanding patterns of cooperation, often through conflict. These counterpoints to regionalism and globalization are not necessarily straightforward or "log-ical." They are typically ambivalent and influenced by the larger pattern they seek to resist or shape. They are usually influenced by globalization, often in unacknowledged or backdoor ways. They assert difference in order to establish sameness, in equal rights or equal treatment.

Growing multiethnicity—manifesting in migration, multiculturalism, identity politics—prompts a new nativism. Cases in point were and are Enoch Powell in the UK, Jean-Marie le Pen in France, and Samuel Hunting-ton and Pat Buchanan in the U.S. Political correctness eats into the perks of privilege, so lambasting political correctness (hate radio, Bill O'Reilly, Rush Limbaugh), immigration, "global jihadists" (Lou Dobbs), and alien cultural influences becomes a new patriot game and a rampart of nostalgia politics. Ironically, though the new nativism seeks to control that which comes in, it pays little heed to that which goes out—in the American case, all the forms of American influence, economic, cultural, and military that affect the world. And for all the attention bestowed on immigration, the other side of the coin is emigration. For instance, "there are more UK nationals living overseas than there are foreign nationals living in the UK."[17] The graying populations in the West and Japan need immigrants to sustain population levels and national economies; in the end, no patriot games can make up for this structural trend, but they can lend a dark edge to social change.

This is not a straightforward field with ethnic exclusivism, fundamen-talism, nativism, and essentialism neatly aligned on one side and cos-mopolitanism, transnationalism, "global souls," and global culture on the other. Universalism usually has parochial roots. Nativism borrows from internationalism. Vernacular interests deploy transnational metaphors to make their case. The new Right in France used the left-wing language of the "right to difference" to redefine and reassert racism. The Tamil Tigers showed Clint Eastwood spaghetti westerns in their training camps to instill an ethos of tough, combat-ready masculinity.[18] Paramilitaries from Chechnya to Bosnia used Rambo images. So-called Muslim fundamentalists are often among the most modern social forces in their use of new technologies, active publishing, social services, civic engagement, and transnational outreach. Localist ethnonationalist movements are often supported by émigrés in distant lands, who themselves have become transnationals yet engage in "long-distance nationalism." Roland Robertson refers to these trends as the "universalization of particularism" (in combination with the "particularization of universalism").[19]

Ethnicity is multipurpose cultural affinity and cultural resources, cultural habitus and vocabulary, emotional and limbic resonance. Since ethnicity implies awareness of other social and ethnic groups, it is relational. The most salient forms of ethnicity—salient because of ethnic competition and conflict—are often held to be inward looking ("ethnic fundamentalism") but are in reality usually bicultural because competition requires awareness of the actions of competing groups. Much that passes for "ethnic conflict" is conflict over political, development, and ecological resources that bears no intrinsic relation to ethnicity. Indigenous peoples probably represent the most classic instance of ethnic exclusivism. Most indigenous peoples are now globally wired in indigenous peoples' networks such as the World Council of Indigenous Peoples established in 1975, the representatives of which meet each August in the UN Conference of Indigenous Peoples in Geneva. Many cooperate with environmental organizations and NGOs, local and distant, and are parties in international law and intellectual property and resource disputes.

Currents of influence crisscross. Socialism borrows from Catholicism and vice versa. Lenin and Che, James Bond and Bruce Lee, images of masculinity derived from Hollywood and Hong Kong movies exercise broad influence. Images of femininity derived from media and beauty contests, fashion, and cosmetics advertising redefine femininity and beauty standards in many cultures. Conversely, haute couture and media borrow local icons (Cleopatra) and images—ethnic designs, lines and styles, or local bangles—to rejuvenate visual and fashion trends. The local, in some form, is in the planetary database and the planetary database is being reworked in the local. The templates of difference take on diverse forms and hues through interplay and cross borrowing between levels, just as marble mingling strata. *Culture*, general software, grows in proportion to *cultures*, local software. Yet *culture* also reinvigorates *cultures*, and global software is nothing without local software. The layers that make up global multiculture include transnational culture, cultures, and deep culture (an overview is in Table 9.1).

Table 9.1. Layers of global multiculture

Layers of culture	Dimensions	Key words
Transnational culture	Translocal influence and cooperation in technology, media, popular culture, art, functional domains, and professions	Planetary database, global cultural supermarket
Cultures	Civilizations, religions Nations Ethnicities, subcultures Localities, cities	Spatially based templates
Deep culture	Human software, human sameness beneath difference	Deep background knowledge

Global multiculture, then, is the growing interplay and mix of units and layers of culture that have long been largely separate. Global multiculture can be understood as neo-medieval, nomadic, and kaleidoscopic. Neo-medievalism is an attractive perspective because it combines changing institutions and structures (overlapping jurisdictions) and changing identities (crisscrossing loyalties) in a single framework. Global multiculture is nomadic because information flows are mobile. It's not place-less but it dislocates and recombines places. Manhattan's Times Square renovated under Mayor Giuliani comes to look like Las Vegas or a Disney town and Las Vegas builds its New York/New York entertainment center.[20] Accelerated globalization multiplies the sources of the self because individuals can access multiple organizational options and identify in multiple ways (as a local, national, regional, world citizen, etc.). This unsettles identity for the points of reference (places, cultures, and values) are in flux and can be accessed from diverse vantage points. These trends are messy and disorganized from the viewpoint of the spatial templates of cultures but from the viewpoint of global multiculture show different kinds of organization. In the maelstrom of the information age, cultures turn into confetti of bits of information and snippets of meaning that are continually decontextualized and recontextualized, fragmented and regrouped, according to fleeting logics. These ephemeral logics may well have changed between the moment of composition and the moment of reception (as in accessing a website or blog). The encyclopedia of human knowledge and the perennial philosophy is rearranged in internet info bits, media sound bites, marketing messages in kaleidoscopic meanings that change with a twist. Global multiculture is a mirror and kaleidoscope of changing times. This is not merely about the loss of fixed moorings and stable meanings and foundations but also about opening up different and possibly deeper strata of meaning and styles of understanding. Confetti culture and snippets of meaning rearranged in kaleidoscopic moments may yield glimpses and understandings of deep culture that were hitherto hidden. Inconvenient truths may yet become convenient.

The conventional discussions of ethnicity and multiculturalism from national viewpoints are incomplete and unreal if they don't take into account overall global changes. It is as if nation states want to have globalization on their terms, domesticated and custom fit, picturesque like theme park multiculturalism, but don't concede the many ways, including back-door ways, in which they shape and interact with globalization and the agency this involves and evokes.

Multicircuit identification and flexible acculturation are cultural adaptations to the new ecology of contemporary globalization. These trends are not new per se, but they are new in degree and scope. In the course of the twentieth century and at the turn of the millennium this gradual shift increasingly takes on the momentum of a quantum leap. This ushers in a social formation that represents a new phase of globalization marked by widening and crisscrossing circles of multicircuit identification—global multiculture. The attempts to reestablish the old divides, to invoke a "clash of civilizations," to revive patriotism and nativism, represent real trends, but since the overall species ecology is changing, the old compartmentalizations don't have time on their side. Because this is not an even field (global culture) and is not likely to become one, we need a different term: global multiculture.

Notes

1. Nederveen Pieterse 2003, ch. 4.
2. Quoted in Winn 2004, 3.
3. Kobrin 1998; Calabrese 1992.
4. AlSayyad and Roy 2006.
5. Carment 1994, 560.
6. AlSayyad 2004, 9.
7. Clark 2006; Volkan and Itzkowitz 1994.
8. Bhagwati 1997, 2003; *Migration in an interconnected world* 2005.
9. Thörn 2006.
10. Anheier and Glasius 2006.
11. For example, Cornwell and Stoddard 2001.
12. Hannerz 1996, 106.
13. D. Carvajal, "Al Jazeera on television is causing trouble for British pubs, but it's not political," *New York Times*, August 21, 2006, C6.
14. See "Globish" at the Wikipedia Web site and in Nerrière 2004.
15. Arquilla and Ronfeldt 2001.

16. Matthews 2000. On non-western contributions to global culture, see Appiah and Gates 1997.

17. As of 2005, four and a half million British passport holders live overseas; Sriskandarajah 2006.

18. Silva 2001.

19. Robertson 1992.

20. AlSayyad 2004.

Bibliography

Note: Articles in newspapers and weeklies are referenced only in the endnotes to each chapter, not in the bibliography.

Abdo, Geneive. *No God but God: Egypt and the triumph of Islam.* New York: Oxford UP, 2000.

Abu-Lughod, Janet L. *Before European hegemony: the world-system, A.D. 1250–1350.* New York: Oxford UP, 1989.

Achcar, Gilbert. *The clash of barbarisms: September 11 and the making of the new world disorder.* New York: Monthly Review Press, 2003.

Adas, Emin. *The prophet and profit: the rise of Islamist entrepreneurs and new interpretations of Islam in Turkey.* University of Illinois at Urbana-Champaign: Ph.D. dissertation, 2003.

Ahmed, Akbar S. *Postmodernism and Islam.* London: Routledge, 1992.

Ahmed, Durre S., ed. *Gendering the spirit: women, religion and the post-colonial response.* London: Zed, 2003.

Ake, Claude. "A world of political ethnicity," in *The historical dimension of development: change and conflict in the South.* The Hague: Ministry of Foreign Affairs, 1994, 49–54.

Alatas, Syed Farid. "A Khaldunian exemplar for a historical sociology for the South," *Current Sociology,* 54, 3, 2006a: 397–411.

———. "From Jāmi'ah to University: multiculturalism and Christian-Muslim dialogue," *Current Sociology,* 54, 1, 2006b: 112–32.

Al-Azmeh, Aziz. *Islams and modernities.* London: Verso, 1993.

———. *Ibn Khaldun: an essay in reinterpretation.* Budapest: Central European UP, 2003.

Alba, R. D. *Ethnic identity: the transformation of white America.* New Haven, Conn.: Yale UP, 1990.

Ali, Y. "Muslim women and the politics of ethnicity and culture in North England," in G. Saghal and N. Yuval-Davis, eds., *Refusing holy orders: women and fundamentalism in Britain*. London: Virago, 1992, 101–23.

AlSayyad, Nezar. "The end of tradition, or the tradition of endings?" in AlSayyad, ed., *The end of tradition?* New York: Routledge, 2004, 1–28.

AlSayyad, Nezar, and Ananya Roy. "Medieval modernity: on citizenship and urbanism in a global era," *Space and Polity*, 10, 1, 2006: 1–20.

AlSayyad, Nezar, and Manuel Castells, eds. *Muslim Europe or Euro-Islam*. Lanham, Md.: Lexington Books, 2002.

Ames, M. M. *Cannibal tours and glass boxes: the anthropology of museums*. Vancouver: U of British Columbia P, 1992.

Amin, Ash. *Ethnicity and the multicultural city: living with diversity*. Liverpool: Economic and Social Research Council Cities Programme, 2002.

Amin, A., and N. Thrift. "Globalization, institutional thickness and local prospects," *Revue d'Economie Régionale et Urbaine*, 3, 1993: 405–27.

Amin, S. *The Arab nation*. London: Zed, 1978.

Amponsem, G. *Global trading and business networks among Ghanaians: an interface of the local and the global*. Bielefeld University: Ph.D. dissertation, 1996.

Anderson, B. "The New World disorder," *New Left Review*, 190, 1992: 3–14.

Anderson, Walter T. "Communities in a world of open systems," *Futures*, 31, 5, 1999: 457–63.

Anheier, H., and M. Glasius. "Introduction," in H. Anheier, M. Glasius, and M. Kaldor, eds., *Global civil society 2005/06*. London: Sage, 2006.

Anzaldúa, G. *Borderland/La Frontera*. San Francisco: Spinsters/Ann Lute, 1987.

Appiah, K. A. *In my father's house: Africa in the philosophy of culture*. Oxford: Oxford UP, 1992.

Appiah, K. A., and H. L. Gates Jr., eds. *The dictionary of global culture*. New York: Knopf, 1997.

Araeen, R. "From primitivism to ethnic arts," *Third Text*, 1, 1989.

Archer-Straw, P., T. Phillips, and J. Mack, eds. *Africa: the art of a continent*. London: Royal Academy of Arts, 1995.

Archibugi, D., and D. Held, eds. *Cosmopolitan democracy: agenda for a new world order*. Cambridge: Polity, 1995.

Armstrong, Karen. "Islam through history," in J. F. Hoge Jr. and G. Rose, eds., *How did this happen? Terrorism and the new war*. New York: Public Affairs, 2001, 53–70.

Arquilla, J., and D. Ronfeldt. *Networks and netwars: the future of terror, crime and militancy*. Santa Monica, Calif.: Rand and National Defense Research Institute, 2001.

Asante, M. K. *Afrocentricity*. Trenton, N.J.: Africa World Press, 2nd rev. ed., 1988.

Atasoy, Seymen. "Globalization and Turkey: from capitulations to contemporary civilization," in Ismael, 1999, 257–70.

Back, L., and V. Quaade. "Dream utopias, nightmare realities: imaging race and culture within the world of Benetton advertising," *Third Text*, 22, 1993: 65–80.

Bajunid, Omar Farouk, ed. "Arab communities and networks in South and Southeast Asia," special focus, *Asian J of Social Science*, 32, 3, 2004: 325–457.

Bakar, Osman. "Islam's destiny: a bridge between East and West," *JUST Commentary*, 33, 1996: 1–5.

Baker, Raymond W. "Egypt in the space and time of globalism," in Ismael, 1999, 243–56.

———. *Islam without fear: Egypt and the new Islamists.* Cambridge: Harvard UP, 2004.

Barber, B. R. *Jihad vs. McWorld.* New York: Times Books, 1995.

Barr, A., and J. Toye. "It's not what you know—it's who you know! Economic analyses of social capital," *Development Research Insights*, 34, 2000: 1–2.

Barraclough, Steven. "Al-Azhar: between the government and the Islamists," *Middle East J*, 52, 2, 1998: 236–49.

Bauman, Z. "Identity: then, now, what for?" in M. Kempny and A. Jawlowska, eds., *Identity in transformation: postmodernity, post-communism and modernization.* Westport, Conn.: Praeger, 2002, 19–31.

Bax, Mart. "Warlords, priests and the politics of ethnic cleansing: a case-study from rural Bosnia-Hercegovina," *Ethnic and Racial Studies*, 23, 1, 2000: 16–36.

Bayart, J-F., S. Ellis, and B. Hibou. *The criminalization of the state in Africa.* London: James Currey, 1999.

Beck, Ulrich. *What is globalization?* Oxford: Blackwell, 2000.

———. *Cosmopolitan vision.* Cambridge: Polity, 2006.

Beeley, B. "Islam as a global political force," in A. G. McGrew and P. G. Lewis, eds., *Global politics.* Cambridge: Polity, 1992, 293–311.

Bell-Fialkoff, A. "A brief history of ethnic cleansing," *Foreign Affairs*, 72, 3, 1993: 110–21.

Benard, Cheryl. *Civil democratic Islam: partners, resources, and strategies.* Santa Monica, Calif.: Rand, 2003.

Bennett, T. *The birth of the museum: history, theory, politics.* London: Routledge, 1995.

Berger, M. "Race and representation: the production of the normal," in *Race and representation.* New York: Hunter College Art Gallery, 1987, 10–16.

Berghe, P. van den. *Race and racism: a comparative perspective.* New York: John Wiley, 1978.

Bernal, Martin. *Black Athena: Afroasiatic roots of classical civilization: the fabrication of Ancient Greece, 1785–1985.* London: Free Association Press, 1987.

Bernard, A., H. Helmich, and P. B. Lehning, eds. *Civil society and international cooperation.* Paris: OECD, 1998.

Bernasconi, R. "'Stuck inside of Mobile with the Memphis Blues again': interculturalism and the conversation of races," in Willett, 1998, 276–97.

Bhabha, Homi K. *The location of culture.* London: Routledge, 1994.

Bhagwati, J. *A stream of windows: unsettling reflections on trade, immigration and democracy.* Cambridge, Mass.: MIT Press, 1997.

———. "Borders beyond control," *Foreign Affairs*, 82, 1, 2003: 98–104.

Blue, Gregory. "Gobineau on China: race theory, the 'yellow peril,' and the critique of modernity," *J of World History*, 10, 1, 1999: 93–139.

Boase, R. *The origin and meaning of courtly love.* Manchester: Manchester UP, 1977.

———. *The troubadour revival.* London: Routledge and Kegan Paul, 1978.

Bonacich, E., and R. P. Applebaum. *Behind the label: inequality in the Los Angeles apparel industry.* Berkeley and Los Angeles: U of California P, 2000.

Borjas, George J. "Globalization and immigration," in Weinstein, 2005, 77–96.

Bose, S. "State crises and nationalities conflict in Sri Lanka and Yugoslavia," *Comparative Political Studies*, 28, 1, 1995: 87–116.

Boubakri, H. "Les entrepreneurs migrants d'Europe: dispositifs communautaires et économie ethnique; le cas des entrepreneurs tunisiens en France," *Cultures et Conflicts*, 33–34, 1999: 69–88.

Boucher, Jerry, Dan Landis, and K. A. Clark, eds. *Ethnic conflict: international perspectives*. Newbury Park, Calif.: Sage, 1987.

Boullata, K. *Faithful witnesses: Palestinian children recreate their world*. Brooklyn, N.Y.: Interlink, 1990.

Bourdieu, P. "Les modes de domination," *Actes de la recherche en sciences sociale*, 2, 2–3, 1976: 122–32.

Bourdieu, P., and J-C. Passeron. *Reproduction in education, society and culture*. London: Sage, 2nd ed., 1990.

Bourhis, R. Y., L. C. Moïse, S. Perreault, and S. Senécal. "Toward an interactive acculturation model: a social psychological approach," *International J of Psychology*, 32, 6, 1997: 369–86.

Boyd, Willard L. "Museums as centers of controversy," *Daedalus*, 128, 3, 1999: 185–228.

Brass, Paul R. *Ethnicity and nationalism: theory and comparison*. New Delhi: Sage, 1991.

———. *The production of Hindu-Muslim violence in contemporary India*. Seattle: U of Washington P, 2003.

Brennan, Timothy. *Wars of position: the cultural politics of left and right*. New York: Columbia UP, 2006.

Britt, D., ed. *Art and power: Europe under the dictators, 1930–45*. London: Thames and Hudson, 1995.

Broertjes, P. I., ed. *Het fenomeen Fortuyn*. Amsterdam: De Volkskrant, Meulenhoff, 2002.

Brookhiser, R. *The way of the WASP*. New York: Free Press, 1991.

Brubaker, Rogers. "Ethnicity without groups," in Wimmer et al., 2004, 34–52.

Buber, M. *I and Thou*. New York: Charles Scribner's Sons, 1970.

Bulmer, M., and J. Solomos, eds. *Ethnic and racial studies today*. London: Routledge, 1999.

Burdsey, D. "'One of the lads'? Dual ethnicity and assimilated ethnicities in the careers of British Asian professional footballers," *Ethnic and Racial Studies*, 27, 5, 2004: 757–79.

Burgess, Chris. "Maintaining identities: discourses of homogeneity in a rapidly globalizing Japan," *Electronic J of Contemporary Japanese Studies*, April 19, 2004, http://www.japanesestudies.org.uk/articles/Burgess.html (January 25, 2007).

Burgin, V., ed. *Thinking photography*. London: Macmillan, 1982.

Burke, Edmund, III. "Islamic history as world history: Marshall Hodgson, 'The venture of Islam,'" *International J of Middle East Studies*, 10, 2, 1979: 241–64.

Burke, P. *Popular culture in early modern Europe*. New York: Harpertorch, 1978.

Burstein, Meyer. "Consistency and precision in public policy," in Saunders and Haljan, 2003, 289–96.

Buruma, Ian. *Murder in Amsterdam: the death of Theo van Gogh and the limits of tolerance*. London: Penguin, 2006.

Cahm, E., and V. Fisera, eds. *Socialism and nationalism in contemporary Europe, 1848–1945*. 3 vols. London: Spokesman, 1980.

Calabrese, Omar. *Neo-Baroque: a sign of the times*. Princeton, N.J.: Princeton UP, 1992.

Calhoun, C., P. Price, and A. Timmer, eds. *Understanding September 11*. New York: New Press, 2002.

Calhoun, Craig. "Nationalism and civil society: democracy, diversity and self-determination," in Calhoun, ed., *Social theory and the politics of identity*. Oxford: Blackwell, 1994, 304–35.

Camilleri, J. A., and C. Muzaffar, eds. *Globalization: the perspectives and experiences of the religious traditions of Asia Pacific*. Petaling Jaya: International Movement for a Just World, 1998.

Can, Wang. *Ethnic groups in China*. Beijing: China Intercontinental Press, 2004.

Carment, D. "The ethnic dimension in world politics: theory, policy and early warning," *Third World Quarterly*, 15, 4, 1994: 551–82.

Cerny, P. G. *The changing architecture of politics: structure, agency, and the future of the state*. London: Sage, 1990.

Chabal, P., and J-F. Daloz. *Africa works: disorder as political instrument*. London: James Currey, 1999.

Cheah, Pheng, and Bruce Robbins, eds. *Cosmopolitics: thinking and feeling beyond the nation*. Minneapolis: U of Minnesota P, 1998.

Chen, Xiangming. *As borders bend: transnational spaces on the Pacific rim*. Boulder, Colo.: Rowman & Littlefield, 2005.

Chen, Yong. *Chinese San Francisco, 1850–1943: a trans-Pacific community*. Edited by G. Chang. Stanford, Calif.: Stanford UP, 2000.

Chicago Cultural Studies Group. "Critical multiculturalism," in Goldberg, ed., 1994, 114–39.

Choenni, A. *Bazaar in de metropool: allochtone detailhandel in Amsterdam en achtergronden van haar locale begrenzing*. Amsterdam: Emporium, 2000.

Chua, Amy. *World on Fire*. New York: Doubleday, 2003.

Clark, B. *Twice a stranger: the mass expulsions that forged modern Greece and Turkey*. Cambridge: Harvard UP, 2006.

Clifford, James. "Four Northwest Coast museums: travel reflections," in Karp and Lavine, 1991, 212–54.

———. "Looking several ways: anthropology and native heritage in Alaska," *Current Anthropology*, 45, 1, 2003: 1–19.

Clifford, J., and G. Marcus, eds. *Writing culture: the poetics and politics of ethnography*. Berkeley and Los Angeles: U of California P, 1986.

Cobas, J. A. "Six problems in the sociology of the ethnic economy," *Sociological Perspectives*, 32, 2, 1989: 201–14.

Cobban, A. *The nation state and national self-determination*. New York: Thomas Crowell, rev. ed., 1970.

Coleman, J. S. "Social capital in the creation of human capital," *American J of Sociology*, 94, 1988: 95–120.

Cooley, J. *Unholy wars: Afghanistan, America and international terrorism*. London: Pluto, 1999.

Cooper, R. *The postmodern state and the world order*. London: Foreign Policy Centre, 2000.

Coquery-Vidrovitch, C. "Du bon usage de l'ethnicité," *Le Monde diplomatique*, July 1994.

Cornell, S., and D. Hartmann. *Ethnicity and race: making identities in a changing world*. Thousand Oaks, Calif.: Pine Forge Press, 1998.

Cornwell, Grant H., and Eva W. Stoddard, eds. *Global multiculturalism: comparative perspectives on ethnicity, race and nation*. Lanham, Md.: Rowman & Littlefield, 2001.

Cotesta, Vittorio. *Sociologia dei conflitti etnici*. Roma: Ed. Laterza, 6th ed., 2005.

Cotthem, C. Villa van. "More than market: the field of business in intercultural space." The Hague: Institute of Social Studies Research Paper, 1999.

Craig, Gordon A. *The Germans*. 1982. Reprint, New York, Meridian, 1991.

Crawford, Darryl. "Chinese capitalism: cultures, the Southeast Asian region and economic globalisation," *Third World Quarterly*, 21, 1, 2000: 69–86.

Crimp, D. "On the museum's ruins," in H. Foster, ed., *Postmodern culture*. London: Pluto, 1985.

Csete, Anne. "China's ethnicities: state ideology and policy in historical perspective," in Cornwell and Stoddard, 2001, 287–308.

Cudd, Ann E. "Psychological explanations of oppression," in Willett, 1998, 187–215.

Cummins, Ian. *Marx, Engels and national movements*. New York: St. Martin's, 1980.

Curtin, P. D. *Crosscultural trade in world history*. Cambridge: Cambridge UP, 1984.

d'Andrea, L., R. d'Arca, and D. Mezzana. *Handbook on the social and economic integration practices of immigrants in Europe*. Rome: CERFE, 1998.

David, Kumar, and Santasilan Kadirgamar, eds. *Ethnicity: identity, conflict, crisis*. Hong Kong: Arena, 1989.

Dávila, A. *Latinos Inc.: the marketing and making of a people*. Berkeley and Los Angeles: U of California P, 2001.

Delbanco, A. "Pluralism and its discontents," *Transition*, 55, 1992: 83–93.

Denitch, Bogdan. *Ethnic nationalism: the tragic death of Yugoslavia*. Minneapolis: U of Minnesota P, 1994.

Denoon, D., M. Hudson, G. McCormack, and T. Morris-Suzuki, eds. *Multicultural Japan: palaeolithic to postmodern*. Cambridge: Cambridge UP, 1996.

Deth, J. W. van, M. Maraffi, K. Newton, and P. F. Whiteley, eds. *Social capital and European democracy*. London: Routledge, 1999.

Deutscher, Isaac. *The non-Jewish Jew and other essays*. London: Merlin Press, 1981.

Dick-Read, R. *The phantom voyagers: evidence of Indonesian settlement in Africa in ancient times*. Winchester: Thurlton, 2005.

Dieleman, F. "Multicultural Holland: myth or reality?" in R. King, ed., *Mass migrations in Europe: the legacy and the future*. London: Belhaven, 1993, 118–35.

Dikötter, F. *The discourse of race in modern China*. Stanford, Calif.: Stanford UP, 1992.

Dobbin, C. *Asian entrepreneurial minorities: conjoint communities in the making of the world-economy, 1570–1940*. Richmond, Surrey: Curzon Press, 1996.

Dodds, J. D., ed. *Al-Andalus: the art of Islamic Spain*. New York: Metropolitan Museum of Art, 1992.

Donald, J., and A. Rattansi, eds. *"Race," culture and difference*. London: Sage, 1992.

Dorronsoro, Giles. *Revolution unending: Afghanistan, 1979 to the present*. Translated by J. King. New York: Columbia UP, 2004.

Draper, Ian. "Britain: acceptance not integration," *Le Monde diplomatique*, March 2005: 5.

Drinnon, Richard. *Facing West: the metaphysics of Indian-hating and empire-building*. Minneapolis: U of Minnesota P, 1980.

Duijzings, Ger. *Religion and the politics of identity in Kosovo*. New York: Columbia UP, 2000.

————. "Ethnic unmixing under the aegis of the west: a transnational approach to the breakup of Yugoslavia," *Bulletin of the Royal Institute for Inter-Faith Studies*, 5, 2, 2004: 1–16.

Duncan, Carol. "Art museums and the ritual of citizenship," in Karp and Lavine, 1991, 88–103.

————. *The aesthetics of power: essays in critical art history*. Cambridge: Cambridge UP, 1993.

Durham, J., and M. T. Alves. "Complaints and discoveries," *Lusitania*, 5, 1993: 130–38.

Dwyer, D., and S. R. Drakakis, eds. *Ethnicity and development: geographical perspectives*. Chichester: Wiley, 1996.

Eaton, Richard M. "Islamic history as global history," in M. Adas, ed., *Islamic and European expansion: the forging of a global order*. Philadelphia: Temple UP, 1993, 1–36.

Edwards, S. E. "Photography and the representation of the other," *Third Text*, 16/17, 1991: 157–72.

Eisenberg, A. "Trust, exploitation and multiculturalism," University of Victoria, British Columbia, 1999, unpublished paper.

Elias, N. *The civilising process*. Translated by E. Jephcott. Oxford: Blackwell, 1994.

Eriksen, T. H. *Ethnicity and nationalism: anthropological perspectives*. London: Pluto, 1993.

Ernst, Carl W. *Eternal garden: mysticism, history, and politics at a South Asian Sufi Center*. Albany: State U of New York P, 1992.

Esman, M. J. "Ethnic politics: how unique is the Middle East?" in Esman and Rabinovich, 1988, 271–88.

————. *Ethnic politics*. Ithaca, N.Y.: Cornell UP, 1994.

————. "Ethnic pluralism: strategies for conflict management," in Wimmer et al., 2004, 203–11.

Esman, M. J., and I. Rabinovich. *Ethnicity, pluralism, and the state in the Middle East*. Ithaca, N.Y.: Cornell UP, 1988.

Esposito, John L. *The Islamic threat: myth or reality?* New York: Oxford UP, 1992.

Ethnic Notions: black images in the white mind. Berkeley, Calif.: Berkeley Art Center, 1982.

Etzioni, Amitai. "Opening Islam," *Society*, 39, 5, 2002: 29–35.

Exotic Europeans. London: South Bank Centre, 1991.

Exotische welten, Europäische phantasien. Stuttgart: Cantz, 1987.

Fabian, J. *Time and the other: how anthropology makes its object*. New York: Columbia UP, 1983.

Falk, R. "False universalism and the geopolitics of exclusion: the case of Islam," Princeton University Center of International Studies, 1996, unpublished paper.

Fallaci, Oriana. *The rage and the pride*. Milan: Rizzoli, 2002.

Fauwe, L. de, and A. van Amerongen. *Kasba Holland*. Amsterdam: Atlas, 2006.

Favell, A. "Globalisation, immigrants and Euro-elites: questioning the transnational social power of migrants," unpublished paper, 2001.

Fedderke, J., R. de Kadt, and J. Luiz. "Economic growth and social capital: a critical reflection," *Theory and Society*, 28, 1999: 709–45.

Feffer, J. *Shock waves: eastern Europe after the revolutions*. Boston: South End, 1992.

Festival of India in the United States, 1985–1986. Edited by L. Frankel. New York: Abrams, 1985.

Findley, Carter Vaughn. *The Turks in world history*. London: Oxford UP, 2005.

Fine, Ben. "Social capital and the realm of the intellect," *Economic and Political Weekly*, March 3, 2001.

Fisman, R. "Preferential credit? Ethnic and indigenous firms vie for equal access," *Development Research Insights*, 34, 2000: 2–3.

Flere, S. "Cognitive adequacy of sociological theories in explaining ethnic antagonism in Yugoslavia," in K. Rupesinghe, P. King, and O. Vorkunova, eds., *Ethnicity and conflict in a post-communist world: the Soviet Union, eastern Europe and China*. New York: St. Martin's, 1992, 251–70.

Fohrbeck, K., and H. Kuijpers, eds. *Van totem tot lifestyle*. Amsterdam: Koninklijk Instituut voor de Tropen, 1987.

Fohrbeck, K., and A. J. Wiesand. *"Wir Eingeborenen": zivilisierte wilde und exotische Europäer/magie und aufklärung im kulturvergleich*. Hamburg: Rowohlt, 2nd ed., 1983.

Fong, Eric, and Linda Lee, eds. "The Chinese ethnic economy," *Asian and Pacific Migration J*, special issue, 10, 1, 2001.

Foqué, René. "Law's concept of a multicultural society," in Saunders and Haljan, 2003, 105–18.

Frank, A. G. *Re Orient: global economy in the Asian age*. Berkeley and Los Angeles: U of California P, 1998.

Frank, Thomas. *One market under god: extreme capitalism, market populism and the end of economic democracy*. New York: Doubleday, 2000.

Fraser, Angus. *The Gypsies*. Oxford: Blackwell, 2nd ed., 1995.

Fraser, Nancy. "From redistribution to recognition? Dilemmas of justice in a 'postsocialist' age," in Willett, 1998, 19–49.

Fukuyama, F. "Social capital and the global economy," *Foreign Affairs*, 74, 5, 1995: 89–103.

Fulford, R. "Into the heart of the matter," *Rotunda*, 24, 1, 1991: 19–29.

Furnivall, J. S. *Netherlands India: a study of plural economy*. Cambridge: Cambridge UP, 1939.

———. *Colonial policy and practice: a comparative study of Burma and Netherlands India*. New York: New York UP, 1956.

Furuchi, Y., and K. Nakamoto, eds. *Asian modernism: diverse developments in Indonesia, the Philippines, and Thailand*. Tokyo: Japan Foundation Asia Center, 1995.

Gagnon, V. P., Jr. *The myth of ethnic war: Serbia and Croatia in the 1990s*. Ithaca, N.Y.: Cornell UP, 2004.

Gans, Herbert. "Symbolic ethnicity: the future of ethnic groups and cultures in America," *Ethnic and Racial Studies*, 2, 1979: 1–20.

Ganster, Paul, and David E. Lorey, eds. *Borders and border politics in a globalizing world*. Oxford: SR Books, 2005.

Gatsché, R. *Inventions of difference: on Jacques Derrida*. Cambridge: Harvard UP, 1994.

Geertz, Clifford. *Islam observed: religious development in Morocco and Indonesia*. Chicago: U of Chicago P, 1968.

———. "Which way to Mecca?" *New York Review of Books*, June 12, 2003: 27–30.

Geisler, Michael E., ed. *National symbols, fractured identities*. Hanover, N.H.: UP of New England, 2005.

Ghai, Yash, ed. *Autonomy and ethnicity: negotiating competing claims in multi-ethnic states*. Cambridge: Cambridge UP, 2000.

Gidley, M., ed. *Representing others: white views of indigenous peoples*. Exeter: U of Exeter P, 1992.

Gilsenan, M. *Recognizing Islam: religion and society in the modern Arab world*. New York: Pantheon, 1982.

Gold, S. J., and I. Light. "Ethnic economies and social policy," *Research in Social Movements, Conflicts and Change*, 22, 2000: 165–91.

Goldberg, David T. "Introduction: multicultural conditions," 1994, in Goldberg, ed., 1994, 1–41.

———, ed. *Multiculturalism: a critical reader*. Oxford: Blackwell, 1994.

Golding, Sue, ed. *The eight technologies of otherness*. London: Routledge, 1997.

Goldstein-Gidoni, Ofra. "The production and consumption of 'Japanese culture' in the global cultural market," *J of Consumer Culture*, 5, 2, 2005: 155–79.

Goldstone, Jack A. "States, terrorists, and the clash of civilizations," in Calhoun, Price, and Timmer, 2002, 139–58.

Göle, Nilufer. "Snapshots of Islamic modernities," *Daedalus*, 129, 1, 2000: 91–117.

Goonatilake, Susantha. "The wandering self between localization and globalization," in Nederveen Pieterse and Parekh, 1995, 225–39.

Gordon, P. H. "Bush's Middle East vision," *Survival*, 45, 1, 2003: 155–65.

Gotham, Kevin F. "Marketing mardi gras: commodification, spectacle and the political economy of tourism in New Orleans," *Urban Studies*, 39, 10, 2002: 1735–56.

Goudsblom, J. *Dutch society*. New York: Random House, 1967.

Graham, Helen, and Jo Labanyi, eds. *Spanish cultural studies: an introduction*. Oxford: Oxford UP, 1995.

Graham, R., ed. *The idea of race in Latin America, 1870–1940*. Austin: U of Texas P, 1990.

Griffin, Keith. "Culture and economic growth: the state and globalization," in J. Nederveen Pieterse, ed., *Global futures*. London: Zed, 2000, 189–202.

Grossberg, Lawrence, Cary Nelson, and Paula Treichler, eds. *Cultural studies*. New York: Routledge, 1992.

Groys, B. *The total art of Stalinism: avant-garde, aesthetic dictatorship, and beyond*. Princeton, N.J.: Princeton UP, 1992.

Guideri, R., and F. Pellizi. "'Smoking mirrors'—modern polity and ethnicity," in R. Guideri, F. Pellizi, and S. J. Tambiah, eds., *Ethnicities and nations: processes of interethnic relations in Latin America, southeast Asia, and the Pacific*. Houston: Rothko Chapel, 1988, 7–38.

Gunn, G. C. *First globalization: the Eurasian exchange, 1500–1800*. Lanham, Md.: Rowman & Littlefield, 2003.

Gupta, S., ed. *Disrupted borders*. London: Rivers Oram Press, 1993.

Gurian, E. H. "Noodling around with exhibition opportunities," in Karp and Lavine, 1991, 176–90.

Haberfellner, R. "Ethnische Ökonomien als Forschungsgegenstand der Sozialwissenschaften," *SWS Rundschau*, 40, 1, 2000: 43–62.

Haberfellner, R., and M. Böse. "'Ethnische' Ökonomien," in H. Fassman, ed., *Abgrenzen, ausgrenzen, aufnehmen: empirische befunde zu fremdenfeindlichkeit und integration*. Klagenfurt: Drava Verlag, 1999, 75–94.

Halabi, Yakub. "Orientalism and U.S. democratization policy in the Middle East," *International Studies*, 36, 1999: 375–92.

Hall, Stuart. "New ethnicities," in Donald and Rattansi, 1992, 52–59.

———. "Who needs identity?" in S. Hall and P. du Gay, eds., *Questions of cultural identity*. London: Sage, 1996.

Halter, Marilyn. *Shopping for identity: the marketing of ethnicity*. New York: Schocken, 2000.

Hamzawy, Amr. "Exploring theoretical and programmatic changes in contemporary Islamist discourse: the journal *Al-Manar al-Jadid*," in A. Karam, ed., *Transnational political Islam*. London: Pluto, 2004, 120–46.

Hannerz, Ulf. *Cultural complexity*. New York: Columbia UP, 1992a.

———. *Culture, cities and the world*. Amsterdam: Centre for Metropolitan Research, 1992b.

———. *Transnational connections: culture, people, places*. London: Routledge, 1996.

Harris, N. *National liberation*. London: IB Tauris, 1990.

Hassan, Riaz. "Globalization's challenge to the Islamic ummah," *Asian J of Social Science*, 34, 2, 2006: 311–39.

Hayden, Patrick, and Chamsy el-Ojeili, eds. *Confronting globalization: humanity, justice and the renewal of politics*. London: Palgrave, 2005.

Hechter, M. *Internal colonialism: the Celtic fringe in British national development, 1536–1966*. London: Routledge and Kegan Paul, 1975.

Hefner, R. W. "Introduction: multiculturalism and citizenship in Malaysia, Singapore, and Indonesia," in R. W. Hefner, ed., *The politics of multiculturalism: pluralism and citizenship in Malaysia, Singapore, and Indonesia*. Honolulu: Hawaii UP, 2001, 1–58.

Hirsi Ali, Ayaan. *The caged virgin: an emancipation proclamation for women and Islam*. New York: Free Press, 2006.

Hobsbawm, E. J., and T. Ranger, eds. *The invention of tradition*. Cambridge: Cambridge UP, 1983.

Hodgson, Marshall G. S. *The venture of Islam: conscience and history in a world civilization*. 3 vols. Chicago: U of Chicago P, 1974.

Hoerder, Dirk. *Cultures in contact: world migrations in the second millennium*. Durham, N.C.: Duke UP, 2002.

Hoffman, L. M. "The marketing of diversity in the inner city: tourism and regulation in Harlem," *International J of Urban and Regional Research*, 27, 2, 2003: 286–99.

Hollander, A. N. J. den, O. van den Muijzenberg, J. D. Speckmann, and W. F. Wertheim. *De plurale samenleving*. Meppel: Boom, 1966.

Hollinger, D. *Postethnic America: beyond multiculturalism*. New York: Basic Books, 1995.

hooks, bell. *Black looks: race and representation*. Boston: South End, 1992.

Horowitz, D. L. *Ethnic groups in conflict*. Berkeley and Los Angeles: U of California P, 1985.

———. "Some realism about constitutional engineering," in Wimmer et al., 2004, 245–57.

Hourani, A., and N. Shehadi, eds. *Lebanese in the world: a century of emigration*. London: IB Tauris, 1993.

Howes, D., ed. *Cross-cultural consumption: global markets, local realities*. London: Routledge, 1996.

Hudson, H. G., Jr. *Blueprints and blood: the Stalinization of Soviet architecture, 1917–1937*. Princeton, N.J.: Princeton UP, 1994.

Hudson, K. "How misleading does an ethnographical museum have to be?" in Karp and Lavine, 1991, 457–63.

Humphrey, M. "Civil war, identity and globalisation," *New Formations*, 31, 1997: 67–82.

Huntington, Samuel P. *The clash of civilizations and the remaking of world order*. New York: Simon and Schuster, 1996.

———. "America in the world," *Hedgehog Review*, 5, 1, 2003: 7–18.

———. "The Hispanic challenge," *Foreign Policy*, March/April 2004a: 30–45.

———. *Who are we? The challenges to America's national identity*. New York: Simon and Schuster, 2004b.

Hymans, J. L. *Léopold Sédar Senghor: an intellectual biography*. Edinburgh: Edinburgh UP, 1971.

Ibrahim, Z. "Ethnicity in Malaysia," in David and Kadirgamar, 1989, 126–42.

Iqbal, A. Muhammad. *The reconstruction of religious thought in Islam*. Lahore: Sang-e-Meel, 1996.

Irwan, A. "Rent and ethnic Chinese regional business networks: Indonesia's puzzling high economic growth," Kuala Lumpur, unpublished paper, 1996.

Isaacs, H. R. *Idols of the tribe: group identity and political change*. Cambridge: Harvard UP, 1975.

Ismael, S. T., ed. *Globalization: policies, challenges and responses*. Calgary, Alberta: Detselig, 1999.

Iyer, Pico. *The global soul: jet lag, shopping malls and the search for home*. New York: Knopf, 2000.

Jahn, J., ed. *Colon: das schwarze bild vom weissen mann*. Munich: Rogner and Bernhard, 1983.

James, C. L. R. *The black Jacobins*. London: Secker and Warburg, 1938.

Jameson, F. *Postmodernism, or the cultural logic of late capitalism*. London: Verso, 1991.

Jayatilleka, Dayan. *Sri Lanka: the travails of democracy, unfinished war, protracted crisis*. New Delhi: Vikas and International Centre for Ethnic Studies, 1995.

Jeganathan, Pradeep, and Qadri Ismail, eds. *Unmaking the nation: the politics of identity and history in modern Sri Lanka*. Colombo: Social Scientists' Association, 1995.

Jenkins, R. "Rethinking ethnicity: identity, categorization and power," *Ethnic and Racial Studies*, 17, 1994: 197–223.

———. "Ethnicity etcetera: social anthropological points of view," in Bulmer and Solomos, 1999, 85–97.

Jennings, F. *The creation of America: through revolution to empire*. Cambridge: Cambridge UP, 2000.

Johnson, C. *Blowback: the costs and consequences of American empire*. New York: Henry Holt, 2000.

Jones, Sian. "Peopling the past: approaches to 'race' and ethnicity in archaeology," in Bulmer and Solomos, 1999, 152–66.

Jonge, Huub de. "Abdul Rahman Basedan and the emancipation of the Hadramis in Indonesia," *Asian J of Social Science*, 32, 3, 2004: 373–400.

Junejo, A. J., and M. Q. Bughio, eds. *Cultural heritage of Sind*. Jamshoro and Hyderabad, Sindh: Sindhi Adabi Board, 1988.

Kalb, D., M. van der Land, R. Staring, B. van Steenbergen, and N. Wilterdink, eds. *The ends of globalization: bringing society back in*. Lanham, Md.: Rowman & Littlefield, 2000.

Kaner, Simon. "Beyond ethnicity and emergence in Japanese archaeology," in Denoon et al., 1996, 46–59.

Kaplan, F. S., ed. *Museums and the making of ourselves: the role of objects in national identity*. London: Leicester UP, 1994.

Kaplan, Robert D. *The ends of the earth*. New York: Random House, 1996.

———. *The coming anarchy: shattering the dreams of the post cold war*. New York: Random House, 2000.

Kapur, D., and J. McHale. *Give us your best and brightest*. Washington, D.C.: World Bank, 2005.

Karp, I. "Culture and representation," 1991a, in Karp and Lavine, 1991, 11–24.

———. "Other cultures in museum perspective," 1991b, in Karp and Lavine, 1991, 373–85.

Karp, I., and S. Lavine, eds. *Exhibiting cultures: the poetics and politics of museum display*. Washington, D.C.: Smithsonian Institution Press, 1991.

Kathib, Lina. "Communicating Islamic fundamentalism as global citizenship," in J. Dean, J. W. Anderson, and G. Lovink, eds., *Reformatting politics: information technology and global civil society*. London: Routledge, 2006, 69–84.

Katunarić, Vjeran. "The meanings of culture in the European core and periphery," in Scaronvob-Ethoki, 1997, 31–40.

Katz, A. "Le musée d'anthropologie, des deux côtés du miroir," in *Le futur antérieur des musées*. Paris: Éditions du Renard, 1991, 25–30.

Kaviraj, S. "On state, society and discourse in India," in J. Manor, ed., *Rethinking third world politics*. London: Longman, 1991, 72–99.

———. "Dilemmas of democratic development in India," in A. Leftwich, ed., *Democracy and development*. Cambridge: Polity, 1996, 114–38.

Kazumichi, K. "The Japanese as an Asia-Pacific population," in Denoon et al., 1996, 19–30.

Kellas, J. G. *The politics of nationalism and ethnicity*. Houndmills: Macmillan, 1991.

Keohane, R. O. "The globalization of informal violence, theories of world politics and the 'liberalism of fear,'" in Calhoun, Price, and Timmer, 2002, 77–91.

Khatib, Lina. "Communicating Islamic fundamentalism as global citizenship," in J. Dean, J. W. Anderson, and G. Lovink, eds., *Reformatting politics: information technology and global civil society*. London: Routledge, 2006, 69–84.

Khun Eng, Kuah-P. "Moralising ancestors as socio-moral capital: a study of a transnational Chinese lineage," *Asian J of Social Science*, 34, 2, 2006: 243–63.

King, Anthony D. *Spaces of global cultures: architecture, urbanism, identity*. London: Routledge, 2004.

Kirshenblatt-Gimblett, B. "Objects of ethnography," in Karp and Lavine, 1991, 386–443.

Klug, Heinz. "How the centre holds: managing claims for regional and ethnic autonomy in a democratic South Africa," in Ghai, 2000, 99–121.

Knight, A. "Racism, revolution, and *indigenismo*: Mexico, 1910–1940," in Graham, 1990, 71–114.

Knippenberg, H., and B. de Pater. *De eenwording van Nederland*. Nijmegen: SUN, 1988.

Kobrin, S. J. "Back to the future: neomedievalism and the postmodern digital world economy," *J of International Affairs*, 51, 2, 1998: 361–86.

Kohei, Hanazaki. "Ainu Moshir and Yaponesia: Ainu and Okinawan identities in contemporary Japan," in Denoon et al., 1996, 117–31.

Kolbert, Elizabeth. "Letter from Rotterdam: beyond tolerance," *New Yorker*, September 9, 2002: 106–14.

Kothari, Rajni. *Rethinking development*. Delhi: Ajanta, 1989.

Kotkin, Joel. *Tribes: how race, religion, and identity determine success in the new global economy*. New York: Random House, 1992.

Kovel, J. *White racism, a psychohistory*. New York: Pantheon, 1970.

Krishna, Anirudh. "Moving from the stock of social capital to the flow of benefits: the role of agency," *World Development*, 29, 6, 2001: 925–43.

Kristeva, J. *Nations without nationalism*. New York: Columbia UP, 1993.

Kukathas, C. "Liberalism and multiculturalism: the politics of indifference," *Political Theory*, 26, 5, 1998: 686–99.

Kuran, Timur. "The religious undertow of Muslim economic grievances," in Calhoun, Price, and Timmer, 2002, 67–74.

———. "The Islamic commercial crisis: institutional roots of economic underdevelopment in the Middle East" (September 2002). USC CLEO Research Paper No. C01–12. Available at SSRN: http://ssrn.com/abstract=276377 or DOI: 10.2139/ssrn.276377 (January 25, 2007).

Kurasawa, Fuyuki. "A cosmopolitanism from below: alternative globalization and the creation of a solidarity without bounds," *European J of Sociology*, 45, 2, 2004: 233–55.

Kwok Bun, Chan, ed. *Chinese business networks: state, economy and culture*. Englewood Cliffs, N.J.: Prentice Hall, 2000.

Kymlicka, Will. "American multiculturalism in the international arena," *Dissent*, Fall 1998: 73–79.

———. "Justice and security in the accommodation of minority nationalism," in May, Modood, and Squires, 2004, 144–75.

Laber, J. "Bosnia: questions about rape," *New York Review of Books*, March 25, 1993: 3–6.

Laguerre, M. S. *The global ethnopolis: Chinatown, Japantown, and Manilatown in American society*. New York: St. Martin's, 1999.

———. *Urban multiculturalism and globalization in New York City: an analysis of diasporic temporalities*. Houndmills: Palgrave, 2003.

Lake, David A. *Ethnic conflict and international intervention*, Institute on Global Conflict and Cooperation Policy Brief no. 3. La Jolla: University of California, 1995.

Lalami, Laila. "The missionary position," *Nation*, June 19, 2006: 23–33.

Lavine, S. D. "Art museums, national identity, and the status of minority cultures: the case of Hispanic art in the United States," in Karp and Lavine, 1991a, 79–87.

———. "Museum practices," in Karp and Lavine, 1991b, 151–58.

Lavine, S. D., and I. Karp. "Introduction: museums and multiculturalism," in Karp and Lavine, 1991, 1–10.

Lederach, J. P. *Preparing for peace: conflict transformation across cultures*. Syracuse, N.Y.: Syracuse UP, 1995.

Lee, R. L. M. "The state, religious nationalism, and ethnic rationalization in Malaysia," *Ethnic and Racial Studies*, 13, 4, 1990: 482–502.

Leonardo, Micaela di. *The varieties of ethnic experience: kinship, class, and gender among California Italian-Americans*. Ithaca, N.Y.: Cornell UP, 1984.

Levitt, Peggy, and N. Nyborg-Sorensen. "The transnational turn in migration studies." Global Commission on International Migration, Geneva, *Global Migration Perspectives* 6, 2004.

Levtzion, N., ed. *Conversion to Islam*. New York: Holmes & Meier, 1979.

Lewis, Bernard. *What went wrong? The clash between Islam and modernity in the Middle East*. New York: Perennial, 2002.

———. *The crisis of Islam: holy war and unholy terror*. New York: Modern Library, 2003.

Lewis, T., F. Amini, and R. Lannon. *A general theory of love*. New York: Vintage, 2000.

Lidchi, Henrietta. "The poetics and the politics of exhibiting other cultures," in S. Hall, ed., *Representation: cultural representations and signifying practices*. London: Sage, 2000.

Lie, John. *Multiethnic Japan*. Cambridge: Harvard UP, 2001.

Light, I., R. Bernard, and R. Kim. "Immigrant incorporation in the garment industry of Los Angeles," *International Migration Review*, 33, 1, 1999: 5–25.

Light, I., and S. J. Gold. *Ethnic economies*. San Diego: Academic Press, 1999.

Light, I., G. Sabagh, M. Bozorgmehr, and C. Der-Martirosian. "Internal ethnicity in the ethnic economy," *Ethnic and Racial Studies*, 16, 4, 1993: 581–97.

———. "Beyond the ethnic enclave economy," *Social Problems*, 41, 1, 1994: 65–80.

Light, Ivan, and Edna Bonacich. *Immigrant entrepreneurs: Koreans in Los Angeles*. Berkeley and Los Angeles: U of California P, 1988.

Light, Ivan, and S. Karageorgis. "The ethnic economy," in Smelser and Swedberg, 1994, 647–71.

Lijphart, Arend. *The politics of accommodation: pluralism and democracy in the Netherlands*. Berkeley and Los Angeles: U of California P, 1975.

———. *Democracy in plural societies: a comparative exploration*. New Haven: Yale UP, 1977.

Lin, Jan. *Reconstructing Chinatown: ethnic enclave, global change*. Minneapolis: U of Minnesota P, 1998.

Linke, Uli. *Blood and nation: the European aesthetics of race.* Philadelphia: U of Pennsylvania P, 1999.

Liu, Hong. "Old linkages, new networks: the globalization of overseas Chinese voluntary associations and its implications," *China Quarterly,* 155, 1998: 582–609.

Lobell, Steven E., and Philip Mauceri. "Diffusion and escalation of ethnic conflict," in Lobell and Mauceri, 2004, 1–10.

———, eds. *Ethnic conflict and international politics: Explaining diffusion and escalation.* New York: Palgrave Macmillan, 2004.

Lonsdale, John. "Globalization, ethnicity, and democracy: a view from 'the hopeless continent,'" in A. G. Hopkins, ed., *Globalisation in world history.* London: Random House, 2002, 196–220.

Lowe, Lisa. "Heterogeneity, hybridity, multiplicity: marking Asian American differences," *Diaspora,* 1, 1, 1991: 24–44.

Lubeck, Paul. "The antinomies of Islamic revival: why do Islamic movements thrive under globalisation?" in R. Cohen and S. Rai, eds., *Global social movements.* London: Routledge, 1999.

Lumley, R., ed. *The museum time machine: putting cultures on display.* London: Routledge, 1988.

Macdonald, S., and G. Fyfe, eds. *Theorizing museums: representing identity and diversity in a changing world.* Oxford: Blackwell, 1996.

Macdonald, Sharon, ed. *The politics of display: museums, science, culture.* London: Routledge, 1998.

Maffesoli, M. "The imaginary and the sacred in Durkheim's sociology," *Current Sociology,* 41, 2, 1993: 59–68.

Makdisi, George. *The rise of colleges: institutions of learning in Islam and the west.* Edinburgh: Edinburgh UP, 1981.

Malkani, Gautam. *Londonstani.* London: Penguin, 2006.

Mamdani, Mahmood. *Good Muslim, bad Muslim: America, the cold war and the roots of terror.* New York: Pantheon, 2004.

Manji, Irshad. *The trouble with Islam today.* New York: St. Martin's, 2nd ed., 2006.

Mann, M. *The sources of social power.* Cambridge: Cambridge UP, 1986.

Manning, Patrick. *Migration in world history.* London: Routledge, 2005.

Marable, Manning. "Black fundamentalism: Farrakhan and conservative black nationalism," *Race & Class,* 39, 4, 1998: 1–22.

Marcus, G. E., and M. M. J. Fischer. *Anthropology as cultural critique.* Chicago: U of Chicago P, 1986.

Marcus, J. "Postmodernity and the museum," *Postmodern Critical Theorizing,* 30, 1991: 10–19.

Matsuda, Takeshi, ed. *The age of creolization in the Pacific: in search of emerging cultures and shared values in the Japan-America borderlands.* Hiroshima: Keisuisha, 2001.

Matthee, R. P. *The politics of trade in Safavid Iran: silk for silver, 1600–1730.* Cambridge: Cambridge UP, 2000.

Matthews, Gordon. *Global culture/individual identity: searching for home in the cultural supermarket.* New York: Routledge, 2000.

Matustík, M. J. B. "Ludic, corporate and imperial multiculturalism: impostors of democracy and cartographers of the new world order," in Willett, 1998, 100–118.

May, Stephen, ed. *Critical multiculturalism: rethinking multicultural and antiracist education*. London: Routledge Falmer, 1999.

May, Stephen, Tariq Modood, and Judith Squires, eds. *Ethnicity, nationalism and minority rights*. Cambridge: Cambridge UP, 2004.

Mayall, J., and M. Simpson. "Ethnicity is not enough: reflections on protracted secessionism in the third world," *International J of Comparative Sociology*, 33, 1–2, 1992: 5–25.

Mazrui, Ali A. "Islamic and western values," *Foreign Affairs*, 76, 5, 1997: 118–32.

McAlear, Donna. *High performance*. London: Organisation for Visual Arts, 1994.

McCormack, Gavan. "Introduction," 1996a, in Denoon et al., 1996, 1–18.

———. "Kokusaika: impediments in Japan's deep structure," 1996b, in Denoon et al., 1996, 265–86.

McElroy, G. C. *Facing history: the black image in American art, 1710–1940*. San Francisco: Bedford Arts, 1990.

McGarry, J., and B. O'Leary, eds. *The politics of ethnic conflict regulation*. London: Routledge, 1993.

McGovern, Mark. "The 'craic market': Irish theme bars and the commodification of Irishness in contemporary Britain," *Irish J of Sociology*, 11, 2, 2002: 77–98.

McLaren, Peter. *Critical pedagogy and predatory culture*. London: Routledge, 1995.

———. *Revolutionary multiculturalism: pedagogies of dissent for the new millennium*. Boulder, Colo.: Westview, 1997.

———. "Wayward multiculturalists: a reply to Gregor McLennan," *Ethnicities*, 1, 3, 2001: 408–20.

McLaughlan, A. *Prejudice and discrimination in Japan: the Buraku issue*. New York: Edwin Mellen Press, 2003.

McLennan, G. "Can there be a 'critical' multiculturalism?" *Ethnicities*, 1, 3, 2001: 389–407.

McNeill, D. "Making social capital work: an extended comment on the concept of social capital, based on Robert Putnam's book," *Forum for Development Studies*, 2, 1996: 417–21.

———. "Social capital and the World Bank," in M. Bøås and D. McNeill, eds., *Global institutions and development: framing the world?* London: Routledge, 2003.

McNeill, William H. *A world history*. Oxford: Oxford UP, 3rd ed., 1979.

Mehta, Uday S. *Liberalism and empire: a study in nineteenth century British thought*. Chicago: U of Chicago P, 1999.

Melucci, Alberto. *Nomads of the present*. London: Hutchinson Radius, 1989.

Mercer, Kobena. "'1968': periodizing postmodern politics and identity," in Grossberg, Nelson, and Treichler, 1992, 424–37.

Mernissi, Fatema. "Palace fundamentalism and liberal democracy," in Qureshi and Sells, 2003, 58–67.

Merriman, N. "The dilemma of representation," in *La nouvelle Alexandrie*. Paris: Direction des Musées de France/Collège International de Philosophie, 1992, 129–40.

Meyer, Carter J., and D. Royer, eds. *Selling the Indian: commercializing and appropriating American Indian cultures*. Tucson: U of Arizona P, 2001.

Meyer, Thomas. *Identity mania: fundamentalism and the politicization of cultural differences*. London: Zed, 2001.

Midgley, J. *Social development: the developmental perspective in social welfare.* London: Sage, 1995.

Migration in an interconnected world: new directions for action. New York: Report of the Global Commission on International Migration, 2005.

Milkman, R., ed. *Organizing immigrants: the challenge for unions in contemporary California.* Ithaca, N.Y.: Cornell UP, 2000.

Miller, C. *Theories of Africans: francophone literature and anthropology in Africa.* Chicago: U of Chicago P, 1990.

Minghuan, Li. *"We need two worlds": Chinese immigrant associations in a western society.* Amsterdam: Amsterdam UP, 2000.

Mitchell, Timothy. "McJihad: Islam in the U.S. global order," *Social Text,* 20, 4, 2002: 1–18.

Mkandawire, Thandika. "The terrible toll of post-colonial 'rebel movements' in Africa: towards an explanation of the violence against the peasantry," *J of Modern African Studies,* 40, 2, 2002: 181–215.

MNghi Ha, Kien. "Ethnizität, differenz und hybridität in der migration: eine postkoloniale perspektive," *Prokla, Zeitschrift für kritische Sozialwissenschaft,* 29, 3, 2000.

Modood, Tariq. "Remaking multiculturalism after 7/7," *Open Democracy,* September 29, 2005.

Mole, J. *Mind your manners: managing business cultures in Europe.* London: Nicholas Brealey, 2nd ed., 1995.

Morris-Suzuki, Tessa. "A descent into the past: the frontier in the construction of Japanese history," in Denoon et al., 1996, 81–94.

Mortimer, E. *Faith and power: the politics of Islam.* New York: Vintage, 1982.

Mosquera, G. "Encounters/displacements: conceptual art and politics," *Third Text,* 24, 1993: 87–91.

Moynihan, D. P. *Pandemonium.* New York: Random House, 1992.

Mudimbe, V. Y. "Letters of reference," *Transition,* 53, 1991: 62–78.

Munjeri, D. "Refocusing or reorientation? The exhibit or the populace: Zimbabwe on the threshold," in Karp and Lavine, 1991, 444–56.

Nag, Sajal. *Roots of ethnic conflict: nationality question in North-East India.* New Delhi: Manohar, 1990.

Nairn, Tom, and Paul James. *Global matrix: nationalism, globalism and state-terrorism.* London: Pluto, 2005.

Nandy, Ashis. "Shamans, savages and the wilderness: on the audibility of dissent and the future of civilizations," *Alternatives,* 14, 1989: 263–77.

Nathans, Eli. *The politics of citizenship in Germany.* Oxford: Berg, 2004.

Neary, Ian. "Burakumin in contemporary Japan," in Weiner, 1997, 50–78.

Nederveen Pieterse, Jan. *Empire and emancipation: power and liberation on a world scale.* New York: Praeger, 1989.

———. "Christianity, politics and Gramscism of the right," in J. Nederveen Pieterse, ed., *Christianity and hegemony.* Oxford: Berg, 1992a, 1–31.

———. *White on black: images of Africa and blacks in western popular culture.* New Haven: Yale UP, 1992b.

———. "Aesthetics of power: time and body politics," *Third Text,* 22, 1993: 33–43.

———. "'Fundamentalism' discourses: enemy images," *Women against Fundamentalism*, 1, 5, 1994a: 2–6.

———. "Unpacking the west: how European is Europe?" in A. Rattansi and S. Westwood, eds., *Racism, modernity and identity: on the western front*. Cambridge: Polity, 1994b, 129–49.

———. "Traveling Islam: mosques without minarets," in Ayse Öncü and Petra Weyland, eds., *Space, culture and power*. London: Zed, 1997, 177–200.

———. "Humanitarian intervention and beyond," 1998a, in Nederveen Pieterse, ed., 1998, 1–22.

———. "Sociology of humanitarian intervention: Bosnia, Rwanda and Somalia compared," 1998b, in Nederveen Pieterse, ed., 1998, 230–65.

———, ed. *World orders in the making: humanitarian intervention and beyond*. London and New York: Macmillan and St. Martin's, 1998.

———. "Europe travelling light: Europeanization and globalization," *European Legacy*, 4, 3, 1999: 3–17.

———. "Europe and its others," in Luisa Passerini and M. Nordera, eds., *Images of Europe*. Florence: European University Institute Working Papers HEC 2000/5, 2000, 35–45.

———. *Development theory: deconstructions/reconstructions*. London: Sage, 2001.

———. "Fault lines of transnationalism: borders matter," *Bulletin of the Royal Institute of Inter-Faith Studies*, 4, 2, 2002: 33–48.

———. *Globalization and culture: global mélange*. Boulder, Colo.: Rowman & Littlefield, 2003.

———. *Globalization or empire?* New York: Routledge, 2004.

———. "Tough liberalism: the Human Development Report and cultural liberty," *Development and Change*, 36, 6, 2005: 1267–73.

———. "Oriental globalization: past and present," in G. Delanty, ed., *Europe and Asia beyond east and west: towards a new cosmopolitanism*. London: Routledge, 2006, 61–73.

Nederveen Pieterse, Jan, and Bhikhu Parekh. "Shifting imaginaries: decolonization, internal decolonization, postcoloniality," in J. Nederveen Pieterse and B. Parekh, eds., *The decolonization of imagination*. London: Zed, 1995, 1–20.

Negra, Diane. "Consuming Ireland: Lucky Charms Cereal, Irish Spring Soap and 1–800-Shamrock," *Cultural Studies*, 15, 1, 2001: 76–97.

Negrin, L. "On the museum's ruins: a critical appraisal," *Theory Culture & Society*, 10, 1, 1993: 97–126.

Nerrière, Jean-Paul. *Don't speak English, parlez globish*. Paris: Eyrolles, 2004.

Newton, K. "Social capital and democracy in modern Europe," in J. W. van Deth, M. Maraffi, K. Newton, and P. F. Whiteley, eds., *Social capital and European democracy*. London: Routledge, 1999, 3–24.

Nicodemus, E. "Meeting Carl Einstein," *Third Text*, 23, 1993: 31–38.

Nimako, K. *Voorbij multiculturalisatie: Amsterdam zuidoost als strategische locatie*. Amsterdam: OBEE Consultancy, 1999.

Nithiyanandam, V. "Ethnic politics and third world development: some lessons from Sri Lanka's experience," *Third World Quarterly*, 21, 2, 2000: 283–312.

Nixon, R. "Of Balkans and Bantustans," *Transition*, 60, 1993: 4–26.

Noor, Farish A. "The caliphate: coming soon to a country near you?" Berlin, unpublished paper, 2000.

Norbu, Dawa. *Culture and the politics of third world nationalism.* London: Routledge, 1992.

Noriega, Chon A. "On museum row: aesthetics and the politics of exhibition," *Daedalus,* 128, 3, 1999: 57–82.

Norton, R. "Ethno-nationalism and the constitutive power of cultural politics: a comparative study of Sri Lanka and Fiji," *J of Asian and African Studies,* 28, 3–4, 1993: 180–97.

Nyamweru, Celia. "Letting the side down: personal reflections on colonial and independent Kenya," in Cornwell and Stoddard, 2001,169–92.

Obbo, C. "Village strangers in Buganda society," in Shack and Skinner, 1979, 227–42.

Oc, T., and S. Tiesdell. "Supporting ethnic minority business: a review of business support for ethnic minorities in city challenge areas," *Urban Studies,* 36, 10, 1999: 1723–46.

Oei Hong Kian. *Kind van het land: peranakan-Chinezen in drie kulturen.* Den Haag: Indonet, 2000.

Oguibe, O. "In the 'Heart of Darkness,'" *Third Text,* 23, 1993: 3–8.

Ohmae, K. *The borderless world: power and strategy in the global marketplace.* London: Collins, 1992.

Oliver, Kelly. "Identity, difference, and abjection," in Willett, 1998, 169–86.

Ong, Aihwa. "Flexible citizenship among Chinese cosmopolitans," in Cheah and Robbins, 1998, 143–62.

———. *Flexible citizenship: the cultural logics of transnationalism.* Durham, N.C.: Duke UP, 1999.

Ooka, E., and B. Wellman. "Does social capital pay off more within or between ethnic groups? Analyzing job searchers in five Toronto ethnic groups," American Sociological Association paper, 1999.

Oommen, T. K. *State and society in India.* New Delhi: Sage, 1990.

———. "New nationalisms and collective rights: the case of South Asia," in May, Modood, and Squires, 2004, 121–43.

Ottati, G. dei. "Trust, interlinking transactions and credit in the industrial district," *Cambridge J of Economics,* 18, 6, 1994: 529–46.

Owusu, T. Y. "The role of Ghanaian immigrant associations in Toronto, Canada," *International Migration Review,* 34, 4, 2000: 1155–81.

Özcan, V., and W. Seifert. "Self-employment among immigrants in Germany: exclusion or path to integration?" *Soziale Welt,* 51, 3, 2000: 289–302.

Pajaczkowska, Claire, and Lola Young. "Racism, representation, psychoanalysis," in Donald and Rattansi, 1992, 189–219.

Pantham, Thomas. "Proletarian pedagogy, Satyagraha and charisma: Gramsci and Gandhi," in R. Roy, ed., *Contemporary crisis and Gandhi.* Delhi: Discovery, 1995, 165–89.

Papastergiadis, Nikos. *The complicities of culture: hybridity and "new internationalism."* Manchester: Cornerhouse, 1994.

Parekh, Bhikhu. "South Asians in Britain," *History Today,* 47, 9, 1997: 65–68.

———. *Rethinking multiculturalism*. London: Macmillan, 2000.

———. *Integrating minorities*. London: Institute of Contemporary Arts, 2001.

The Parekh Report. *The future of multi-ethnic Britain*. Report of the Commission on the Future of Multi-Ethnic Britain. London: Runnymede Trust, 2000.

Parry, Benita. "The contradictions of cultural studies," *Transition*, 53, 1991: 37–45.

———. "Resistance theory/theorising resistance or two cheers for nativism," in P. Hulme, ed., *Post-colonial theory and colonial discourse*. Manchester: Manchester UP, 1993.

Paul, James C. N. "Ethnicity and the new constitutional orders of Ethiopia and Eritrea," in Ghai, 2000, 173–96.

Pearce, Susan M., ed. *Art in museums*. London: Athlone, 1995.

Pécuod, A. "Entrepreneurship and identity: cosmopolitan and cultural competencies among German-Turkish businesspeople in Berlin," *J of Ethnic and Migration Studies*, 30, 1, 2004: 3–20.

Perera, Nihal. "The making of a national capital: conflicts, contradictions, and contestations in Sri Jayawardhanapura," in Geisler, 2005, 241–72.

Peters, Michael A. "Between empires: rethinking identity and citizenship in the context of globalization," in Hayden and el-Ojeili, 2005, 105–22.

Petras, James. *The Power of Israel in the United States*. Atlanta: Clarity Press, 2006.

Philips, Melanie. *Londonistan: how Britain is creating a terror state within*. London: Gibson Square, 2006.

Phillips, R. B. "Why not tourist art? Significant silences in native American museum representations," in G. Prakash, ed., *After colonialism*. Princeton, N.J.: Princeton UP, 1995, 98–125.

Picton, J. "In vogue, or the flavour of the month: the new way to wear black," *Third Text*, 23, 1993: 89–98.

Piguet, E. *Les migrations créatrices: étude de l'entreprenariat des étrangers en Suisse*. Paris: L'Harmattan, 1999.

Pinglé, Vibha. "Identity landscapes, social capital and entrepreneurship: small business in South Africa," unpublished paper, 2000.

Pitman, Bonnie. "Muses, museums, and memories," *Daedalus*, 128, 3, 1999: 1–32.

Pollock, Sheldon. "Cosmopolitan and vernacular in history," *Public Culture*, 12, 3, 2000: 591–626.

Pomeranz, Kenneth. *The great divergence: China, Europe and the making of the modern world economy*. Princeton, N.J.: Princeton UP, 2000.

Portes, A. "The social origins of the Cuban enclave economy of Miami," *Sociological Perspectives*, 30, 4, 1987: 340–72.

———. "The informal economy and its paradoxes," in Smelser and Swedberg, 1994, 426–50.

———, ed. *The economic sociology of immigration*. New York: Russell Sage, 1995.

———. "Transnational communities: their emergence and significance in the contemporary world-system," in R. P. Korzeniewicz and W. C. Smith, eds., *Latin America in the world economy*. Westport, Conn.: Greenwood Press, 1996, 151–68.

———. "Globalization from below: the rise of transnational communities," in Kalb et al., 2000, 253–70.

Portes, A., and P. Landolt. "The downside of social capital," *American Prospect*, 26, 1996: 18–21, 94.

Portes, A., and J. Sensenbrenner. "Embeddedness and immigration: notes on the social determinants of economic action," *American J of Sociology*, 98, 6, 1993: 1320–50.

Posey, D. A. "Traditional resource rights," in L. van der Vlist, ed., *Voices of the earth: indigenous peoples, new partners and the right to self-determination in practice*. Amsterdam: Netherlands Centre for Indigenous Peoples, 1994, 217–39.

Prazauskas, Algis. *Ethnicity, nationalism and politics*, Working Paper 280. The Hague: Institute of Social Studies, 1998.

Premdas, Ralph R. "Balance and ethnic conflict in Fiji," in J. McGarry and B. O'Leary, eds., *The politics of ethnic conflict regulation*. London: Routledge, 1993, 251–74.

Prior, Nick. *Museums and modernity: art galleries and the making of modern culture*. Oxford: Berg, 2002.

Prösler, M. "Museums and globalization," *Sociological Review Monograph*, 1996, 4.

Putnam, R. D. *Making democracy work: civic traditions in modern Italy*. Princeton, N.J.: Princeton UP, 1993.

——. *Bowling alone: the collapse and revival of American community*. New York: Simon and Schuster, 1999.

Qureshi, Emran, and Michael A. Sells, eds. *The new Crusades: constructing the Muslim enemy*. New York: Columbia UP, 2003.

Race and representation: art/film/video. New York: Hunter College Art Gallery, 1991.

Ramesh, Jairam. *Making sense of Chindia: reflections on India and China*. New Delhi: India Research Press, 2005.

Ramet, Sabrina P. "Nationalism and the 'idiocy' of the countryside: the case of Serbia," *Ethnic and Racial Studies*, 19, 1, 1996: 70–87.

Ramsay, Anil. "The Chinese in Thailand: ethnicity, power and cultural opportunity structures," in Cornwell and Stoddard, 2001, 51–72.

Rapport, Nigel, ed. *British subjects: an anthropology of Britain*. Oxford: Berg, 2002.

Rashid, Ahmed. *Taliban: the story of the Afghan warlords*. London: Pan Macmillan, 2001.

——. *Jihad: the rise of militant Islam in Central Asia*. New Haven: Yale UP, 2002.

Rashid, S., ed. *"The clash of civilizations"? Asian responses*. Karachi: Oxford UP, 1997.

Rath, Jan. "The informal economy as bastard sphere of social integration: the case of Amsterdam," in E. Eichenhofer, ed., *Migration und Illegalität*. Osnabrück: Rasch Verlag, 1999, 117–36.

——, ed. *Immigrant businesses: the economic, political and social environment*. London and New York: Macmillan and St. Martin's, 2000.

Ray, L. J. *Rethinking social theory: emancipation in the age of global social movements*. London: Sage, 1993.

Redfield, R. *Peasant society and culture*. Chicago: U of Chicago P, 1956.

Reynolds, Craig J. "Thai identity in the age of globalization," in Reynolds, ed., *National identity and its defenders: Thailand today*. Chiang Mai: Silkworm Books, 2002, 308–38.

Richards, Paul. *Fighting for the rain forest: war, youth and resources in Sierra Leone*. Oxford: James Currey and Heinemann, 1996.

Riggs, F. W. "Ethnonationalism, industrialism, and the modern state," *Third World Quarterly*, 15, 4, 1994: 583–610.

———, ed. *Ethnicity: concepts and terms used in ethnicity research.* Honolulu: International Social Science Council Committee on Conceptual and Terminological Analysis, 1985.

Ringer, B. B. *"We the people" and others: duality and America's treatment of its racial minorities.* New York: Tavistock, 1983.

Robertson, R. *Globalization: social theory and global culture.* London: Sage, 1992.

Robison, L. J., A. A. Schmid, and M. E. Siles. "Is social capital really capital?" *Review of Social Economy*, 60, 1, 2002.

Rodrik, Dani. "Feasible globalizations," in Weinstein, 2005, 196–213.

Roediger, David R. *The wages of whiteness: race and the making of the American working class.* London: Verso, 1992.

Rogoff, I. "From ruins to debris: the feminization of fascism in German-History Museums," in Sherman and Rogoff 1994, 223–49.

Roosens, E. E. *Creating ethnicity: the process of ethnogenesis.* London: Sage, 1989.

Rose, R., W. Mishler, and C. Haerpfer. "Social capital in civic and stressful societies," *Studies in Comparative International Development*, 32, 3, 1997: 85–111.

Roseberry, W. "Multiculturalism and the challenge of anthropology," *Social Research*, 59, 4, 1992: 841–58.

Rosenau, J. N. *Turbulence in world politics.* Brighton: Harvester, 1990.

Roth, Alisa. "Germany's cold shoulder," *Nation*, May 27, 2002: 20–22.

Roth, J. H. "Political and cultural perspectives on 'insider' minorities," in J. Robertson, ed., *A companion to the anthropology of Japan.* Malden, Mass.: Blackwell, 2005, 73–88.

Rothchild, Donald. "Liberalism, democracy and conflict management: the African experience," in Wimmer et al., 2004, 226–44.

Rubin, W. *"Primitivism" in twentieth century art: affinity of the tribal and the modern,* 2 vols. New York: Museum of Modern Art, 1984.

Rupesinghe, K., and S. Kothari. "Ethnic conflicts in South Asia," in David and Kadirgamar, 1989, 248–76.

Rupesinghe, Kumar, and Valery A. Tishkov, eds. *Ethnicity and power in the contemporary world.* Tokyo: United Nations UP, 1996.

Rydell, R. W. "Museums and cultural history," *Comparative Studies of Society and History*, 34, 2, 1992: 242–47.

———. *World of fairs: the century-of-progress expositions.* Chicago: U of Chicago P, 1993.

Sadowski, Yahya. *The myth of global chaos.* Washington, D.C.: Brookings Institution Press, 1998.

Said, Edward W. *Covering Islam.* New York: Pantheon, 1981.

———. *Culture and imperialism.* New York: Knopf, 1993.

———. "The clash of definitions," in Qureshi and Sells, 2003, 68–87.

Salih, Mohamed M. A. "Taking ethnicity seriously: another development and democracy in Africa," unpublished paper. The Hague: Institute of Social Studies, 1999.

Samman, Khaldoun. *Cities of God and nationalism: Mecca, Jerusalem, and Rome as contested world cities.* Boulder, Colo.: Paradigm, 2007.

Sánchez, Rosario. "On a critical realist theory of identity," in L. M. Alcoff, M. Hames-García, S. P. Mohanty, and P. M. L. Moya, eds., *Identity politics reconsidered.* London: Palgrave, 2006, 31–52.

Sangren, P. S. "Rhetoric and the authority of ethnography: 'postmodernism' and the social reproduction of texts," *Current Anthropology*, 29, 3, 1988: 405–35.

Sansone, Livio. *Schitteren in de schaduw: overlevingsstrategieën, subcultuur en etniciteit van Creoolse eren uit de lagere klasse in Amsterdam, 1981–1990*. Amsterdam: Spinhuis, 1992.

———. *Blackness without ethnicity: constructing race in Brazil*. New York: Palgrave, 2003.

Satha-Anand, C. "Spiritualising real estate, commoditising real estate: the Muslim minority in Thailand," in Camilleri and Muzaffar, 1998, 135–46.

Satloff, Robert. *The battle of ideas in the war on terror*. Washington, D.C.: Washington Institute for Near East Policy, 2004.

Saunders, Barbara, and David Haljan, eds. *Whither multiculturalism? A politics of dissensus*. Leuven: Leuven UP, 2003.

Saunders, Frances S. *Who paid the piper: the CIA and the cultural cold war*. London: Granta Books, 1998.

Sayeed, Khalid Bin. *Western dominance and political Islam: challenge and response*. Karachi: Oxford UP, 1997.

Sayyid, S. *A fundamental fear: Eurocentrism and the emergence of Islamism*. London: Zed, 2nd ed., 2003.

Scaronvob-Ethoki, Nada, ed. *The cultural identity of central Europe*. Zagreb: Institute for International Relations and Culturelink, 1997.

Scarre, C., ed. *Past worlds: atlas of archaeology*. Ann Arbor, Mich.: Borders Press and HarperCollins, 2003.

Scheff, T. J. "Emotions and identity: a theory of ethnic nationalism," in Calhoun, 1994, 277–303.

Schmidt, D. "Unternehmertum und Ethnizität—ein Seltsames Paar," *Prokla, Zeitschrift für kritische Sozialwissenschaft*, 29, 3, 2000: 120–36.

Schutte, G. "Tourists and tribes in the 'new' South Africa," *Ethnohistory*, 50, 3, 2003.

Seagrave, S. *Lords of the Rim*. London: Corgi Books, 1996.

Seeck, A., ed. *"Rohe barbaren" oder "edle wilde"? der europäische blick auf die "andere welt."* Göttingen: Institut für Angewandte Kulturforschung, 1991.

Shack, W. A. "Introduction," in Shack and Skinner, 1979, 1–17.

Shack, W. A., and E. P. Skinner, eds. *Strangers in African societies*. Berkeley and Los Angeles: U of California P, 1979.

Sharabi, H. *Neopatriarchy: a theory of distorted change in Arab society*. New York: Oxford UP, 1988.

Shaw, T. "Ethnicity as the resilient paradigm for Africa: from the 1960s to the 1980s," *Development and Change*, 17, 4, 1986: 587–606.

Shepperson, Arnold. "AmaBokkebokke! National symbols and the cultural task beyond apartheid," *European J for Semiotic Studies*, 8, 2–3, 1996: 395–411.

Sheridan, A. *Michel Foucault: the will to truth*. London: Tavistock, 1980.

Sherman, D. J., *Worthy monuments: art museums and the politics of culture in nineteenth-century France*. Cambridge: Harvard UP, 1989.

Sherman, D. J., and I. Rogoff, eds. *Museum culture: histories, discourses, spectacles*. London: Routledge, 1994.

Shibutani, T., and Kian Kwan, eds. *Ethnic stratification*. New York: Macmillan, 1965.

Shohat, Ella. "Gender and culture of empire: toward a feminist ethnography of the cinema," *Quarterly Review of Film and Cinema*, 13, 1–3, 1991: 45–84.

Shohat, Ella, and Robert Stam. *Unthinking Eurocentrism*. London: Routledge, 1994.

Shweder, Richard. "'What about female genital mutilation?' and why understanding culture matters in the first place," in Shweder, Minow, and Markus, 2002, 216–51.

Shweder, Richard, Martha Minow, and Hazel Rose Markus, eds. *Engaging cultural differences: the multicultural challenge in liberal democracies*. New York: Russell Sage, 2002.

Siddiqui, Muhammad Ali. "Nostalgia and much more," in Siddiqui et al., 1997, ix–xviii.

Siddiqui, Muhammad Ali, et al. *Common heritage*. Karachi: Oxford UP, 1997.

The significance of the silk roads in the history of human civilizations. Osaka: National Museum of Ethnology, 1992.

Silva, Jani de. *Globalization, terror and the shaming of the nation: constructing local masculinities in a Sri Lankan village*. Victoria, B.C.: Trafford, 2005.

Silva, P. L. de. *Political violence and its cultural constructions: representation and narration in times of war*. London: Macmillan, 2001.

Smart, Alan. "Gifts, bribes and guanxi: a reconsideration of Bourdieu's social capital," *Cultural Anthropology*, 8, 3, 1993: 388–408.

Smelser, N. J., and R. Swedberg, eds. *The handbook of economic sociology*. Princeton, N.J.: Princeton UP, 1994.

Smith, Anthony D. "Ethnic identity and world order," *Millennium*, 12, 2, 1991: 149–61.

———. "Chosen peoples: why ethnic groups survive," *Ethnic and Racial Studies*, 15, 3, 1992: 436–55.

Smith, Michael Peter. "Postmodernism, urban ethnography, and the new social space of ethnic identity," *Theory and Society*, 21, 1992: 493–531.

Smooha, S. "The model of ethnic democracy: Israel as a Jewish and democratic state," *Nations and Nationalism*, 8, 4, 2002: 475–503.

Smooha, S., and T. Hanf. "The diverse modes of conflict-regulation in deeply divided societies," *International J of Comparative Sociology*, 33, 1–2, 1992: 26–47.

Snow, Philip. *The star raft: China's encounter with Africa*. Ithaca, N.Y.: Cornell UP, 1988.

Sollors, Werner, ed. *The invention of ethnicity*. New York: Oxford UP, 1989.

Spivak, Gayatri C. *In other worlds*. London: Routledge, 1987.

———. *Outside in the teaching machine*. London: Routledge, 1993.

Stannard, K., ed. *Insight Guides: Jordan*. Singapore: APA Publications, 1994.

Stavenhagen, Rodolfo. "Ethnodevelopment: a neglected dimension in development thinking," in R. Apthorpe and A. Kráhl, eds., *Development studies: critique and renewal*. Leiden: E. J. Brill, 1986, 71–94.

Stavrianos, L. S. *Global rift: the third world comes of age*. New York: Morrow, 1981.

Stearns, P. W. *Cultures in motion: mapping key contacts and their imprints in world history*. New Haven: Yale UP, 2001.

Steger, Manfred B. "American globalism 'Madison Avenue-style': a critique of U.S. public diplomacy after 9–11," in Hayden and el-Ojeili, 2005, 227–41.

Stein, H. F., and R. F. Hill. *The ethnic imperative: examining the new white ethnic movement.* University Park: Pennsylvania State UP, 1977.

Stein, L. "Erste Konferenz der europäischen Ethnographie-Museen," *Mitteilungen aus dem Museum für Völkerkunde Leipzig,* 55, 1993: 60–61.

Steiner, Stan. *The vanishing white man.* New York: Harper and Row, 1976.

Steyn, Melissa. *"Whiteness just isn't what it used to be": white identity in a changing South Africa.* Albany: State U of New York P, 2001.

Stojan, W. M. "Searching for identity: Austria in Europe," in Scaronvob-Ethoki, 1997, 41–44.

Stölzl, C., ed. *Deutsches Historisches Museum: ideen kontroversen perspektiven.* Frankfurt, 1988.

Storper, Michael. "Lived effects of the contemporary economy: globalization, inequality and consumer society," in J. Comaroff and J. L. Comaroff, eds., *Millennial capitalism and the culture of neoliberalism.* Durham, N.C.: Duke UP, 2001, 88–124.

Subrahmanyam, Sanjay. "Connected histories: notes towards a reconfiguration of early modern Eurasia," *Modern Asian Studies,* 31, 3, 1997: 735–62.

———. "Hearing voices: vignettes of early modernity in south Asia, 1400–1750," *Daedalus,* 127, 3, 1998.

Sugimoto, Yoshio. *An introduction to Japanese society.* Cambridge: Cambridge UP, 2nd ed., 2003.

Tambiah, S. J. "Transnational movements, diaspora, and multiple modernities," *Daedalus,* 129, 1, 2000: 163–94.

Tate, G. *Flyboy in the buttermilk.* New York: Fireside, 1992.

Taylor, Jane. *Petra and the lost kingdom of the Nabateans.* London: IB Tauris, 2001.

Taylor, Jean G. *The social world of Batavia: European and Eurasian Dutch in Asia.* Madison: U of Wisconsin P, 1986.

Taylor, R. "Political science encounters 'race' and 'ethnicity,'" in Bulmer and Solomos, 1999, 115–23.

Temple, J., and P. Johnson. "Social capability and economic development," paper. Oxford: Nuffield College, 1996.

Theye, T., ed. *Wir und die wilden: einblicke in einer kannibalische Beziehung.* Reinbeck: Rowohlt, 1985.

Thörn, Håkan. *Anti-apartheid and the emergence of global civil society.* London: Palgrave, 2006.

Thornton, W. H. *Fire on the rim: The cultural dynamics of east/west power politics.* Lanham, Md.: Rowman & Littlefield, 2002.

Tilly, Charles. *The politics of collective violence.* Cambridge: Cambridge UP, 2003.

Timm, E. "Kritik der 'ethnischen Ökonomie,'" *Prokla, Zeitschrift für kritische Sozialwissenschaft,* 29, 3, 2000.

Tiryakian, Edward A. "Three metacultures of modernity: Christian, gnostic, chthonic," *Theory Culture & Society,* 13, 1, 1996: 99–118.

———. "Assessing multiculturalism theoretically: *e pluribus unum, sic et non,*" *International J on Multicultural Societies,* 5, 1, 2003: 20–39.

Tishkov, V. A. "Ethnic conflicts in the context of social science theories," in Rupesinghe and Tishkov, 1996, 52–68.

Todorov, T. *La conquête de l'Amérique: la question de l'autre.* Paris: Éditions du Seuil, 1988.

Tomaselli, Keyan G., and Alum Mpofu. "The rearticulation of meaning of national monuments: beyond apartheid," *Culture and Policy*, 8, 3, 1997: 57–76.

Torpey, J. *The invention of the passport: surveillance, citizenship and the state*. Cambridge: Cambridge UP, 1999.

Toulmin, S. *Cosmopolis: the hidden agenda of modernity*. Chicago: U of Chicago P, 1990.

Toyota, M. "Contested Chinese identities among ethnic minorities in the China, Burma, and Thai borderlands," *Ethnic and Racial Studies*, 26, 2, 2003: 301–20.

Truettner, W., ed. *The west as America: reinterpreting images of the frontier, 1820–1920*. Washington, D.C.: Smithsonian Institution Press, 1991.

Tseng, Yen-Fen. "Chinese ethnic economy: San Gabriel Valley, Los Angeles County," *J of Urban Affairs*, 16, 2, 1994: 169–89.

——. "The mobility of entrepreneurs and capital: Taiwanese capital-linked migration," *International Migration*, 38, 2, 2000: 143–68.

Turner, Bryan S. *Max Weber: from history to modernity*. London: Routledge, 1992.

——. *Orientalism, postmodernism and globalism*. London: Routledge, 1994.

Turner, T. "Anthropology and multiculturalism: what is anthropology that multiculturalists should be mindful of it?" in Goldberg, ed., 1994, 406–25.

Turton, D., ed. *War and ethnicity: global connections and local violence*. New York: Rochester UP, 1997.

UNDP. *Arab human development report*. New York: UNDP, 2003, 2004.

Uphoff, N., and C. M. Wijayaratna. "Demonstrated benefits of social capital: the productivity of farmer organizations in Gal Oya, Sri Lanka," *World Development*, 28, 11, 2000: 1875–90.

Uvin, Peter. "Ethnicity and power in Burundi and Rwanda: different paths to mass violence," *Comparative Politics*, 31, 3, 1999: 253–72.

Uyangoda, Jayadeva. "Ethnic conflict, ethnic imagination and democratic alternatives for Sri Lanka," *Futures*, 37, 9, 2005: 959–88.

Vail, L., ed. *The creation of tribalism in Southern Africa*. London: James Currey, 1989.

van Brakel, Jaap. "Varieties of multiculturalism: no need for a shared language," in Saunders and Haljan, 2003, 145–66.

van de Putte, Andre. "The nation-state and multicultural society," in Saunders and Haljan, 2003, 61–82.

Van Hear, Nicholas. *New diasporas*. Seattle: U of Washington P, 1998.

Vanvugt, E. *Een propagandist van het zuiverste water: H. F. Tillema en de fotografie van tempo doeloe*. Amsterdam: Mets, 1993.

Varadarajan, Tunku. "A Patel motel cartel," *New York Times Magazine*, July 4, 1999: 36–39.

Varshney, Ashutosh. *Ethnic conflict and civic life: Hindus and Muslims in India*. New Haven: Yale UP, 2nd ed., 2002.

Veenhof, Klaas. "'Modern' features in old Assyrian trade," *JESHO*, 40, 4, 1997: 336–66.

Veiter, T. *Nationalitätenkonflikt und volksgruppenrecht im 20. Jahrhundert*. 2 vols. Munich: Bayerische Landeszentrale für politische Bildung, 1977 (2nd ed., 1984).

Verdery, Katherine. "Ethnicity, nationalism, and the state: ethnic groups and boundaries past and present," in H. Vermeulen and C. Govers, eds., *The anthro-*

pology of ethnicity: beyond "ethnic groups and boundaries." Amsterdam: Spinhuis, 1994.

Vertovec, S. "Transnationalism and identity," *J of Ethnic and Migration Studies*, 27, 4, 2001: 573–82.

Volkan, V. D., and N. Itzkowitz. *Turks and Greeks: neighbours in conflict*. Huntingdon: Eothen Press, 1994.

Waever, Ole. "Securitization and desecuritization," in R. D. Lipschutz, ed., *On security*. New York: Columbia UP, 1995.

———. "European security identities," *J of Common Market Studies*, 34, 1996: 103–32.

Wagner, Ulla. "Problems of time, place and voice," unpublished paper. Stockholm: National Museum of Ethnography, 1997.

Waldinger, R. "The 'other side' of embeddedness: a case-study of the interplay of economy and ethnicity," *Ethnic and Racial Studies*, 18, 3, 1995: 555–80.

Waldinger, R., H. Aldrich, and R. Ward. *Ethnic entrepreneurs: immigrant business in industrial societies*. Newbury Park, Calif.: Sage, 1990.

Walker, Dennis. *Islam and the search for African American nationhood*. Atlanta: Clarity Press, 2005.

Wallerstein, Immanuel. *The decline of American power*. New York: New Press, 2003.

Wallis, B. "Selling nations: international exhibitions and cultural diplomacy," in Sherman and Rogoff, 1994, 265–82.

Wamba-Dia-Wamba, E. "Philosophy in Africa: challenges of the African philosopher," in T. Serequeberhan, ed., *African philosophy: the essential readings*. New York: Paragon, 1991, 211–46.

Wang, Fu-chang. "The development of political opposition in Taiwan, 1986–1989." Pittsburgh: American Sociological Association Annual Conference, 1992.

Warde, A. "Eating globally: cultural flows and the spread of ethnic restaurants," in Kalb et al., 2000, 299–316.

Waters, Mary C. *Ethnic options: choosing identities in America*. Berkeley and Los Angeles: U of California P, 1990.

———. "Ethnic and racial groups in the USA: conflict and cooperation," in Rupesinghe and Tishkov, 1996, 236–62.

Weeramantry, C. G. *Islamic jurisprudence: an international perspective*. New York: St. Martin's, 1988.

Weindbaum, M., and S. Hughes. *The bamboo network: How expatriate Chinese entrepreneurs are creating a new economic superpower in Asia*. New York: Free Press, 1996.

Weiner, M., ed. *Japan's minorities: the illusion of homogeneity*. New York: Routledge, 1997.

Weinstein, Michael M., ed. *Globalization, what's new?* New York: Columbia UP, 2005.

Werbner, Pnina. "What colour 'success'? Distorting value in studies of ethnic entrepreneurship," in H. Vermeulen and J. Perlmann, eds., *Immigrants, schooling and social mobility: does culture make a difference?* London and New York: Macmillan and St. Martin's, 2000, 34–60.

———. "Metaphors of spatiality and networks in the plural city: a critique of the ethnic enclave economy debate," *Sociology*, 35, 3, 2001: 671–93.

Wertheim, W. F. "The trading minorities in Southeast Asia," in Wertheim, *East-west parallels*. The Hague: Van Hoeve, 1964, 39–82.

———. *Indonesië van vorstenrijk tot neo-kolonie*. Amsterdam: Boom, 1978.

West, Cornel. "The postmodern crisis of the black intellectuals," in Grossberg, Nelson, and Treichler, 1992, 689–705.

———. *Race matters*. New York: Vintage, 1994.

———. "The million man march," *Dissent*, Winter 1996: 97–98.

Whitney, J., ed. *Doing business in Japan: an insider's guide*. Tokyo: Key Porter, 1994.

Whitrow, G. J. *Time in history: views of time from prehistory to the present day*. London: Oxford UP, 1988.

Wieviorka, Michel. "The making of differences," *International Sociology*, 19, 3, 2004a: 281–97.

———. "The stakes in the French secularism debate," *Dissent*, Summer 2004b: 71–73.

Willett, Cynthia, ed. *Theorizing multiculturalism*. Oxford: Blackwell, 1998.

Williamson, S. *Resistance art in South Africa*. Cape Town: David Philip, 1989.

Willis-Braithwaite, D. *Picturing us: African American identity in photography*. New York: New Press, 1993.

Wilson, A. Jeyaratnam. *Sri Lankan Tamil nationalism*. New Delhi: Penguin, 2000.

Wilson, F. *Mining the museum: rethinking the institution*. New York: New Press, 1993.

Wilson, M. "Strangers in Africa: reflections on Nyakyusa, Nguni, and Sotho evidence," in Shack and Skinner, 1979, 51–66.

Wimmer, Andreas. "Introduction: facing ethnic conflicts," in Wimmer et al., 2004, 1–20.

Wimmer, Andreas, R. J. Goldstone, D. L. Horowitz, U. Joras, and C. Schetter, eds. *Facing ethnic conflicts: toward a new realism*. Lanham, Md.: Rowman & Littlefield, 2004.

Winn, Neil. "Introduction," in Winn, ed., 2004, 1–7.

———, ed. *Neo-medievalism and civil wars*. London: Frank Cass, 2004.

Woolcock, M. "Social capital and economic development: towards a theoretical synthesis and policy framework," *Theory and Society*, 27, 2, 1998: 151–208.

World Bank. *The initiative on defining, monitoring and measuring social capital*, Social Capital Initiative Working Paper 1, Washington D.C., 1998.

Yengoyan, Aram A. "Universalism and utopianism," *Comparative Study of Society and History*, 39, 4, 1997: 785–98.

Yen Liang, Chiu. "Taiwan's aborigines and their struggle towards racial democracy," in David and Kadirgamar, 1989, 143–54.

Yiftachel, Oren, and Asad Ghanem. "Understanding 'ethnocratic' regimes: the politics of seizing contested territories," *Political Geography*, 23, 2004: 647–76.

Yogasundram, Nath. *A comprehensive history of Sri Lanka from prehistory to tsunami*. Colombo: Vijitha Yapa Publications, 2006.

Yoshino, Kosaku. *Cultural nationalism in contemporary Japan*. London: Routledge, 1995.

———, ed. *Consuming ethnicity and nationalism: Asian experiences*. Honolulu: U of Hawaii P, 1999.

Young, Iris M. *Justice and the politics of difference*. Princeton, N.J.: Princeton UP, 1990.

———. "Unruly categories: a critique of Nancy Fraser's dual systems theory," in Willett, 1998, 50–67.

———. "Two concepts of self-determination," in May, Modood, and Squires, 2004, 176–97.

Yunnan Nationalities Villages. Kunming: Haigeng Kunming Yunnan, n.d.

Zhao, Gang. "Reinventing China: imperial Qing ideology and the rise of modern Chinese national identity in the early twentieth century," *Modern China*, 32, 1, 2006: 3–30.

Zizek, Slavoj. "Multiculturalism or the cultural logic of multinational capitalism," *New Left Review*, 225, 1997.

———. "Passion: regular or decaf?" *In These Times*, February 27, 2004.

Zolberg, V. "The collection despite Barnes: from private preserve to blockbuster," in Pearce, 1995, 94–108.

Zukin, S. *Landscapes of power: from Detroit to Disney World*. Berkeley and Los Angeles: U of California P, 1991.

Index

237

About the Author

Jan Nederveen Pieterse is professor of sociology at the University of Illinois at Urbana-Champaign and specializes in globalization, development studies, and intercultural studies. Recent books are *Globalization or Empire?* (2004), *Globalization and Culture: Global Mélange* (2003), and *Development Theory: Deconstructions/Reconstructions* (2001). Additional information about the author can be found on the internet at http://netfiles.uiuc.edu/jnp/www/.